MANAGING EMERGING

EMERGING

RISK

The Capstone of Preparedness

MANAGING
EMERGING
RISK

The Capstone of Preparedness

KEVIN D. BURTON

CRC Press
Taylor & Francis Group
Boca Raton London New York

CRC Press is an imprint of the
Taylor & Francis Group, an **informa** business

CRC Press
Taylor & Francis Group
6000 Broken Sound Parkway NW, Suite 300
Boca Raton, FL 33487-2742

First issued in hardback 2017

© 2012 by Taylor & Francis Group, LLC
CRC Press is an imprint of Taylor & Francis Group, an Informa business

No claim to original U.S. Government works

ISBN 13: 978-1-138-41398-6 (hbk)
ISBN 13: 978-1-4398-2641-6 (pbk)

Visit the Taylor & Francis Web site at
http://www.taylorandfrancis.com

and the CRC Press Web site at
http://www.crcpress.com

CONTENTS

ACKNOWLEDGMENTS

This book and the author have benefited from the wise council of many close peers and working emergency management professionals who remain in the shadows, as is the state of our current profession, doing the good work that they do. The author owes a debt of gratitude to these professionals, as does our nation. Unsung heroes and silent operations are not appropriate to such an important profession, in my opinion.

The author would like to thank the countless personal advisors who drove this project to completion. Among them, Jeff Bearce, a solid friend who holds a PhD in Philosophy from the University of California, Berkeley, patiently explored with me confounding questions regarding the ethics of emergency response and the sophistry of mastery. Andrew Granger trusted me to take a leap of faith into the unknown and stood by me in so many ways over the past ten years. John Whitaker with his wife Rachel provided the grounding necessary to balance life with work. All of you and many others made this book possible with your gentle support.

My father, Dr. George Burton, acted as a critical reader, deep thinker, and friend throughout the process—probing the logic and presentation of the material every step of the way and, in the process, transforming our relationship from one of father and son to that of informed peers taking one another's counsel. My wife, Adriana, believed in me and helped me find the room to make this book a reality; my daughter Athena put sunshine on the edge of every cloud and the wisdom of innocence at my fingertips. This book is dedicated to my family, who defined me and supported me in the process of writing it. To them I owe many thanks.

A great portion of gratitude is owed to the tireless efforts of editor Jason Philo who was able to make sense of my sentences. Ronnie Richmond, my friend and the illustrator of this book, was able to visualize the abstract and bring the creative design of learning to my attention. My publisher, CRC Press and Mark Listewnik, urged me to write what I know, defying the status quo and setting out on a journey of rethinking risk. I cannot thank all of you enough.

ABOUT THE AUTHOR

Since 1994, Kevin D. Burton has been an active practitioner of the Business Continuity and Disaster Recovery disciplines. As a senior consultant at one of the "Big Two" Disaster Recovery consultancies, he had the responsibility of servicing the unique needs of E-businesses and highly mature n-tiered application architecture frameworks in the late 1990s. During this period, his clients included May Company Stores, Cattelus Corporation, Sun America Financial, Homestore.com, Indymac Bank, Dole Foods, SAIC and People Soft.

In the summer of 2001, he found himself advising the CEO of Toyota Motor Sales as an expert in Information Technology Strategy and Governance with respect to Business Continuity and Disaster Recovery. After 9/11, his role was enlarged and he became responsible for building a sustainable governance process for business resiliency worldwide and delivering a redundant data center solution for Toyota's U.S. operations.

Building on the concept that 9/11 pushed Disaster Recovery practitioners into the realm of emergency management within the private sector, Mr. Burton began to develop a broader, more holistic approach to private sector emergency management and created a small firm called Burton Asset Management. As the Principal of Burton Asset Management, he has served as an executive coach, trusted advisor, and program manager for Oakley, The Arizona Department of Transportation, Maricopa County Department of Health, Pulte Homes, Standard Pacific Homes, and Triad Financial Corporation. In addition, he enjoys deep relationships with consultancies in the disaster recovery community, including IBM, SunGard and Gartner Group. He directly advised the Gartner Group and Cisco Systems in and around global systems deployment and risk management for American Express, Caterpillar, and Baxter Pharmaceuticals.

His experience ranges from G100 companies with revenues in the billions to regionalized medium businesses and local small businesses with 5–25 employees. His projects consistently include architecting and delivering business and technical requirements for strategic, sustainable and cost effective disaster recovery. His broad range of experience has helped clients address many issues to increase their IT process efficiencies or to address business process needs, staff and governance issues, and business-to-IT communication. Direct relationships with agencies in the public sector and other organizations have a built-in tradition of employee safety, risk mitigation and a clear foresight into the risk of today as well as tomorrow.

Articles by and about Mr. Burton and his company have been published in *GQ Australia, Continuity Insights,* and *Disaster Recovery Journal.* Apple Computers recently profiled Burton Asset Management because of the company's innovative approach to risk management.

Today, Mr. Burton is an avid practitioner, speaker, and student in the field of emergency management who consults for Honeywell, Inc. and other companies in the defense industry and travels extensively around the globe, managing emerging risk.

In Mr. Burton's first published textbook, he develops a theme that has emerged from his clinical experience, namely, that a new paradigm for evaluating, let alone "connecting the dots," is necessary if we are to successfully deal with *emerging* threats. This paradigm relies heavily on lessons that can be learned from what (at least at first) may seem to be a strange bedfellow: the marketing industry.

He introduces a whole new lexicon of terms that will intrigue and inform the reader: Possibility vs. Probability Thinking, scenario planning, storytelling, the Disaster Halo Effect, Process Emergence, Zero Sum Scenarios, User Bias, Power Users, memes and meme clusters, cool hunters, Pattern Recognition techniques, Areas of Dominant Influence, Reverse Engineering, Swarm Effects, Kiddie Tactics, and the development of the Brand of Self.

To the extent that these ideas and concepts are implemented, the almost paranoid feeling about impending threats, i.e. "They' ... re he ... re!" can be replaced with the more positive notion, "We're ready!"

1

Imagine This

1.1 ABOUT THE SCENARIOS

These fictitious scenarios draw on contemporary cultural themes and events. They are built to test the currently accepted and normal view of what is possible, and what practitioners may have yet to respond to. They press the advantage toward attackers or Mother Nature: they are emergent in nature. The reader will be introduced to new nodes of social settings and new modes of attacks—new, perhaps, because practitioners have never considered them in the context of a threat.

While these scenarios may be incredible, they are, like all good scenarios, *stories* about futures we have yet to inhabit based on our current reality.

1.2 THE PHOENIX RAVE MASSACRE

Jimmy Burgess tasted blood in his mouth. It was a metallic, acrid taste. Like the time he bit his tongue when he crashed on his skateboard last year trying to get vertical. There was smoke everywhere, and he could not see his hand in front of his face. He started coughing and spit out a thick phlegm of blood onto the floor. Kids were all over the place. Some girls were crying. A lot of them were moaning or yelling for help. The thumping of the music was replaced with a throb in his head and loud ringing in his ears.

Jimmy stood up and looked around. The rave looked like a battlefield. He was pressed next to the bar at the back of the warehouse, and where the stage used to be there was nothing but a smoking crater. After that, closer to him, there were bodies trapped under parts of the warehouse roof and lighting trusses. Jimmy figured at least 3,000 kids were dead, or dying, between the space of the back of the warehouse and where the stage used to be. What happened? He thought there was some kind of huge explosion from under the stage. All he recalled was hearing a giant BOOM and then waking up on the floor.

It looked like dozens of people were trying to get out of the building through the only exit that he could see—the same entrance that everyone came in through, but there was trouble and lots of screaming. Jimmy heard several popping noises. "Is someone shooting fireworks?" he thought to himself. The crowd surged toward the door, and got pushed back. It reminded him of a Who concert he had heard about. Getting his cell phone to call 911, he noticed several others were doing the same, at least the ones who were not freaking out.

***

Officer Chris Harris ran into the parking lot of the warehouse when he heard the explosion. When he had passed by an hour ago, he noticed that there was an ambulance and two off-duty cops working security in the parking lot. They always had to keep an ambulance outside these parties; kids were always getting too drunk or overdosing on Ecstasy. He stopped dead in his tracks when he saw something that he could not

2

even believe was real. Both of the off-duty officers were firing automatic rifles into the swarm of kids trying to escape the smoldering, smoking building. Officer Harris stood at the entrance of the parking area in shock as he watched 15 kids crumble while they were torn apart by AK-47 fire. He did not move until one of the fake officers turned his gun and cracked off several rounds in his direction. "Those aren't real cops? Are they!?"

***

As Jimmy looked around at the confusion and carnage around him, he realized there were tears running down his cheeks. His flash mob site, gogoraveaz.com, had promoted this party like crazy. He had been tipped off that the band Ruff Tank was going to do a surprise performance. Usually, the crowd was between 3,000 and 4,000 kids for just a good DJ. Tonight, there were a lot more people at the rave because he used Twitter, Facebook, and a cool video of Ruff Tank he embedded from YouTube to get the word out. It was not his official job or anything, but everyone knew him as the go-to guy for the biggest and best parties. "Oh, God … this is all my fault."

A girl, stumbling back from the surging crowd at the exit, screamed at him, "The cops are shooting at us!" He looked at the faces around him. He could hear people saying on their phones that there were cops shooting at them from outside the building. He looked over at the exit, and watched as the crowd surged toward the door, away from the smoke and flame, then back from the door, as the popping sound would increase. Putting two and two together, he realized people were being shot at from the outside.

***

As Officer Harris was calling in the explosion and gunfire, emergency response vehicles were pulling onto the street outside the parking area around the warehouse. He peeked around the corner, his duty weapon drawn, and winced when a chip from the concrete wall that surrounded the lot struck his cheek. Two rounds whizzed past him, but the first one had been close. He was ready to fire on one of men with the AK, but his shift supervisor called him back to the command vehicle 300 feet up the street. "Harris! Get out of there, and get your ass here now!" He ran to his commander's car.

The first words out of his commander's mouth were, "How many are there?"

3

"Two. I saw two guys with AK-47s. They're dressed like us." The commander hesitated. Officer Harris repeated, "They're dressed like cops."

Swearing under his breath, the commander asked, "What are they doing?" The relentless gunfire in the background made the question seem rhetorical to him, "Ummm, they're killing kids who are trying to escape the burning building! You know, the one that just blew up!?" The SWAT van and Bomb Squad pulled up behind the commander's black Crown Victoria.

The SWAT team jumped out of their van with weapons ready. As Officer Harris was walking with his supervisor toward the SWAT Commander, the Bomb Squad behind him suddenly took cover. The SWAT team went into action as someone yelled, "Drop your goddam weapon and get on the ground, fucker!" Officer Harris turned around and saw one of the fake cops approaching them from the parking area of the warehouse. Like hornets, the SWAT team flew into action as the point man ordered the gunman on his knees.

In just seconds, two men were tackling the fake cop to the ground. Two seconds more, and three more men were on the scene securing the area. Pushing and shouldering their way around, one officer thrust his knee into the perp's back, another one forced his boot into the back of the gunman's knee, crushing it. Three other SWAT officers swept their M16s over the rooftops and around the alleyways surrounding them.

When the fake cop detonated the vest he was wearing, he instantly killed the two officers restraining him and knocked down the three perimeter SWAT officers with human and metal shrapnel. Officer Harris was far enough away that he was not injured, but as he instinctively dropped for cover, it did not stop him from feeling the heat, smelling the burning flesh, and tasting the blood that had vaporized with the blast. Nearby, the SWAT Commander warned his team, "Suicide vests—they're wearing PIEDs!" (Personalized Improvised Explosive Devices).

The bomber's unforeseen action immediately changed the scale and the response protocol for the entire operation. While automatic gunfire clattered every few minutes and calls continued to flood into 911 from surviving teenagers, an hour was spent setting up a perimeter and bringing in a hostage negotiator. Ten minutes later, the negotiator and SWAT Commander agreed that deadly force was appropriate because they were still losing hostages.

***

From inside the building, Jimmy called his mom. She was out on a date so he left her a message. "Mom," he said into his phone, "listen, I went to this big rave—like a concert thing, and ..." he started weeping. "Mom, some bad things are happening here right now and I just want you to know it's not my fault, but ... I just wanted to see how many people I could get to come to the show using ... using the Internet." He did not know how to explain social networking. Shots rattled at the entrance and people were screaming again, and Jimmy knew she would hear them on her phone. "I love you, Mom," Jimmy gulped back tears. "And, I'm sorry." He hung up.

***

Finally, the SWAT team was able to make their move on the parking lot. To Officer Harris's surprise, the other terrorist ran toward the kids who were trying to get out of the warehouse. He ran and pushed his way into the crowd of teenagers. Diving into them, they screamed as he continued to fire rounds into their torsos. When he sufficiently buried himself in the depths of the panicked teenagers, he detonated.

In slow motion, Officer Harris and the other first responders watched everything happen. During that infinite silence after the blast, they stood dazed, not believing their eyes. With all of their plans, protocols, and safety measures, they could only stand silently. They watched the smoldering exit of the warehouse. They heard crying and whimpering from inside.

***

When Jimmy heard the gunfire getting louder, he ran away from the door. After the blast, he turned back and looked at the dead teenagers and the ugly aftermath of the explosion. Between sobs, he said to himself, "Why did I promote this so much? How many would still be alive now if it weren't for me?" Kids started running back into the warehouse, away from the only way out and back into the smoke-filled space. One of them swore at the cops as he passed. "He seems as good a one to follow as anyone else," Jimmy thought as began to succumb to the mob mentality.

***

It took the hostage negotiator 30 minutes to convince the teenagers inside that the shooting was over and that it was safe to come out. Meanwhile, the SWAT team worked to clear the perimeter of the building. Fire and rescue soon had kids coming out of the building, and they were treating

5

smoke inhalation, first- to third-degree burns, and massive trauma survivors. Patrol officers helped identify the dead and collect whatever remains could be found.

Officer Harris looked at the ambulance in the parking lot and saw that no one was there. "Why isn't anyone using that ambulance? In fact, now that I think about it, I haven't seen anyone there all night." Asking around, he could find no one who belonged to that ambulance. "This is weird … it's not right," and he started trying to get into the vehicle.

***

Jimmy could not say for sure if he was happy to see all the cops in the parking lot. But he was glad that the fireman came in and just threw him over his shoulder to get him out of the building. The fresh air tasted good. The fireman sat him down and called for an EMT.

Getting oxygen and being treated for minor cuts, Jimmy looked around at the full parking lot. He began to weep again. "There was only supposed to be fun here tonight. We were only going to dance and get laid. It was just fun … All of these people, how many are my Facebook friends? All the pain and suffering these kids are dealing with because of me! There must have been 5,000 people here tonight!"

Looking around he saw some guys in suits flashing a badge at one of the SWAT guys near the parking lot entrance. "Here they come now, looking for me for making this event so popular. I'll bet they think I helped plan this. Yes, I feel badly about this, but I would never do this! It's not my fault people shared what I was telling them. It's not my fault that this took off so fast."

***

Officer Harris did not have enough time to understand what he was looking at when the world ended. The abandoned ambulance exploded in a bright flash of blue-green light. The blast of the heat and shrapnel ripped through the parking lot, flipping nearby cars and throwing kids, policemen, firemen, and EMTs to the ground in a sick, human halo effect. The flash was the last thing Officer Harris and most of the others saw. The shockwave from the blast traveled faster than their nerve impulses could carry pain messages to their brain. The closest were the luckiest. Those concentrically farther out died more slowly and painfully. Jimmy never saw his mother. There were no remains found of Officer Harris. Most murdered in the blast could not have an open casket funeral.

6

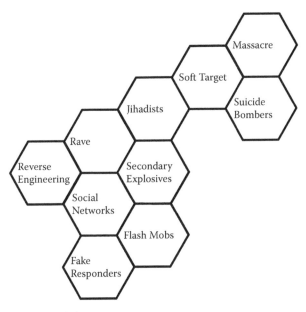

Figure 1.1   Elements of the rave massacre.

The Aftermath

The total death toll of the Arizona Rave Massacre was 3,670 people, with more than 75 of these being first responders. (Figure 1.1).

A prominent jihadist group claimed responsibility for the attack. They credited three unknown radical Muslims and a gullible, prominent rave promoter for carrying out the attack. In terms of lives lost, this was the second-worst terrorist attack in U.S. history.

In the News: Stories that Support the Scenario
- **October 16, 2008; Phoenix, Arizona**: The FBI has sharpened its scrutiny of some Phoenix-area Muslim leaders because of their links to two controversial incidents and a federal probe into the financing of terrorist groups. One incident involves Akram Musa Abdallah, who had been using his company as a front for funneling money to Hamas in the West Bank. The other is a shooting incident involving 20 young, Muslim males, armed with assault rifles, a shotgun, a sniper rifle, and handguns. For more than an hour, the shooters blasted away at a granite rock and empty cans in front of a hill. Officials estimate the fusillade totaled 500 to

1,000 rounds. Five of the shooters left before police arrived. Police detained 10 adults and five minors, including one who was only 11 years old.[1]

- **March 18, 2009; Phoenix, Arizona**: Michael Booher, who served four years in prison for coercing a seven-year-old to urinate on his genitals, now obtains permits for rave parties he allows at his warehouse. This prevented him from having problems with the city, like getting shut down by the fire marshal—for a while, anyway.[2]

- **January 26, 2009; Chicago, Illinois**: Chicago police arrested a 14-year-old boy for allegedly impersonating one of their own. The boy, who has been charged as a juvenile for impersonating an officer, walked into the Grand Crossing District station, 7040 S. Cottage Grove Ave., dressed in a Chicago police uniform, police spokeswoman Monique Bond said. The boy, who reported for duty about 1:30 p.m., partnered with another police officer for about five hours. If a 14-year-old boy can impersonate an officer for five hours, then it is realistic that the two attackers in our scenario can appear as real police officers to innocent kids.[3]

- **January 11, 2010; Phoenix, Arizona**: Phoenix was abuzz with Cardinals Football fever as people gathered at light rail stations at the east and west ends of the light rail line. The event leaders, identified by the red scarves tied to their bags, inconspicuously navigated the nervous crowds, answering questions and reviewing the action plan. At 2:00 p.m., participants began filling the light rail trains. There were so many participants in the East Valley that they had to be divided into two trains. Even with the group split up across three trains (the third being the West Valley train), there was standing room only in the cars. As the trains began to move, the pants came off. Nonparticipants reacted first with looks of confusion, which turned into shock, often followed by laughter; a group called Improv AZ created the flash mob. Flash mobs have attracted as many as 5,000 participants.[4]

Most cities and municipalities require that all events held in public spaces, and special events in private rental spaces, be permitted and regulated. Often the permitting process requires proof of insurance for the event, proof that no traffic complications will arise from the event, and that special security needed for the event will be provided. At events that serve alcohol, a provisional alcohol permit may be required as well.

Unscrupulous, or poorly informed, warehouse property owners disregard these regulations when they sublet their properties to so-called "promoters" who are throwing warehouse parties or raves.

Furthermore, in most counties and municipalities, including the Phoenix area, no criminal background checks are conducted on the promoters of the parties themselves, or the owners of the properties at which such parties take place.

In Practice: Data that Supports the Scenario

After-hours parties, warehouse parties, raves, or other dance parties can crop up in virtually any city, at any time. They are largely unregulated and gather large crowds that congregate and party with little oversight.

The rave scene in Phoenix, AZ, has been vibrant for at least five years. The average rave can attract from 1,500 to 4,000 people. Hand-flyers, word-of-mouth, text messages, and popular social networking tools promote these events. They are typically hosted in warehouses or other open spaces.

1.3 THE SAINT LOUIS EARTHQUAKE SCENARIO

Arthur Mellons knew that the proposed location for the city's new Emergency Operations Center (EOC) was not safe. First, those in favor argued that a riverfront location was beneficial for reasons of "accessibility." Next, even though all of the geological surveys, studies, and the Hazards US-Multihazard (HAZUS-MH) data had shown that almost all of the Saint Louis area was susceptible to liquefaction in earthquakes with a magnitude of 7.5 and peak ground acceleration (PGA) of 0.2, if you lowered the PGA of the quake to 0.1 the building area would be deemed safe. Moreover, this was a good piece of land. The location brought the price in under budget, and the state was giving additional incentives to build there.

Moving the peak ground acceleration down to 0.1 and underestimating data provided by the United States Geological Survey (USGS) was wrong, and Arthur knew it. Changing the numbers that way would put the EOC in harm's way. That said, it was not like Arthur was the only one making the decision. The city and state planners knew the numbers too, but they kept them behind closed doors after that last meeting. With the money they saved on the site, the City of Saint Louis Emergency Management Agency (CEMA) was successful in creating an Emergency

Management Campus that rivaled the one they had toured in the Federal Emergency Management Agency's (FEMA) Region VII in Kansas City. Arthur accepted the approval of the EOC and simply hoped he would never see a day when the political miscalculation was challenged.

***

One Year Later …

"If the Arch can twist and bend like that without cracking in half, the EOC will be fine," Arthur kept telling himself as he lay on his back while the ground beneath him heaved and buckled for 45 seconds. The shaking was so intense that the twisting, heaving Arch above him popped off panels to reveal the twisting stairwell inside. Yet the Arch stood.

Two sharp cracking noises, followed by a low rumble, seemed to end the earthquake and Arthur rose shakily to his feet. Looking south he could see that the bridges were still intact and crossing the river, but most likely damaged. To his west, his car was pushed halfway into the Jefferson National Expansion Memorial area by a semi. Behind that, a more horrific scene unfolded; the Saint Louis skyline was a diorama of crumbling brick and shattered glass buildings. Most of those buildings had not been retrofitted for a quake of this size. Smoke columns rose in the distance.

Arthur knew the quake had to be at least a 7.0. He turned slowly around and took in the dazed tourists, the now still Arch, the bridge, and the river. The river itself seemed to be moving backward, a boiling mess of gray-red water. "I've got to get to the EOC!" Arthur thought and turned back for his car. After two steps, he realized that the car was going nowhere, and he would have to hoof it up past the Jefferson Memorial to the little plot of land by the river. The "Little Lie" tightened his stomach.

It was the same feeling he had two weeks ago when they inaugurated the Emergency Operations Center. The "Little Lie" tightened his stomach when the ribbon was cut. "Should I have blown the whistle on this whole project? Would it have been worth being blacklisted?"

As he started running north past the Jefferson Memorial, he knew he was about to find out just how wrong that choice of his higher ups was. He was looking at his feet, careful not to trip over the large cracks in the sodden earth as he ran, and slammed right into a brick of a man.

Looking up, he realized it was his friend John Hendricks from the Saint Louis Police Department (SLPD). John was a massive guy. Six foot two and 220 pounds of muscle. He made a hell of a cop. "Hey!" he shouted as Arthur stumbled back. "Hey, Arthur!"

10

"What's going on?" Arthur asked, but John held up a finger to silence him and turned up his radio. He had it on the unified communication frequency, and reports were already flooding in. A mandatory evacuation of the park grasses of the Jefferson National Expansion Memorial and downtown Saint Louis had been ordered. A 45-second-long earthquake of 7.7 magnitude had hit the Midwest. The earthquake was a ground thrust along the New Madrid Fault Line. Based on the size of the event, the President had already declared the region a national disaster area, setting in motion the Federal response capability. Arthur and John looked at each other.

The radio report continued: FEMA had been mobilized; the area affected spanned four different FEMA regions. Tennessee, Arkansas, and Southern Missouri were the most severely impacted states. The damages in the Saint Louis area were obvious. The power was off. There were leaks in natural gas pipelines. No bridge, highway, or viaduct had failed, but the damages to all were severe. The building collapses were widespread in downtown Saint Louis. As predicted by the models, the intensity and peak ground movement associated with this earthquake caused liquefaction in several areas. Just north of the city two huge landslides had created an artificial basin. Due to the landslides, the river flow downstream was reduced to 30%. The artificial basin was filling fast. Local response seemed to be working smoothly as assessment teams were already en route.

Arthur thought that the new EOC had to be working, and for a moment, the "Little Lie" let him be. The landslides were half-a-mile upstream. Only one of the ramps to the highway had collapsed.

Arthur looked out at the river. It seemed to be nearly drained of water. The banks of the river were exposed. "Holy ..." he nudged John who looked at it and shook his head. "I've got to get up to the EOC." John nodded and looked toward the city. "You wanna come with?" Arthur offered.

John shook his head, and looked up the hill toward the crumbled city. "You're right, there are people in there that need your help," Arthur told him. "There sure are," John says. "I gotta get going." John started jogging up the hill toward the city, and Arthur took off running for the EOC.

Rounding the bend to the Jefferson Memorial building, Arthur was panting. He started up the small hill that took him to the EOC on the other side. He noticed a film crew from the local news channel had set up there with their cameras pointed down toward the EOC. He ran faster.

As he crested the hill, he looked down in horror. The EOC was sunken in the earth at least three feet. The roof was caved in. The

11

building was in ruins. As he watched, an aftershock rumbled and a wall of gray earth and water cascaded down the riverbed and swamped into the low-lying area where his EOC once stood. The side of the building was dragged away with two CEMA trucks and several of his employees; his eyes begin to well up as the "Little Lie" took hold of him and pushed him to the ground.

Amy Werthers, the local news station reporter, tapped him on the shoulder; a cameraman pointed a camera in his face. "What do you think about the earthquake and flood?" She asked Arthur, "Did we fail to connect the dots when we built the new Saint Louis Emergency Operations Center?" Arthur looked at her, becoming sick as the "Little Lie" unraveled like a snake in his belly. "Dots? What dots?" he asked.

The "Little Lie" was somehow behind him as the floodwaters wrenched the Arch from its foundation, twisted it into the murk, and slammed it into the bridge.

The Aftermath

The aftermath of the earthquake was breathtaking. Nearly 715,000 buildings were damaged in the eight-state area. About 42,000 search-and-rescue personnel working in 1,500 teams were required to respond to the earthquake. Damage to critical infrastructure (essential facilities, transportation, and utility lifelines) was substantial in the 140 impacted counties near the rupture zone, including 3,500 damaged bridges and nearly 425,000 breaks and leaks to both local and interstate pipelines. Approximately 2.6 million households were without power after the earthquake. Nearly 86,000 injuries and fatalities resulted from damage to infrastructure. Nearly 130 hospitals were damaged. Moreover, roughly 15 major bridges were unusable. Three days after the earthquake, 7.2 million people were still displaced and 2 million people sought temporary shelter. Direct economic losses for the eight states total nearly $300 billion, while indirect losses would be at least twice this amount (Figure 1.2).

The flash flood in Saint Louis caused 400 deaths and 2,000 injuries. The loss of the CEMA EOC set back the local response for five days. Ninety percent of the equipment deployed in the first hour of the response was lost or damaged. The City of Saint Louis Emergency Management Agency (CEMA) capabilities were reduced to 20%. Ultimately, the 101st Airborne Division was called into the city to restore order and allow for a sustained response to the disaster.

Figure 1.2   Elements of the earthquake scenario.

In the News: Stories that Support the Scenario

- **April 18, 2008; 4:37 a.m.:** A 5.2 magnitude earthquake rattled Southern Illinois and eastern Missouri. A 4.5 magnitude after-shock came at 10:14 a.m. In Saint Louis, the only reported damage was of concrete that fell from the 72-year-old South Kings Highway viaduct over the Union Pacific line at Shaw Boulevard. City engineers closed the bridge to inspect it, and then reopened some of the six lanes about 6:30 a.m.[5]

- **USGS Historical Earthquakes:** "New Madrid Earthquakes 1811–1812. This sequence of three very large earthquakes is usually referred to as the New Madrid earthquakes, after the Missouri town that was the largest settlement on the Mississippi River between St. Louis, Missouri, and Natchez, Mississippi. On the basis of the large area of damage (600,000 square kilometers), the widespread area of perceptibility (5,000,000 square kilometers), and the complex physiographic changes that occurred, the New Madrid earthquakes of 1811-1812 rank as some of the largest in the United States since its settlement by Europeans. They were by far the largest east of the Rocky Mountains in the U.S. and Canada. The area of strong shaking associated with these shocks is two to three times as large as that of the 1964 Alaska earthquake and 10 times as large as that of the 1906 San Francisco earthquake. Because there were no seismographs in North America at that time, and very few people in the New Madrid region, the estimated magnitudes of this series of earthquakes vary considerably and depend on modern researchers' interpretations of journals, newspaper reports, and other accounts of the ground shaking and damage. The magnitudes of the three principal earthquakes of 1811-1812 ... are the preferred values taken from research involved with producing the 2008 USGS National Seismic Hazard Map."[6]

In Practice: Data that Supports the Scenario
The first recorded earthquakes in U.S. history are the 1811-12 New Madrid Fault earthquakes. Between December 12, 1811, and February 7, 1812, a magnitude 8.0 earthquake was the largest ever recorded in the lower 48 states. Four major earthquakes all above an estimated 7.3 magnitude occurred in the area between Saint Louis and the modern city of Memphis during this period. Only the sparse population present in the area limited the damages.

The geological results of the 1812 quake are still visible: new lakes were created; the Mississippi River changed its course, and the ground warping of this course change created uplifts, subsidence, and six-foot sand blows (large patches of sand created by the liquefaction that creates strata in the ground). One of the characteristics of this fault is that noticeable events are not as frequent as with the California quakes. The lack of activity has caused a lackadaisical response to retrofitting buildings and preparing for a catastrophic event. The latest attempt by FEMA to accelerate response and planning activities around a New Madrid Scenario is called the NMSZ New Madrid Seismic Zone (NMSZ) Catastrophic Earthquake Disaster Response Planning Initiative.

1.4 GOING GREEN, ECOTERRORISTS AND A FIRST STRIKE ADVANTAGE

Special Agent Jack Terry was onto something. His intelligence was good. The data coming from the U.S. Department of Homeland Security (DHS) and several FBI bulletins were convincing. His Earth Liberation Front (ELF) undercover agent recovered reliable information about the group's intentions in the coming weeks. He knew that these environmentalists were about to take things too far in the interests of environmental conservation.

"I've got to get the department on alert and get authorization to start monitoring ELF more closely," Jack said to himself. "I'm not the best at PowerPoint, but I know I can put this information together in such a way that they'll see the threat for themselves and we'll stop these ecoterrorists in their tracks."

After the presentation, his boss told him, "Nice job, Jack … ecoterrorists bring down Seattle! I can see it now," as he arced his arm through the air.

"I don't get it," thought Jack. "The HAZMAT teams, Radiological Assistance Program, the Atmospheric Release Advisory Capability people, the Accident Response Group, The King County Fire Marshal and Police … every one of them thought I was crazy! They just hate the FBI, so they're going to 'shoot the messenger!'" He was so pissed off he did not even notice his work phone was ringing.

***

When Andy Hawthorne joined his friends at their first ELF meeting outside Seattle, he did not think he was being used. They were into saving the earth from the rampant pollution and manmade CO_2 that was ruining the forests, oceans, and the whole planet for everyone. He felt like everyone at the meeting was cool. They were all just a bunch of 20-somethings who worked at different companies in and around Seattle, just trying to get by after graduating. Tonight's meeting was very different from anything they had ever done. Tonight, they were outside the third datacenter he had shown them two weeks ago; they were chopping at a fiber optic trunk line with an axe.

***

Rene Montero was freaked out. She was going to be so busted by her boss when he came in. This was not a simple disaster recovery test failure; heck, they had those all the time. This was … this was the entire recovery center being taken off-line. There was no inbound Internet or data connection whatsoever. Synchronous backups were failing all over the 40,000-square-foot facility. Here, a user acceptance test for that big shipping company just went completely offline there was no way for the users to connect to the test data. She went out and checked the demarcation box, and all the trunks were in order. There was no blackout, and the generator was not even on. She looked at her cell phone and thought about calling the carriers, but she would have to go in and get the lists because she did not have the after-hours numbers.

***

Christy Gild smiled at Andy when they were done chopping through the third trunk line located in the middle of the woods outside the recovery center. It had only taken them six minutes to drive from one recovery center to the next. Andy knew where they all were because he was asked to tour them with his boss at the paper company. This was just before he started writing the disaster recovery plans he was hired to complete.

Christy was cute. He would not have come with them tonight if it was not for her. The leader of the group, Bryant, made him nervous. The guy was too radical and intense about everything, but Christy's smile made it tolerable for him, and when she grabbed his hand and said, "Come on!" he forgot about everything else. They ran toward the edge of the hill they were on so that they could look out over the city. "Watch," she whispered, and he thought she might kiss him. The rest of their small "assault team" came up behind them and stood silently.

The explosion was a big, great ball of fire that mushroomed up and spread over a building just at the edge of the city. "General Lumber," Christy said, "the biggest logger in Seattle." Jimmy turned and stared at her. She nodded and went on, "There goes their data center." Before Jimmy could speak, a second explosion went off deeper in the city. "Oh my God ..." Jimmy said, but Christy grasped his hand harder and hopped up and down with excitement, "Union Bank, right on time!" The little group let out a cheer.

The third explosion looked like it was right in the heart of the city. "And there goes SIX," Christy said. They were off and running. "What's SIX?" Andy shouted as they piled into the van. "SIX, S.I.X. the Seattle Internet Exchange." Christy was grinning from ear to ear. "Down on Sixth Street. It's like the 20th biggest Internet switch in the whole world!" Christy squealed. The van took off, and they were tossed back into their seats.

***

By the time Rene made her way back through the raised floor area of the giant recovery center's data center and into the network operations center, Bob McEnroe was already holding two phones to his ear and three others were ringing incessantly. Bob looked at her with total dismay and

16

pointed at a phone. Rene picked it up and the voice on the other end said, "This is Jackie from Max Data Declarations, I have an Emergency Disaster Declaration from Tiny Toys in Seattle, ETA is…."

Rene cut her off, "But!" The voice at the other end of the line hesitated, and then said quietly, "It looks like you guys are going to have multiple declarations tonight, our call center just lit up like a Christmas tree." Rene made an effort to remain calm and drew a deep breath, "We can't take declarations for recovery right now," she said as calmly as she could. "We're offline."

***

Jack was out of his chair and running down Sixth in time to see the massive bomb at the Seattle Internet Exchange go off. Most people just called it the Westin Building, but Jack knew better. It was a major exchange for traffic on the Internet, one of the biggest in the world, routing e-mails, financial transactions, and even military data from as far away as Hong Kong and Tokyo. Sure, the one in the Bay Area was bigger, but this was the failover for most of the West Coast; it handled a ton of the traffic coming into North America from all points west. Based on the size of the explosion and the color, he knew it was a fertilizer bomb.

Jack's gut told him ELF was behind this, and he was determined to prove it if it was the last thing he did as an FBI agent.

***

Christy punched Andy in the arm as the van rounded a corner and they cruised toward the coffee shop. "I hope you have cash," she said, "because there's no credit cards allowed tonight!" Andy just gaped at her. "What did we just do?" he finally let out.

"We just took out the two biggest polluters in Seattle and made sure that China's economy slowed down for at least a month." The van skidded to a stop in front of the coffee shop and Andy got out. As the crew piled out behind him, he started walking away.

"Hey, Andy! Where you going?" Christy yelled after him. He did not bother to answer.

***

By the time Rene and Bob were done convincing the folks at Data Max that they were completely offline, the scale of the disaster was clear. Every company in the Northwest was being sent to Denver or Phoenix to recover their data. ATMs, e-commerce, electronic banking, check imaging and

17

clearing, supply chain management systems … whole companies were offline and now had to deal with four to six hours of travel time before they could even begin the work of rebuilding their data center's capabilities. Those were the ones that were not synching data to the Seattle Data Max site. They learned that three other companies, normally their competitors in the disaster recovery business, were offline in Seattle too. "We've always been too lax on security," Rene mused.

Jack's boss was setting up a command center on the perimeter of the SIX. Half of the building's façade was missing. It looked like the Oklahoma City bombing, but with more wires and cable. Jack approached his boss as he was finishing barking orders at the local police department. When he turned to Jack, his face was grim. "They cut the fiber optic trunks to all the disaster recovery centers in Seattle before they did this. Those are some sophisticated terrorists."

Jack shook his head. "Or some sophisticated hippy kids," Jack offered. His boss stared at him for a long beat, sizing him up. "They also blew up the data centers at General Lumber and Union Bank," his boss said evenly. Jack nodded again, keeping his mouth shut. "You think it was those kids from the ERR?"

"The ELF," Jack corrected him. "Yeah, whatever. You think this is them?" Jack's boss waved his hand behind him in the general direction of the carnage that once was SIX. Jack nodded. "Then why the hell didn't you warn us?" His bossed growled. Jack said as calmly as he could, "Remember that presentation I gave on radical elements in the green movement three weeks ago?"

"That!?!" Jack's boss barked, "That wasn't a briefing, Jack, you were just spitting out data—there was nothing actionable." Jack remained calm, "I was trying to warn everyone—" Jack's boss cut him off, "Jack, you didn't tell us a thing! You showed us something that some local college kids had been doing, but there was no real threat in the data you showed us!" He slammed his fist on the hood of his car.

Jack, frustrated with the lack of vision in his team spewed out, "If you had half a brain in your head, you would have seen what I saw in that presentation! It was obvious these punks were up to something, and if you'd listen to your gut once in a while you would have known that!"

"Your gut?! Your gut … look, Jack, you know as well as I do that you don't get anywhere in this field without listening to your gut, but you can't just go around showing a fancy slide show and expecting people to just 'know what you mean.' You're a good agent, Jack, but you failed everyone if you were trying to tell us something was going on. You have to say,

'Something is going on!' If you want the team behind you, you have to learn how to show us how things are coming together and what might happen next!" The commander was furious, "Now we've got these amateur kids blowing up three data centers and, as I understand it, just knocked out the Internet for the entire Northwest."

"At least *I* got their story right," Jack said. "What!?!" as the commander shoved him, "What did you say!?" Jack stepped back and shook his head. "Sir, *I* knew what was going on. And because you didn't pick up on it, they took the first strike advantage."

The commander shoved Jack to the ground and snarled, "What good is knowing if you don't do a damn thing about it!" Turning away while he pulled a Marlboro from his pocket and lit it, he ordered Jack back to the office to start processing paperwork.

The Aftermath

The Earth Liberation Front communiqué on the attack said: "We support the struggle and actions of our friends and comrades of 'Tree Arrow Cell' against evil in all its forms. It is time that General Lumber, Union Bank, and its bastard owners and their brainless servants are held accountable for exploiting, violating, and destroying large portions of our forests. The attacks on the recovery centers are to make sure it will hurt for a long time. Innocent lives lost are always painful and regrettable, but they are collateral damage if seen from the perspective of our struggle to liberate Mother Nature from the greedy leeches that are exploiting HER."

A total of nine ecoterrorists were found responsible for the attack that changed the perception of this type of threat forever (Figure 1.3). Twenty-six employees and five bystanders were killed in the attacks. The injured numbered more than 100. Material damages to Data Max and the other recovery centers were overwhelming. The economic damage of this event was felt around the world. The NYSE had to suspend trading for more than three days. Jack McEnroe retired the day they asked him to lead the investigation of the ELF. After his initial failure to communicate his story, he did not think he was capable of leading the investigation.

In the News: Stories that Support the Scenario
- **January, 9, 2009; Santa Clara, California**: A total of ten fiber optic cables were deliberately cut in three different locations in the Santa Clara and San Jose areas. This event left thousands of people in three counties without cell phone, Internet, and landline service

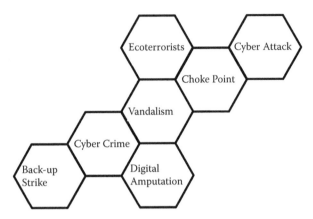

Figure 1.3   Elements of the ecoterrorist attack.

for much of the following day; 911 services were also affected. Among the other impacts were loss of services for Verizon, Verizon Wireless, Sprint wireless, T-Mobile, and AboveNet customers. An estimated 1.5 million users were affected in some way. ATM and credit card processing stopped during the outage.[7]

- A network outage of this magnitude was likely orchestrated by someone who not only knew which manholes provided access to AT&T fibers, but also knew which places on the network were most vulnerable and could cause the most damage. AT&T is offering a $250,000 reward to anyone who can provide information that leads to the arrest and conviction of the vandals. Regardless of whether the cables were cut by disgruntled employees or random vandals, this incident highlights the potential for such an attack to be carried out in a coordinated fashion and/or on a broader scale, by foreign or domestic terrorists.[7]
- In 2006 and 2008, the U.S. Department of Homeland Security sponsored exercises—Cyber Storm I and II, respectively—designed to test the responsiveness of government agencies and private sector assets to coordinated attacks. The latter test simulated a physical telecom and Internet disruption, coupled with "cyber attacks" on critical controls.[8]

In Practice: Data that Supports the Scenario
The scenario above was set in the Pacific Northwest, the cradle of domestic environmental activism. The data warehouses, or recovery centers,

that provide backup services for all the major business continuity and disaster recovery (BC/DR) providers serving this region are clustered in three metropolitan areas: Denver, San Francisco, and Seattle.

Even if our overall preparedness has improved and matured over the years, are we ready for these new forms of vandalism/terrorism that combine low-tech data disruptions with high-tech hacking? The jury is still out. One thing is for sure: Cyberspace is now the playground of criminality, and a faceless crime is hard to trace. The Santa Clara outage is still unsolved.

The FBI considers Ecoterrorism (animal and earth rights extremists) the most serious domestic threat we face. More than 2,000 acts of terror have been committed, causing losses of more than $110 million since 1979. The targets are international corporations, lumber companies, animal testing facilities, and genetic research firms. Yet, Ecoterrorism has never been perceived as a critical threat by our society. This can be explained by different reasons. First, environmentalism, and animal and natural habitat conservation, are seen as legitimate concerns in our society. Large swaths of society, even if they condemn violent acts, feel sympathetic with these issues and some romanticize ecoterrorists as nature's warriors.

The tactics employed, and the focus on property damage, rather than harming people, has diffused societal outrage and kept Ecoterrorism out of the sensationalistic 24-hour news cycle. It is also important to note that society perceives the threats associated with the use of low-tech and known devices, like those employed by the ecoterrorists, as less risky than unknown or high-tech threats, such as genetic research and chemical plants.

The strength of the ecoterrorist movement is difficult to assess. Their organizational models revolve around largely decentralized and loosely affiliated cells, which makes intelligence gathering and prevention very difficult. A few organizations, such the Animal Liberation Front (ALF), the Earth Liberation Front (ELF), and even Greenpeace, walk a fine line between legality and instigation of civil protest and violent acts. Their models foster direct action that can lead loners or new cells to take matters into their own hands.

1.5 THE NARCO-JIHAD STRIKE

It was hot, nearly 102°F in the blazing sun radiating off the large cement walkways and hardscapes of the Governor's Square. Arizona could be so incredibly hot, especially in September because you wanted it to be over.

Emergency Management Director Jason Timbers was trying to find a few moments of inner calm, crossing the public square in front of the federal courthouse in downtown Phoenix. The last three weeks had been crazy for him and all the people involved with the planning of the trial against José "Toby" Aznar, the famous narcotics trafficker.

"I have a bad feeling about all this anger for what's supposed to be just a trial against a criminal. I really don't understand why this trial has got people so worked up," he thought.

The Governor's Square and the streets nearby were filled with Minuteman militias, the tea party faithful, and anti-immigration militants on one side, and cartel members (who sneaked into the United States for the occasion), immigrants (legal and illegal), and immigration rights advocates on the other side. The tension had been building up for some time, but in the last three weeks it had reached unexpected levels. The recent years of Arizona legislation concerning immigration had not helped the situation, and the area seemed tense to Jason.

***

At the same time, the mayor of Phoenix was in his office joking with the new intern. The stress of the last three weeks had not fazed his naturally good-humored self. After all, everyone had worked hard to organize and prepare for what was the most important trial in the state's history. The planning went smoothly, and he was satisfied and confident that all the possible precautions and measures had been taken to prevent any incident. He had already forgotten the big fights with Emergency Management Director Timbers three weeks ago.

***

Frank Jackson was at the Joint Force Office (JFO) across the Square from the Federal Courthouse. He was one of the FBI agents deployed for this "special event." "Is everything ready? Do we have all the cameras on? Are the drones operational?" He chattered his orders while scanning the "screen wall" that consisted of 20 flat-panel displays that were showing the images of the 60 surveillance cameras and the major news networks that were broadcasting the event live. "Prepare for the worst!" he was thinking, "These people don't have a clue what this all means."

***

When the armored convoy carrying Aznar entered the Square, the crowd fell silent for a few seconds as everybody stared at the long line of black vehicles. Jason, as well, turned his head toward the incoming convoy. Out of the corner of his eye, he perceived a bright flash, and before he had time to respond, he found himself forced to the ground by a series of powerful explosions.

The explosions alarmed the crowd, and instantly, people began screaming. Everyone in the Square began running for their lives, stampeding over the injured bodies on the ground, without knowing exactly where to go or what was going on. With every new explosion, scores of people were injured or killed by shrapnel.

***

Jason was still lying on the ground when the explosions stopped. Shaking off the blasts, he tried to clear his head from the deafening ringing in his ears. He talked to himself as he made his way back to the Incident Command (IC) trailer located on the other side of the Governor's Square. "If they only paid attention to what we had said in the briefing. But *no*. This was another big news event for Arizona, the toughest state on Immigration Reform. This was more important than the first NBA title, or the future of the tourism industry in the state. These must be the Syrian Katyusha artillery rockets; they must have mounted them on pickup trucks. Shit! If they only had listened to us!" thought Jason as he entered the trailer.

Frank's eyes were moving nonstop from the screens to the other people in the room; all the "higher ups" that planned the event were there. His expression was a mask of anger, frustration, and disbelief at what he was seeing unfold on the screens. "They're using the same ammunition that Hezbollah used in Northern Israel in 2006; a mix of explosives and steel balls, or metal fragments that are lethal, just like I told you!"

"At least the Secret Service or the FBI is already here," Jason thought as he and Frank were watching four black SUVs arrive on the scene at full speed, blocking the convoy that was trying to take refuge inside the courthouse carport. "Are those yours, Kevin?" asked Jason as he approached.

"No, I thought they were yours," Kevin Clark replied.

They all watched as a total of 16 people exited the vehicles, all in black SWAT-like fatigues. The TV cameras broadcasted the event in real time. The commandos in black uniforms started to move toward the motorcade. Jason took a good look at them and realized, "There is something wrong. Two of them are carrying RPGs! Shit! They must be part of the Zetas! This is exactly what Frank had warned our bosses about! The Zetas are

23

going to try to kill Aznar before he can testify and name other major drug traffickers."

***

Jason was no longer thinking; he left the trailer and began running as years of instinct and training kicked muscle memory into gear. He ran toward the convoy. Over the sound of explosions, he was yelling at the police escort group to take cover, but it was too late. A Zeta opened fire on the convoy and on anything moving in its general direction. A few policemen tried to defend the convoy, but they were quickly overwhelmed by the firepower of the commandos. Concrete and hot steel flashed around Jason's face, and he held his arm up to cover the sting of hot cement hitting his jaw.

Within mere minutes, the Zetas had massacred the entire convoy, killing Aznar and his lawyers. The screaming sirens in the distance did nothing to stop them from driving their trucks out of the Square and toward the streets of surrounding Phoenix. Jason watched in disbelief as they left the Square almost entirely undisturbed. As quickly as they came, they had disappeared, retreating deeper into the downtown area, shooting at anything in their way. The entire event was broadcast on national television. The United States could only look on in shock.

Jason ran back to the IC and spoke quickly with Frank from the FBI. The FEMA Incident Commander was yelling commands in near panic. All of the medical emergency first responders were activated within minutes. Stricken officers and members of the groups at the rally were soon met with the Emergency Medical Attention they needed. Camera crews clambered to get the shots of the life-saving actions now taking place in the battlefield that was once the front of the Federal Courthouse building. Stunned federal and state employees wandered out onto the Square in shock.

"It's a miracle you survived that,'" Frank whispered to Jason. Jason nodded, looking out at the crowd of wounded, dead, and those attending to them. A legitimate SWAT team arrived and surrounded the entrance of the Federal Courthouse. "You know, I listened to your part of the briefing about the Zetas. I didn't believe you, but I was amazed at the military sophistication they had," Jason said.

Frank nodded again, somberly, a calmness settling around him as the damage he could foresee but not forestall unfolded in front of them. "They fight battles like this every day, in border towns from California to Texas. This time they brought the battle to us." The light shifted as the

24

sun started moving behind one of the taller buildings and cast a shadow across the ever-growing group of first responders doing their work in the killing field just outside the window. Amongst the prone bodies of the demonstrators a young child, maybe ten or eleven years old stood swaying. Frank noticed him as a fireman ran past him to attend to the more severely injured.

"Look at that," Frank said to Jason. Jason turned and watched as the boy lifted what looked like a penlight and shone it at a fire truck in the middle of the Square. "What the ..." Frank said. Jason could barely make out the pinpoint of laser light dancing on the side of the truck. Soon the light settled. Frank grabbed Jason and threw him to the ground as a guided missile blasted into the side of the fire truck and expanded out and down in a 60-foot radius, tossing debris and vehicles into the air, shattering the façade of the Federal Building and blowing out all of the glass in every building within two miles. Hundreds were dead instantly.

Within seconds, the death toll leapt astonishingly from 180 to 670 deaths, and the numbers kept growing. Phoenix's hospitals were already overwhelmed. There were not enough ambulances, ER beds, or even blood, to take care of the injured.

Jason got to his feet and yelled at everyone in the room; "Dammit! We told you three months ago that your Hospitals could not handle an incident of this proportion. They are already stretched as it is. I remember telling you that the Hospital system could handle only a surge of patients up to 150–200 people. I also told you that with all of this publicity, and the immigration/racial turmoil, people would come out and demonstrate on the square. Now let's hope that it's not too late, and the situation won't get any worse!"

"How could it get any worse?" Kevin Clark from the Secret Service asked, in shock. "I mean, what was that?" Jason looked at him in awe— *was this guy even in the same briefing as he was three weeks ago?*

"That!?! That was a CCS-C3 Silkworm Missile, and it just killed hundreds of people!" Frank yelled.

The room fell silent.

Frank turned away, angered by the sense of helplessness he felt from what they all witnessed. "That was an act of war," he said quietly.

***

The police poured into the main Square to try to cordon off the crime scene. First responders were doing their best, but it was clear that there were not enough responders for all of the injured people. As Frank and Jason arrived at the Square to see the damage for themselves, they sensed the tension between the "Anglos" and the "Latinos." Jason had tried to calm the crowd a couple of times already, but the situation was on the verge of degrading further at any moment. To aggravate the situation, Frank's FBI guys were cordoning the crime scene and arguing with the locals, slowing the arrival of much needed ambulances. Usually in these situations, the need to preserve the forensic evidence of the crime scene, and the needs of the emergency responders conflicted; it was no different in this situation.

Frank took the call from the FBI Headquarters in Washington, DC, and his boss was furious. "For chrissake, Frank! I don't want excuses! You explain to me now, why after months gathering intelligence on the cartel's intentions, on their capabilities, and on their plans, we managed to be so unprepared for this?" Frank waited a long minute before answering, "At the kickoff meeting we presented the data: the intelligence that was supporting the arrival of new types of weapons from the Middle East, the idea that the Aznar testimony was perceived by the cartel as a life or death issue for the cartels ... all the other clues. We explained to you how the Zetas were changing tactics and buying weapons from the Middle East." Frank's boss yelled into the phone, "That's why I sent you there! You and your friend Jason were two of the most senior people at the planning meeting in Phoenix—didn't you get your message across? What the hell were those protesters doing there?"

Frank was resigned to being dressed down by the Director and held the phone away from his ear.

On one of the monitors, news crews were showing clashes between Mexican-Americans and white militias in the streets and images of the explosion.

Frank finished his call with the Director and turned to Jason; "Jason, what do you think our strategy needs to be here?"

"Do you still have a job?" Jason asked sarcastically. "For the moment," Frank responded.

Jason nodded. "OK. We need to escalate our response to the next level if we want to avoid the same kind of ethnic war between Mexican immigrants and the rest of the population. We need a Presidential Declaration— that means we need to get the Governor involved."

Frank answered bitterly, "Jason, if they didn't believe us three weeks ago at the briefing, when we showed them the data and intelligence we gathered about the light, truck-mounted artillery rockets, and the change

26

in strategy, do you think they will believe us now? We told them everything: how they could attack, this new 'Italian mob' ideology/strategy that the cartel was implementing in their operations, the consequences given the patterns of social tensions among the different ethnic groups, and overradicalized political factions. We told them what the risks were and they didn't take us seriously, now we're going to tell them that if they don't call in the Army and the National Guard we can risk some kind of balkanization of the Southwest? Do you really believe that they will do as we tell them?"

Jason looked back out the window at the carnage. "I hope to God they do."

The Aftermath

Governors of Texas, Arizona, New Mexico, and California have declared a state of emergency and deployed the National Guard to calm the rioting between Latinos and whites (Figure 1.4). The major border crossings of Laredo, El Paso, and Tijuana were attacked by bands of illegal immigrants and were closed for three days.

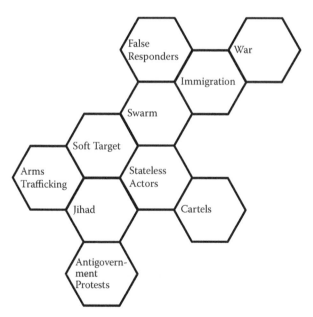

Figure 1.4 Elements of the narco-jihad event.

In the News: Stories that Support the Scenario
- The U.S. Joint Operating Environment (JOE) 2008 Report states that a failed Mexico may present a greater threat to the United States than Pakistan.[9]
- **The *El Paso Times*, January 25, 2009**; Mexico's ambassador to the United States, Arturo Sarukhan, rejected the notion that Mexico might be on the verge of collapse, saying that the U.S. Joint Operating Environment (JOE) 2008 Report was "plainly preposterous" and poor analysis.[10]
- Retired U.S. Army Gen. Barry R. McCaffrey, the former director of the U.S. Office of National Drug Control Policy, said in a separate analysis on Mexico that the government "is not confronting dangerous criminality—it is fighting for its survival and could lose effective control of large swaths near the U.S. border."[11]
- The National Drug Threat Assessment for 2009 says that Mexican drug-trafficking organizations now "control most of the U.S. drug market," with distribution capabilities in 230 U.S. cities. The cartels also "maintain cross-border communication centers" that use "Voice Over Internet Protocol, satellite technology (broadband satellite instant messaging), encrypted messaging, cell phone technology, two-way radios, scanner devices, and text messaging, to communicate with members" and even "high-frequency radios with encryption and rolling codes to communicate during cross-border operations."[12]
- While declaring that the cooperation between U.S. and Mexican law enforcement officials is at its "best level ever," Mexican Attorney General Eduardo Medina Mora urged the U.S. Congress to pass the Merida Initiative, the Mexico law enforcement aid package. While the money is important, he argued, the critical component is the commitment it would represent in terms of U.S. assistance in the drug war. "I have said to my American counterparts that this war cannot be won by either one of us alone," Mora added. "If we do not win it together, we will lose it together." The former U.S. drug czar, Barry McCaffrey, agreed. "This is the most alarming situation I've seen in Mexico in 15 years," he warned. "Our own interests are at stake. We must stand with these people; they're literally fighting for their lives."[13]

In Practice: Data that Supports the Scenario
When we talk about mobs and drug trafficking, we tend to focus on the numbers: how many deaths, how many tons of cocaine, how much money

a year. We look at these breathtaking numbers from the cartel wars on the Mexican border with astonishment and incredulity. What these numbers do not always convey, or what we do not want to see, are the long-term consequences that the drug mobs have on the society, culture, and institutions of the nations in which they take root. Even when "U.S. and Mexican officials describe the drug cartels as a widening narco-insurgency,"[14] our response falls back to the orthodoxy of the law enforcement perspective and the experiences that the United States and our South American allies have gained since the 1980s in the numerous "War on Drugs" campaigns that we have staged.

The situation is so serious that the Pentagon and a wide array of commentators and officials have voiced concerns over the possibility that Mexico will become a failed state in the very near future. Underneath these concerns, there are some fundamental issues, some of which have been compounded by the post-9/11 environment.

First, the Mexican cartels have gained control of the distribution of drugs within the United States, making the Mexican drug lords a U.S. internal problem. The violence related to the ongoing war has spilled well into the Southwestern United States post-9/11; elevated security at the U.S./Mexican border has made trafficking more remunerative, but more difficult, and has enhanced competition for safe routes in the United States among the cartels. As a byproduct, this has created a cocaine market in Europe through Africa, and has combined al-Qaeda and cartel interests in gun and money trade.

The War on Drugs and increased pressure on the cartels has also forced cartels to differentiate their illicit activity into racketeering and ransom kidnapping in the United States. This undermined the social pact in Mexico in which police, political powers, and civil society turned a blind eye on the cartels so long as they and their communities were "indirectly" benefiting economically from the trafficking. Violence was kept to a minimum level, and Mexican territory was used just as a staging area in the drug routes to the U.S. market.

Second, the U.S. intelligence community is very wary of the possibility of a tactical alliance between the cartels and Islamic terrorism. This threat is real. In recent history, drug trafficking and terrorist movements had symbiotic lives: The Shining Path in Peru, FARC in Colombia, the Taliban and al-Qaeda, in Afghanistan. Other types of alliances, connections, or strategies have linked organized crime and terrorist movements. The Red Brigades, Basque Homeland and Liberty (ETA), Irish Republican Army (IRA), and Hezbollah, all had, or have, connections with "mobs"

29

or employed criminal activities as a means to finance their activities. The alliance between Hugo Chavez and the Iran Islamic Republic has heightened these concerns.

Furthermore, Mexico is the second largest U.S. trading partner. The economies of the two countries are so intertwined that, as the recent economic downturn of 2008 has shown, any sudden change in the economic landscape has huge repercussions on both sides of the border. The remittance of Mexican immigrants in the United States is the second largest item in the Mexican economy. In the last two years, these remittances have shrunk, exacerbating the economic crisis in Mexico. The current downturn will make any type of rescue aid from the United States impossible in the case of a deep financial crisis in Mexico, but if the crisis should happen, it will further damage the U.S. economy.

The debate on immigration has become a polarizing issue and has created extreme positions. Populist pundits on one side have helped create resentment toward immigrants. These feelings, which border on xenophobia and racism, dwell on the sense of economical insecurity and social anxiety in the U.S. middle class. On the other side, there has been a resurgence of Latino/Mexican nationalism that brings into discussion not only the assimilation process of immigrants into U.S. society, but also the way in which the Southern part of the U.S. territory has been acquired and who has the natural right to it. In the middle of this discussion, there is a growing Hispanic American population and at least 12 million undocumented immigrants, 56% of which are Mexican.

As already stated, the Homeland Security community has adopted the conventional approach in preparing for a potential Mexican failure. They are planning to provide care for up to 2.5 million Mexican refugees without having them swell the ranks of the undocumented, to provide security to the U.S. border communities, to persecute criminals on both sides of the border, and to intervene in Mexico maintaining the simulacra of two different equal nation-state entities. Does this approach exhaust all the reasonably conceivable scenarios? Is it possible that a "Commander Arkan" would materialize on the U.S.–Mexican border?

Zeljko "Arkan" Ražnatović is mostly unknown to the general public in the United States. His persona and hideous actions, sadly so real, seem out of an action novel. He was born in the former Federal Republic of Yugoslavia to a prominent military family with personal ties to the former country's intelligence: its chief was his father's best friend. Smart and rebellious, he became a career criminal: a hit man for the Yugoslavian secret service, soccer hooligans leader, paramilitary commander, and war criminal during the Yugoslav Wars. He was able to ride the economic and social discontent using soccer, religion, ethnic and racial conflict, and his personal leadership fueled by the "Tony Montana" mobster mythology. The xenophobic Minuteman Civil Defense Corps on one side, and nationalistic and ethnic movements such as the *Movimiento por La Liberation de Aztlan* on the other, are already fertile ground where new types of scenarios could sprout.

1.6 CONCLUSION

Each scenario in this chapter is framed in views borrowed from theories on a new social and market economy we will be exploring in this book. In some cases, the scenarios may have already been considered by practitioners, but by linking them to new tactics and new realities we will be taking them to another level of complexity.

It may seem like we are pulling out all of the stops to create a "perfect storm," but we are just conforming to the inherit complexity of reality. September 11, 2001 and Hurricane Katrina were perfect storms that evolved into complex realities. To quote Malcolm W. Nance, from the *Terrorist Recognition Handbook*, Second Edition, "Common sense is the most disregarded intelligence analysis tool in our arsenal."[15] We are applying various techniques, common to classic disaster scenario planning, in which there are secondary, tertiary, and additional domino effects resulting from the original event. These scenarios can be read as plots for tabletop exercises as well as risk assessments on the current, or soon to be current, threat spectrum.

In the chapters that follow, the reader will be presented with trends and tools that can be used in emergency and crisis management to develop and foresee exactly the types of scenario described. We will also add our view on how to think about these types of events as "worst-case scenarios" and to contemplate their origination from a new perspective. The goal is that the context of these scenarios will start to form based on new insights into how we work with scenario planning and will be easier for the reader to digest.

The reader's first reaction to the opening scenarios in this chapter may be, "That would never happen...." Or, "If there were that many moving parts combined into the perfect storm, it is clear that our response capability would be overwhelmed." The point of this book is that risks *are* emerging and morphing ... and are sometimes multiphased. Perfect storms happen all the time, and they are usually defined as such only in retrospect. At the very least, the reader should be aware of these potentials and not be surprised or caught unprepared by them in the future. Critical thinking about how one might respond, think on the fly, improvise, and plan differently is exactly what these scenarios are designed to inspire.

In Chapter 2, we will establish that hindsight bias has hurt our ability to plan and respond to the unexpected. This book is not suggesting that hindsight bias will be easily overcome by applying creative foresight and new approaches to our practice. Nor is the book suggesting that any of the myriads of challenges in our field, from information sharing to addressing internal civil unrest within the bounds of the Posse Comitatus Act will be easy. Our hope is that this book will educate and inspire critical thinking in our field about what it means to reconsider emergency management scenarios, given theories from several disciplines with unique expertise, so that better scenario planning can be presented and applied in our field in a new way.

REFERENCES

1. Sean Holstege and Dennis Wagner. "Leaders Face Increased FBI Scrutiny," *The Arizona Republic.* Nov. 16, 2008, http://www.azcentral.com/arizonarepublic/news/articles/2008/11/16/20081116scrutiny1116.html (accessed October 6, 2011).
2. Stern, Ray. "Sex Offender Still a Fixture of Downtown Warehouse Rave Scene; City Ponders Yanking Use Permit," *The Phoenix New Times.* March 18, 2009, http://blogs.phoenixnewtimes.com/valleyfever/2009/03/sex_offender_still_a_fixture_o.php (accessed October 6, 2011).
3. Rozas, Angela, Gomer, Jeremy, Ahmed, Azam. "14-year-old Boy Impersonates Cop, Police Say," *Chicago Tribune.* January 26, 2009, http://articles.chicagotribune.com/2009-01-26/news/0901250331_1_police-officers-chicago-police-boy (accessed October 6, 2011).
4. Carter, Ruth. "Recap: No Trou for You!" Improv AZ. January 11, 2010, http://improvaz.com/2010/01/no-pants-az-2010-recap-no-trou-for-you (accessed October 6, 2011).
5. The USGS, Earthquake Hazards Program. April 18, 2009. Summary Report. http://earthquake.usgs.gov/earthquakes/eqinthenews/2008/us2008qza6/ (accessed October 6, 2011).
6. The USGS, Historical Earthquakes. "New Madrid 1811-1812 Earthquakes." Earthquake Summary, (last modified May 4, 2011). http://earthquake.usgs.gov/earthquakes/states/events/1811-1812.php.

7. Diaz, Sam. "AT&T offers $100K Reward in Fiber Optic Vandalism; Notes Second Incident." ZDNet Between the Lines. April 9, 2009. http://www.zdnet.com/blog/btl/at-t-offers-100k-reward-in-fiber-optic-vandalism-notes-second-incident/16106 (accessed October 6, 2011).
8. Government Accountably Office. "Cybersecurity: Continued Attention Needed to Protect Our Nation's Critical Infrastructure." July 26, 2011. http://www.gao.gov/new.items/d11865t.pdf (accessed October 6, 2011).
9. The Joint Operating Environment, "Challenges and Implications for the Future Joint Force," JOE 2008, http://www.globalsecurity.org/military/library/report/2008/joe2008_jfcom.htm (accessed October 6, 2011).
10. Washington Valdez, Diana, "Experts Say Government Stable Despite Mounting Border Violence," *The El Paso Times*. February 2, 2009. http://www.elpasotimes.com/news/ci_11606866 (accessed October 6, 2011).
11. The Velvet Rocket. "Is Mexico a Failed State?" May 10, 2010. http://the-velvetrocket.com/2010/05/10/is-mexico-a-failed-state/ (accessed October 6, 2011).
12. National Drug Intelligence Center, "National Drug Assessment 2009," NDIC, March 25, 2009. NDIC.http://www.justice.gov/ndic/pubs31/31379/ (accessed October 6, 2011).
13. Potter, Mark, "Mexican Drug War Alarming U.S. Officials," RLD Blog, NBC News. June 25, 2008. http://worldblog.msnbc.msn.com/_news/2008/06/25/4376042-mexican-drug-war-alarming-us-officials (accessed October 6, 2011).
14. Steve Booth and William Fainaru. *The Washington Post*. April 2, 2009. http://www.washingtonpost.com/wp-dyn/content/article/2009/04/01/AR2009040104335.html (accessed July 4, 2011).
15. Nance, Malcolm. *Terrorist Recognition Handbook: A Practitioner's Manual for Predicting and Identifying Terrorist Activities, Second Edition*. Boca Raton: CRC Press, 2008; p. 247.

2

The New Face of Risk and the Market State

2.1 KEY TERMS

2.2 CHAPTER OBJECTIVES

After reading this chapter, you will be able to:

- Describe the evolution of disaster preparedness in history.
- Describe the professional practices that are incorporated into the overall role of an emergency manager in the United States today.
- Describe the meaning of the *Disaster Halo Effect* and the role of *emergence* in emergency management planning.
- Describe the impact on emergency management of the shifting geopolitical landscape in which preparedness is based on the worldview that the emergency manager operates in the *market state* as opposed to the *nation-state*.

2.3 OVERVIEW: THE NEW FACE OF RISK AND THE MARKET STATE

Managing risk and the notion of *preparedness* has been part of the human condition for many centuries. Preparedness for war, natural disasters, and today terrorism, has evolved with the threats (both perceived and real) that mankind faces. The current state of preparedness in the United States is shaped by threats once readied for in the past and those threats that *should* be readied for in the future. Two drivers in the practice of emergency management and preparedness today constitute our view of the future and *the new face of risk*:

- The **Disaster Halo Effect**, the recognition that modern threats exhibit more than one "event" and multiple outcomes that can be viewed as being emergent (or evolving) and,

- The worldview of the nation as a **Market State** in which nationalism is replaced with a globalized approach focused on the trading of goods, services, and ideas among **nation-states**.

While it is often assumed that the current amalgamation of approaches to threats and preparedness used in the practice of emergency management is effective, reflecting on recent catastrophic events (both man-made and natural) reveals that the current practice of emergency management is pressed to grow and mature. To do so we must review the historical roots of preparedness that emergency management draws upon, as well as the contemporary events that are pressing the practice of emergency management to change, including the focus on terrorism in the post-9/11 American era, the impact of the Disaster Halo Effect, and the rise of the Market State.

The key lessons of this chapter are that emergency management is a growing and maturing practice that is influenced by the past as well as the present (Figure 2.1). Current events have proven to exhibit the Disaster Halo Effect; therefore, the current approach to preparedness must evolve to better foresee, plan for, and mitigate a *modern* set of entangled events. The role of geopolitics, in the form of Market State thinking, will inform a *new set of rules* as emergency managers practice in an ever-changing landscape. To understand the new rules of risk, the history of disaster preparedness must be considered.

2.4 THE HISTORY OF PREPAREDNESS

The historical roots of our field can be found in the concepts of **contingency planning** and **scenario planning**. Contingency planning is the act of preparing for an unforeseen change in circumstances so that one will not be caught off guard. Contingency planning involves both the ability to

Figure 2.1 Key concepts in this chapter include the history of emergency management including 9/11, the Disaster Halo Effect, and the worldview of the Market State.

foresee circumstances other than those currently at hand, and to "tuck in" or store emergency materials and resources based on those unforeseen circumstances. Similarly, scenario-based planning considers outcomes and alternatives other than the obvious or expected outcome at hand and is used as a tool to aid in preparing for the unforeseen.

In early incarnations of war planning, the ability to spring forth from adversity with determination was viewed as the reward of good planning. Early practitioners of **creative foresight** saw good planning as a rigorous means to an end by protecting what they valued most along the way. The act of creative foresight is building scenarios and imagining situations and circumstances that are unexpected, yet likely, and should serve to further the creation and delivery of new planning models. Early practitioners used contingency and scenario planning as a creative means for staying competitive in the face of adversity and protecting their armies, their wealth, or their status.

Contingency Planning as a Strategic Concept in the Sixth Century BCE

Sun Tzu introduced the concept of scenario planning and contingency planning to military thinking more than 2,600 years ago in his book *The Art of War*. Several of these military strategies included simple concepts such as backups (weapons caches), scenario planning (imagining unforeseen events), and the building of a competitive advantage based on planning for the unknown. He taught that strategy is about responding swiftly and appropriately to changing conditions, rather than simply working through a task list. For Sun Tzu, traditional military planning involved working in a controlled environment. However, he saw that in a dynamic environment, competing plans collided to create situations that often left military leaders unprepared. Military strategies based on contingency planning and creative foresight were viewed by Sun Tzu as being better prepared for the uncertainties of war and, therefore, had to be more agile on the battlefield. His contingency plans were truly flexible scenarios designed to provide the optimum response to changing conditions, and the reward for this planning was winning the battle.

Scenario Planning as a Military Concept 1950–1970

The scenario planning concept reemerged during the Cold War Era as a method for military planning. Following World War II, the specter of nuclear holocaust brought with it a new threat and the need for contingencies and creative foresight. The basic method of scenario planning used an early model of **game theory** (the simulation of military scenarios that combined known facts with plausible variables based on social, technical, economical, and political trends). Herman Kahn introduced the concept of scenario planning and **war games** during the Cold War Era. These war games were often tabletop exercises that tested the limits of the military's imagination and abilities by presenting new contexts in which a war might be fought. In the 1960s, Kahn founded the Hudson Institute and refined scenarios as a tool for business prognostication. He became one of the United States' top futurists.

Scenario Planning and Contingency as a Business Concept: 1970–2000

Scenario planning took on a new dimension in the early 1970s with the work of Pierre Wack, who was a planner in the London offices of Royal Dutch Shell. Wack and his scenario planning team realized that the Organization of Petroleum Exporting Countries (OPEC) could demand much higher prices and disrupt Shell's business. The only uncertainty was *when*, not if. Wack described the full ramifications of possible oil price shocks and warned management that the oil industry might become a low-growth industry.

The contingencies foreseen by Wack and his team helped Shell's managers imagine the decisions they would have to make as a result of an unlikely event occurring. In October 1973, after the Yom Kippur War in the Middle East, there was an oil price shockwave felt around the world. Of the major oil companies, Shell was the only company prepared for the change by having focused more of its operations on downstream reserves and holdings. The company's management responded quickly and, in the following years, Shell moved from one of the weaker oil companies in terms of profit, to becoming the second largest oil company in the world—and the most profitable.

To operate in an uncertain world, business managers needed the ability to question their assumptions about the way that world worked so that they could see things more clearly. The purpose of scenario planning was (and still is) to help executives change their view of reality, to match it more closely with reality as it is, and to propose other possible realities that might come to be. The end result is not always an accurate picture of tomorrow, but it always leads to better decisions about how to operate in the future.

Based on Wack's insights into future market dynamics, corporations stood up and took notice. Later, the Shell scenario planning group envisioned a future in which Shell would not have access to the data (which controlled oil prices and sales) housed on their mainframe computers. Because Wack had been accurate in the past, Shell invested in the creation of information technology backups.

> Scenario Planning is a discipline for rediscovering the original entrepreneurial power of creative foresight in the contexts of accelerated change, greater complexity, and genuine uncertainty.
>
> —Pierre Wack, Royal Dutch Shell, 1984[1]

The use of an offsite storage facility to protect computer backups and vital organizational records by a commercial user, previously used for government documents only (the original Iron Mountain), was one direct result of Wack's scenario planning. Thus, the modern industry of **Business Continuity and Disaster Recovery** (BC/DR) was born. While the definitions of BC/DR vary, for the purposes of this book we set forth the following definitions:

Business Continuity should be understood to mean the acquisition and organization of tasks and materials needed to work around a business interruption in the *absence of technology and computing systems*. *Disaster Recovery* is the focal area of disaster response that deals with technology and business computing systems recovery. The two practices rely on one another, but may have completely different needs and approaches.

Business continuity and disaster recovery spawned completely new industries in the period between the early 1970s and today that were focused on building business contingency plans, data backup and recovery tactics, and strategies.

In the mid-1970s SunGard began as a subsidiary of the oil giant Sun Oil Company, providing remote-access data processing for Sun's Information Services (SIS). A pivotal moment came in the late-1970s when Sun's business had become heavily dependent on computer systems and the company realized that they could lose up to $3 million by the third day if their computer systems failed. SIS President John Ryan had his division develop a disaster recovery plan and business contingency plan for Sun Oil Co., which included daily backups to tape that were stored at an off-site location that could be loaded onto an alternate mainframe should Sun's mainframe computer fail.

In 1978, SIS was approached by a group of Philadelphia businesses searching for a similar disaster recovery solution, which led to SunGard Recovery Services becoming a commercial hot site provider. By the end of 1979, there were more than 100 providers of computer backup services located across the United States.

Over the next ten years, from 1980–1990, the industry grew to generate $240 million in annual subscription fees. Vendors marketed their services as "hot sites" which were designed to provide stand-by computer resources, in the event that one or more subscribers required an alternative computer center to process critical applications. This requirement was usually prompted by an actual or perceived event that could render a subscriber's computer systems inoperable. The activation of the hot site services was initiated through the formal declaration of a disaster. The definition of "disaster" varied by client and, subsequently, hot site providers allowed broader interpretations. For example, some clients have activated their hot site subscriptions during power outages, while other clients activated their subscriptions to simply provide backup during a planned relocation of their data center.

Between 1990 and 2000, the BC/DR industry was composed of 31 major companies, which represented the majority of the hot site providers. Collectively, they generated subscription fees in excess of $620 million annually. The industry had seen substantial consolidation since 1989 that ultimately created a situation in which two companies dominated the market: IBM and SunGard. These companies controlled more than 80 percent of the market in both revenue and subscriber base in the hot site arena.

Financially oriented firms tended to utilize hot sites more frequently due to the critical nature of their operations. In fact, more than 65 percent of all hot site recoveries involved these types of firms. Over the past 30 years, the majority of recoveries have occurred at Comdisco, IBM, and SunGard. These three vendors alone have supported more than 67 percent of all disaster recoveries at hot sites.

Slowly, the perception that creative foresight and contingency planning could provide a competitive advantage for organizations was fragmented away into emergency planning and was simply being responsive to disasters. Many organizational leaders viewed hot site agreements as "expensive insurance policies" and FEMA warned the public to be ready for events that we could hardly imagine.

In the early 1990s, business continuity was positioned mainly in terms of disaster recovery. In the event of a major disaster, technology assets (e.g., systems, networks, applications, and data) were to be "recovered" at an alternate location. The typical recovery time objective (RTO)—i.e., the desired time to recover applications—or acceptable transaction loss—was 24 hours. Most of the enterprises that implemented disaster recovery plans did so because they were in highly regulated industries such as banking and other financial service sectors. In most enterprises, however, BC/DR planners spent their time trying to raise awareness of the need to protect enterprise assets (often unsuccessfully) and fighting organizational apathy toward disaster recovery planning.

By the mid-1990s, business continuity initiatives had expanded to include the recovery of critical work processes. For example, many enterprises recognized that recovering their call center technology was pointless if they lacked personnel to staff the call center itself, or a workplace in which to locate it. Business continuity planning and disaster recovery scenarios remained largely unchanged, as did recovery time objectives.

In the late 1990s, practitioners in the field of BC/DR were viewed as a "necessary evil" of private and public sector life. They became a failsafe for unforeseen catastrophic events and the documenters of audit materials. Of course, many practitioners actually responded to disasters and/or saved their businesses from calamity; however, many *more* sat for years, suffering as they planned and waited for catastrophes that were never visited upon them or their clients. Most of our history of preparing for the potential upsides of good planning, creative foresight, and reaping the rewards of good planning was long forgotten.

The trend toward an expansion of business continuity planning initiatives gathered momentum in the late 1990s. This trend was driven in part by preparations for a potential year 2000 crisis. The year 2000 crisis, or "Y2K" event, was a problem created by a lack of foresight. Many enterprise-level computer programs were not written to "roll over" to a year date ending in 00, as only two character spaces were provided in many programs for the year field and 00 could be interpreted as 2000, or 1800. One result of the year 2000 remediation effort was a massive enterprise investment in re-engineering business processes and implementing integrated enterprise resource planning systems. As they prepared their year 2000 contingency plans, many enterprises began to understand that if their critical systems and applications failed, their business processes would fail along with them, thereby stopping sales, shipping, and manufacturing processes.

The inevitable result would be a severe negative impact on the profitability and possible survival of the enterprise. With this new understanding of their vulnerabilities, enterprises invested heavily in BC/DR between

1997 and 2000. RTOs for mission-critical business processes were reduced to less than 24 hours and sometimes much less; recovery point objectives (RPO) were often set to protect systems up to the point of disaster (i.e., no loss of work or transactions). A *recovery point objective* is an acceptable amount of data lost within a defined time frame. Moreover, the growing interdependencies among internal processing systems and external service providers began to increase the complexity of recovery. However, the other outcome was that any remediation efforts that succeeded were credited to strong computer programming teams that corrected the erroneous code; the over-hyped end-of-the-world scenarios were credited to overly excited BC/DR practitioners who championed the arrival of Y2K as justification for a field that continued to drift slowly away from foreseeing events and avoiding them through planning and moved toward predicting the catastrophic and responding to it.

The Internet, e-business, and the systems that supported them achieved critical mass in 1999 and caused fundamental changes in the way enterprises thought about BC/DR. Enterprises began re-engineering their business processes yet again, this time aligning them with those of their customers, suppliers, and business partners. As a result, RTOs and RPOs were reduced still further as a standard, and in some cases reached zero. (A zero RTO means zero downtime, or 24/7 continuous systems availability). Furthermore, scenario plans broadened to take on new e-business-specific risks, including downtime, caused by:

1. Operational risk (e.g., the three-day Microsoft Web site outage in January 2001)
2. Security risk (e.g., the denial-of-service attacks against Web sites and networks)
3. Lack of capacity (e.g., the spikes in business volumes caused by Victoria's Secret's Internet fashion show)
4. Application failure (e.g., the full-day London Stock Exchange outage in April 2000)
5. Partner/outsourcer unavailability (e.g., the Internet Service Provider network failure or failed links between an enterprise's Web site and its partners' sites)
6. Loss of physical structures (e.g., the facilities lost to wildfires at the Los Alamos National Laboratory)

In the new e-business world, enterprises became deeply concerned about any risk of downtime. Furthermore, any downtime resulted in negative media coverage, which would severely impact the enterprise's image and reputation, as well as its continuing viability. Yet few response plans created during this era actually engaged marketing professionals to craft pointed messages about responses to emergency events, or any form of strong public relations strategies that would offset the resulting negative press caused by such an event. A simple "check box" approach was taken that included contacting a Press and Information Officer (PIO) and having them manage crisis response communications on the fly.

The events of September 11, 2001, had a significant impact on the requirement for sound business disaster planning (see Figure 2.2). Many of the organizations with offices in the World Trade Center (WTC) had BC/DR plans in place as a result of the bomb attack on the North Tower (Tower 1) in 1993. There were a number of stories on the news that following weekend (September 15–16, 2001) about organizations located in the Twin Towers that were fortunately operational at their contingency locations.

By September 14, Comdisco had fielded 73 disaster declarations from 36 companies; primarily financial services firms in the New York area. Comdisco clients filing disaster declarations included 20 security firms, 12 banks, two insurance companies, and the New York Board of Trade.

In a way, the 9/11 terrorist attacks were thought to have completed a 20-year evolution in contingency planning, but they also changed everything (Figure 2.2). The dramatically heightened recognition of the importance of BC/DR was *thought* to indicate a period of increased budgets for dedicated, nonshared recovery solutions for business applications and systems of all types. Planners would have the opportunity to integrate BC/DR into the project life cycles of business processes and applications. Old and new risks would be addressed where they should be— in the business requirements phase of a project, not as an afterthought when production had been completed. Most importantly, there would be newfound business continuity planners who could not only foresee and plan for negative events, but add competitive advantages in their plans; thus, the downstream effects of such an event would not have long ranging Disaster Halo Effects, but would rather yield positive business value during and after an event. After 9/11, enterprise decision makers finally seemed to understand why business continuity was important—the very survival of their enterprises depended on it.

Surprisingly, the period immediately following 9/11 *did not* accelerate business continuity, disaster recovery, or proactive planning as

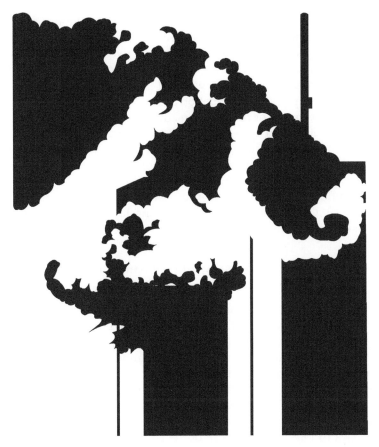

Figure 2.2 It was believed that, after 9/11, Business Continuity and Disaster Recovery in the private sector would be changed forever and completely rethought—but it was not.

expected. Business continuity and disaster recovery planners continued to struggle upstream against corporate apathy, lack of executive support, and—perhaps—even shock. The focus from contingency planning and creative foresight as a positive force for adding value to the enterprise of emergency response had moved so far from its origins that the "expensive insurance policy" stigma remained in place. Practitioners in the field often spoke at conferences about the heroics of first responders such as firefighters, police, and FEMA despite the fact that most in this community, as public sector employees, were rarely in attendance.

Realizing an opportunity existed in ad hoc point solutions and hardware sales, many hardware and software vendors moved into the private sector BC/DR space offering easy, inexpensive fixes for a fearful business world. Post-9/11, the private sector emergency managers fragmented into Business Continuity practitioners who did not agree with hardware solutions being put in place by information technology disaster recovery planners. These private sector practitioners, in turn, often neither agreed, nor coordinated with, security, health, or safety teams, and the private sector practitioners started moving toward the public sector. In short, the focus from contingency planning being a valuable, insightful tool for businesses had fragmented, and in some cases, had been lost all together.

In addition, over the same 30-year period, the public sector, specifically the U.S. Government, was also reacting to new threats through a series of developments in the areas of creative foresight and planning.

Scenario Planning and Contingency as a Government Concept: 1970–2000

From Kahn's early work in war gaming and game theory, the military, the Central Intelligence Agency (CIA), and the Federal Bureau of Investigation (FBI), continued work in the areas of contingency planning and the use of creative foresight. The CIA, created in 1947 under the National Security Act, was the formalization of the Office of Strategic Services (OSS), and is currently chartered with gathering intelligence for the United States on its enemies abroad. The FBI, formed under the United States Department of Justice in 1935, has roots in other agencies in the U.S. justice system dating back to 1908. Under title 28 of the United States Code, Section 533, the primary function of the FBI is to support the United States Attorney General as he or she may "appoint officials to detect … crimes against the United States."[2]

During the period from 1970 through 2000, both the CIA and the FBI were deeply involved in protecting U.S. interests, both domestic and foreign, and deployed a multitude of tactics in the areas of espionage, intelligence gathering, and creative foresight to thwart wartime or criminal activities across a broad range of threats. These threats required surveillance, intelligence, and action by the agencies to assure the safety of Americans. There were many accounts of the use of creative foresight and mechanisms for gathering information on the nature of these threats, and speculation by the two agencies' parts on the impact of varied plots and strategies that might be deployed by our enemies.

During this period, the CIA found itself interacting with rapidly changing geopolitical actors and landscapes. During the Soviet War in Afghanistan that lasted from 1979 until 1989, the CIA monitored and actively supported activities by the Islamist Mujahedeen Resistance similar to the tactics the United States faced during the Vietnam conflict. These tactics were very different than the conventional warfare tactics of World War I and II in that there were often proxy wars, acts of terror, and radical approaches to using smaller forces to disrupt larger conventional armies.

Ultimately, the collapse of the Soviet Union in December 1991 eliminated the largest Cold War threat to the United States. However, it also introduced a series of new nation-states with the will and power to do harm to the United States. The CIA remained actively involved in monitoring these regions through the use of intelligence gathering and other clandestine activities. In a sense, the collapse of the Soviet Union increased the workload of the CIA immensely as small regional conflicts arose, and new, more agile threats emerged.

Certainly, one of the FBI's most seminal cases during this period was the bombing of Oklahoma City's Alfred P. Murrah Federal Building. On April 19, 1994, Timothy McVeigh and an accomplice perpetrated the second deadliest terror attack on U.S. soil, exceeded only by the attacks of 9/11; 168 people were killed in the bombing. McVeigh was quickly apprehended and ultimately sentenced to death for his crime. It is a classic study of the Criminal Justice System and the FBI working together in a case that shocked the United States and was, perhaps, a precursor of things to come.

Meanwhile, during the same 30-year period from 1970 through 2000, the Federal Emergency Management Agency (FEMA) was formed and underwent many changes. From the time it became an independent agency under the 1978 Reorganization Plan No. 3 and was activated by President Jimmy Carter through Executive Order, the agency responded to many disasters including the Love Canal toxic waste incident in 1978, and the Three Mile Island nuclear accident in 1979. James Lee Witt, the Director of FEMA under President Bill Clinton, worked diligently toward focusing the mission of FEMA on natural disaster preparedness and away from civil defense activities that were viewed as competing interests. Witt's contribution to disaster planning and emergency management was immense, including the notion of all hazards planning, in which he invested considerable agency resources. **All hazards planning** meant considering *all threats and scenarios equally* and preparation for *any possibility.*

We should be prepared for whatever type of event that we may face. That is an all hazards plan. If not, shame on us. That is our responsibility.

— James Lee Witt, Former Director of FEMA[3]

Scenario Planning and Contingency Planning at the Beginning of a New Millennium

In the private sector, disaster recovery and business continuity planners struggled with tight budgets and a poor appetite for spending in the post-Y2K business environment. This low priority persisted even as the practice of viewing business preparedness as the act of creating a "three-legged stool" consisting of disaster recovery, business continuity, and employee safety was starting to emerge. In the public sector, the responsibility of preparedness was divided among the CIA, FBI, and FEMA, with little interagency cooperation and less understanding of the roles of each agency. Of course, all of that was about to change.

The 9/11 Attack and the U.S. Public Sector

The attacks of September 11, 2001, confounded the private sector as vendors of hardware solutions, planning tools, and consulting firms jockeyed for position to capitalize on the new fears businesses faced as a result of terror. However, the U.S. Government was not slow to act. The attacks illuminated holes in the fabric of the FBI, CIA, and FEMA in preparedness. On October 8, 2001, the Office of Homeland Security was created by the Executive Order of President George W. Bush. In November of 2002, the Homeland Security Act created the **U.S. Department of Homeland Security** (DHS).

Some 22 agencies were incorporated into the DHS including FEMA, the Customs Service, the Secret Service, the Transportation Security Agency, and many others. The DHS's most current mission statement is, "We will lead the unified national effort to secure America. We will prevent and deter terrorist attacks and protect against and respond to threats and hazards to the Nation. We will secure our national borders while welcoming lawful immigrants, visitors, and trade."[4]

The DHS is tasked with the varied and competitive tasks of civil defense *and* natural disaster preparedness, much like FEMA was before. However, today FEMA is a subset of the larger DHS apparatus and often finds itself at odds with other subagencies beneath the DHS umbrella. It

48

is also important to note that the DHS does not include the FBI, but rather *partners with* the FBI to conduct fact-finding missions and develop intelligence on potential threats.

2.5 TODAY'S EMERGENCY MANAGEMENT STAKEHOLDERS

Today, emergency management practice includes stakeholders from Homeland Security, professionals and consultants, emergency management students (graduate and undergraduate) and professionals, security managers, city, state and federal officials, contingency planners, disaster recovery and business continuity experts, and others who are interested in the current state of emergency preparedness in both the private and public sector. It also includes stakeholders who interact with these groups from the FBI and other intelligence agencies (Figure 2.3).

Perhaps the most interesting group of stakeholders is the layperson who seeks to understand emergency preparedness for personal or business reasons. The breadth of fields in which the interested layperson works and their depth of influence in the discipline cannot be overlooked as it is often a business analyst or a sharp observer of current events who is the most deeply invested in emergency planning in both the public and private sectors. For brevity, the term emergency manager applies to all of these stakeholders within this text. To a large extent, any interested and informed person who cares about the future and the ability to survive it is an emergency manager in their own right.

There is a sense that, after the shock of 9/11, more threats are coming in the Market State era. This new relationship between trade and emergency preparedness has forced the study of emergency management into the public domain and made the field of study applicable from Wall Street to Main Street to Pennsylvania Avenue. Trade itself, on its current globalized, Internet-enabled, high-speed vector is the cornerstone of the Market State. Looking back at the seminal moments of change in preparedness, it is the changing perception of emerging threats that have most impacted the practice of emergency management.

Former DHS Chief Tom Ridge said at a speech in Miami-Dade County, Florida, "We cannot let anything impede the ability of brave men and women to save the lives of citizens as well as their own."[5] Later, the head of the DHS, Janet Napolitano—who has made similar comments on cyber security and other terror threats—said about the H1N1 virus, "To

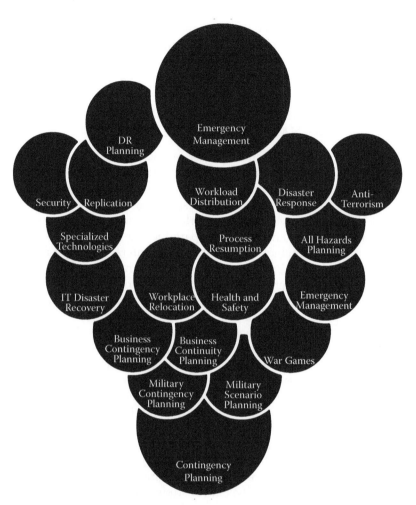

Figure 2.3 The evolution of the emergency management profession. Throughout the history of emergency management, practitioners in the field have worked in various disciplines and held many job titles.

my mind, its purpose goes with something that I've thought all along: that securing America is a shared responsibility. DHS can't do it alone. You need the private sector. You need the academic world. You need the non-governmental organizations."[6] The reality is that the voices of public discontent regarding Homeland Security, the DHS, and Anti-Federalism from extreme groups that see the government as an "evil empire" are so disconcerting that the basic, ethical message that good scenario planning, emergency response awareness, and planning for business and individuals is highly ethical, patriotic, and protects personal value has nearly been buried. Some of these radical groups would even have us believe that the *more patriotic* thing to do during a large-scale disaster would be to resist any government aid!

The simple fact is, talking heads and politicos aside, the United States must realize that when faced with catastrophic disasters or terror attacks, we are all emergency planners—for our country, our communities, our families, and our businesses. *We are all stakeholders in emergency management and we can face that fact now, or wait until a multi-State event reminds us. Just ask any Japanese citizen who experienced the 9.0 earthquake in March 2011.*

2.6 THE FIRST EVENT SCENARIO AND DISASTER HALO EFFECT

One of the changing perceptions of threats today is that disasters and terror attacks exhibit a Disaster Halo Effect (see Figure 2.4). The Disaster Halo Effect is the recognition that modern threats exhibit more than one "event" and multiple outcomes that can be viewed as being emergent (evolving). Often multiple outcomes, or *consequences*, are manifested from a single event; the event we call the **First Event Scenario** in this book. These multiple outcomes can be more dangerous, more costly, and ultimately even more catastrophic than the trigger event itself. The Disaster Halo Effect is based on the notion of emergence, which is studied in the field of social sciences and computer sciences and is used to explain complex and novel systems.

September 11, the Boxing Day Tsunami, Hurricane Katrina, the terror attacks on Mumbai, and the Siege at Beslan are all illustrative of how terror attacks and natural disasters evolve and their effects spread. Consider all of the terrorist attacks and natural disasters studied—then try and find one that *did not* exhibit the Disaster Halo Effect. When is a catastrophic earthquake just an earthquake? Rarely. There are always emergent components to catastrophic events. Emergency managers have started to consider that the domino effect found in events like these is becoming more frequent, and they are right. The Disaster Halo Effect is becoming the norm *because of the increased complexity of our planet and the interaction of our modern technologies and social structures*; yet many emergency management

51

Figure 2.4 The Disaster Halo Effect looks beyond the primary, secondary, and tertiary events of the First Event and includes *all* the events that ripple outward from a disaster.

practitioners are surprised by the Disaster Halo Effect and do not incorporate it into their recovery planning. Specifically:

1. Emergency management professionals are often surprised by the radical novelty of the natural disasters or terror attacks they face, mostly due to previous expectations created by **hindsight bias**. Hindsight bias is the tendency to say, "I've never seen it that way before, so it couldn't be that way now." For example, the fact that the earthquake in Chile that occurred February 27, 2010, *did not* create a tsunami that struck Hawaii was novel because it did not match emergency managers' expectation of *what should happen* based on previous events.

2. Emergency management professionals are often surprised by the *coherence* or *correlation* that catastrophes exhibit. Thinking that water scarcity and civil unrest are the unexpected outcomes of a large-scale event versus *expecting there will be* multiple coherent outcomes as a result of the First Event Scenario is one example. The on-the-ground reality is that the availability of fuel will increase the giving of aid, which will impact the likelihood of civil unrest.

Notions like these seem to evade the typical emergency manager. Often, emergency managers do not see these correlations and bring them together into a single view of catastrophes or attacks. Yet, time and again, the correlations exist.

3. Emergency management professionals are often surprised by the global or macro-level sub-events of the events they plan for and respond to. However, if the first 10 years of the new millennium has proven anything to the emergency management community, it is that the world is more connected, more integrated, and more reliant on other nations' attitudes, approaches, and support, or lack thereof, during these events. In addition, natural hazards are being tracked globally now more than ever and there is a globalized, worldwide scientific review of these events that makes few, if any of them, local.

4. Emergency management professionals see the evolution of disasters and terror attacks as the product of a dynamic process, but are wary of approaching catastrophe with a wide-angle view that considers that most, if not all events, exhibit the Disaster Halo Effect.

5. Emergency management professionals *do* perceive that the complexity of modern attacks and disasters is demonstrable and obvious, but seem confounded by this observation. They continue to deal with events as one-off issues, as opposed to one major event with multiple emergent issues imbedded within.

On the one hand, emergency management professionals seem to perceive that catastrophes are evolutionary and dynamic. On the other, there is a lack of terminology or an attitude of attack that reflects a mastery of the Disaster Halo Effect in the field. Often, the scope of emergency management scenarios are ratcheted down, budgets are restricted, and myopic views of "what would really happen" hamstring efforts to plan for and mitigate what has happened time and again—the Disaster Halo Effect in natural catastrophes and terror attacks.

In 2008, the DHS's Michael Chertoff gave a speech at the Wharton School of Risk Management in which he remarked that, "The problem is that responding to disasters after they occur is not risk management. That's suffering the consequences of unmanaged risks."[7] Risk management and emergency management share this problem of hindsight bias and a lack of command around the Disaster Halo Effect. Many programs, systems, and practices are in place to improve the emergency managers' ability to look forward and plan for terrorist attacks and catastrophic disasters, but the past nine years have shown that emergency managers can be caught off guard by these events. *There is a tendency to look back at emergencies after they have occurred as opposed to looking forward—anticipating and preparing for them.*

The Disaster Halo Effect is one of the looming issues facing our field. To better understand the Disaster Halo Effect, consideration should be given to the concept of **emergence**. Jeffrey Goldstein provides an excellent contemporary definition of characteristics of emergence: "The common characteristics are: (1) radical novelty (features not previously observed in systems); (2) coherence or **correlation** (meaning integrated wholes that maintain themselves over some period of time); (3) a global or macro level (i.e., there is some property of "wholeness"); (4) the product of a dynamic process (it evolves); and (5) "ostensive" (it can be perceived). For good measure, Goldstein throws in supervenience—downward causation."[8] Radical novelty, correlation, global dynamic, and perceivable are all terms emergency managers should consider when dealing with the new face of risk.

Taking a moment to consider these terms, the shape of the new face of risk begins to take form. **Supervenience** is the concept that something is literally coming out of something novel, additional, or unexpected, and is the relationship between *super*, meaning on, above, or additional, and *venire*, meaning to come. The idea that emergence is supervenient is to say that emergence always includes outputs that are unexpected, yet correlate to the First Event Scenario. **Radical novelty** is the concept that an event or thing is more than simply new or "novel"—it is totally unexpected and unique to the event. The term **global dynamic** suggests a shift in thinking toward the scope of events in an ever-shrinking world with heightened interdependencies. Finally, **perceivable** means all of these emergent qualities can be seen, measured, and documented. Taken together, these hallmarks of emergence shape a new perspective from which to consider disasters.

The basis of sound planning and first response lie in the foundational understanding of risk itself and that risk has become *emergent*. The pioneer psychologist G. H. Lewes coined the term "emergent," regarding which he says:

> Every resultant is either a sum or a difference of the co-operant forces; their sum, when their directions are the same—their difference, when their directions are contrary. Further, every resultant is clearly traceable

in its components because these are homogeneous and commensurable. It is otherwise with emergence, when, instead of adding measurable motion to measurable motion, or things of one kind to other individuals of their kind, there is a co-operation of things of unlike kinds. The emergent is unlike its components insofar as these are incommensurable, and it cannot be reduced to their sum or their difference. [9]

Later, Goldstein adds supervenience, or **downward causation**, to complete his definition of emergence. Downward causation is the idea of self-organization and the causal impact of large-scale events on small-scale events. Goldstein is presenting a kind of "domino effect" theory in his work, which expands on the notion of "one thing leading to another" and sets forth the simple concept that, in nature, one thing leads to *many* others because it is convenient and perhaps, even necessary.

For example, emergence would view the falling of the Twin Towers as more than just one thing leading to another. There is no set sequence to emergence, but a trigger event that has multiple and random outcomes—from the second tower falling to the lung disease and other ailments found in our heroic first responders to that event years later. Goldstein's theory is much closer to the truth about disasters and terror attacks than the simple notion of primary, secondary, and tertiary impacts. It considers all outcomes as likely *and* random given a large enough first event.

The Disaster Halo Effect exhibits all the hallmarks of emergence and has a supervenient quality, which is the quality of large-scale events causing multiple smaller events. This is particularly noteworthy for emergency management professionals. Supervenience is the backbone of rapidly evolving, quick, and highly dynamic events. If something can be influenced by a larger force and is quick and easy to do, then it will be used and used by many—in terrorism and in emergency response. Terrorists will leverage the supervenient to their advantage, as will Mother Nature (after all, water does flow downhill), and when possible, *the emergency management professional should too.*

In the 2009 Santa Clara cable outage, when vandals cut emergency 911 lines, first responders used the social media tool Twitter to update as many people as they could, as fast as they could, about the situation. This is an excellent example of the supervenient in practice by emergency management professionals. The larger scale idea of Twitter was used to respond to a smaller scale challenge—communication during an outage. Emergence cannot be undersold or disregarded. It is a fact of life for emergency management professionals and rears its head as the Disaster Halo Effect, and/or our response to it.

Globalization, technological acceleration, the media, and other factors have all been applied to justify the intense novelty and emergent quality of contemporary events. However, little has been done to test the limits of the field's ability to predict, plan for, and respond to them. Emergency managers are much better prepared to cope with the modern reality of the new face of risk *if they are taking the Disaster Halo Effect into account* and utilizing it in scenario building, planning, and response. Returning to a myopic view and single event-based approach is no longer tenable. Neither is limiting the field of practice to doomsday scenarios that add little benefit to the organizations we support.

2.7 THE RISE OF THE MARKET STATE

The other changing perception of threats today is that disasters and terror attacks take place in a new geopolitical landscape referred to as the Market State. The Market State is a worldview of the nation in which nationalism is replaced with a globalized approach focused on the trading of goods, services, and ideas among nation-states. The Market State is defined as nation-states that "are becoming increasingly skillful in enlisting the support of market forces to achieve their own objectives."[10] The Market State concept is reflected in the writings of many knowledgeable authors.

This notion that the state is a market and, therefore, is measured by the goods, services, ideas, and ideologies it transfers to and from other nations has created some of the most thought-provoking books of our generation. Consider Thomas Friedman's *The World is Flat*, in which he lays claim to a new market era in which he starts thinking, "How can I use my own network—or the network of others—to take the streaming video coming off that drone and feed it, live, to flat-screen TVs in the CIA, the DIA, the NSA, Army intelligence, and Air Force intelligence, and then integrate each of those analysts into a single chat room, so they can type their response to what they are seeing and what sort of threat it poses, and that chat will come up alongside the screen, so we all can analyze it together?"[11]

In Friedman's proposal, the data is the goods. The trans-silo sharing (CIA, DIA, NSA, and so forth) of that data is made possible by placing a higher value on the goods, and the transfer of those goods, than it does on the silos. The data coming in from the drones becomes a commodity to such a high degree that the internal silos are broken away and the Market State reacts in an agile and competitive, not reactive, fashion. The notion that a flat world creates a more interactive, competitive, and data-rich information-sharing environment as a clear byproduct of the Market State can be witnessed today by anyone. However, emergency managers have been slow to respond to this new perception of national identity *and* the threats and risk that come with it. In addition, the potential upside scenarios that would be incumbent on the classic school of contingency planning are now absent from any variant of emergency management practice when they are needed the most in the Market State era.

A shift to the Market State era means that the interplay between nations and their leaders is based in market thinking and informs decisions and the distribution of aid. It also means that stateless actors can "market" their ideologies and tactics across borders more readily. Consider the rapid response of Venezuela's leader toward Haiti after the 2010 earthquake that rocked that region. Was it a marketing ploy? Was it a method of *trade* more than a means toward humanitarian aid? Many would argue that it was. What is assumed is that after the aid would come ideology, and ultimately politics, based on the market exchange of goods and services between the two nations.

Consider this report from CBS News: "Venezuela has stepped up its aid effort to Haiti as a second earthquake rocked the Caribbean country again today. This follows a 7.3 magnitude earthquake, which destroyed the Haitian capital, Port-au-Prince, last week leaving at least 75,000 people confirmed dead, 250,000 injured, and millions homeless. 'It seems that the United States is militarily occupying Haiti, taking advantage of the tragedy, 6,000 soldiers have arrived. Thousands are disembarking in Haiti as if it were a war,' Chávez said during his weekly television program 'Alo Presidente' on January 18. A few days later on January 25, President Hugo Chavez refused to respond to calls by rich nations for Venezuela to forgive the debt Haiti owes it. In the wake of a massive, deadly earthquake that hit impoverished Haiti on January 12, several industrialized countries and international organizations have called for countries owed money by Haiti to write the debts off. Haiti's debt with Venezuela is among the biggest, at $167 million, according to a report at the end of 2008 from the International Monetary Fund. 'Some are using this issue to make Venezuela appear to be an insensitive country … saying it has to announce (the nation's plans regarding Haiti's debt) plans,' Chavez said."[12]

On the other hand, consider the participation of the Yakuza (Japanese Mafia) in the 9.0 earthquake that struck on March 11, 2011. Jake Adelstein of *The Daily Beast* wrote in his article "Yakuza to the Rescue," "There is an unwritten agreement amongst the police and the Yakuza groups that is acceptable for them to perform volunteer activities during a crisis but not to seek publicity for it." He also quoted a Yakuza member saying, "Please don't say any more than we are doing our best to help. Right now, no one wants to be associated with us and we'd hate to have our donations rejected out of hand," and "There are no Yakuza or *Katagi* (ordinary citizens) or *Gaijin* (foreigners) in Japan right now. We are all Japanese. We all need to help each other."[13]

Does current emergency management offer more value when positioned as the "coin of the realm" for nations at risk? Have we marketed the value of a strong, safe, secure, and prosperous United States with any meaning or effect? Strong emergency management *is* a democratic imperative, yet few of us challenge the armchair naysayers and conspiracy theorists. Without a concentrated effort in the United States to rebrand emergency management as the hallmark of patriotism and democracy, and position a new contingency planner in the private sector that delivers true business value, you can bet that the United States will not successfully compete in the Market State world as a first-place nation for very long.

To better understand the shift to a Market State world, Figure 2.5 illustrates the role of history and various eras of sociopolitical orientations:

In a stateless world, hunter/gatherers protected territories. In the Feudal State world, kings and lords protected farmlands and property. In the Empire State world, emperors and kings protected vast expanses of claimed land called "empires." In a nation-state world, nations and "superpowers" protected national interests using the threat of war. In a Market State world, nation-states in the form of unions protect the trade of commodities, commerce, and aid.

The lower panels in Figure 2.5 suggests a shift in global priorities to a focus on politics, values, dependence, and religion driven by market incentives at the state level and, thus, the Market State emerges.

Figure 2.5 Moving to the Market State. In this figure of the Market State, the top panels show the goods controlled, and the bottom panels show the range of control.

2.8 EMERGENCY MANAGEMENT
AND THE MARKET STATE

Nationalism, values, religion, and messaging play a role in predicting and responding to both natural and man-made disasters in a Market State world. When emergency managers consider the term "marketing," they may have a hard time reconciling it with their daily practice in the field. You may ask yourself, "How do marketing concepts and this idea of a Market State affect me?"

Marketing consists of the commercial functions involved in transferring goods, be it products or ideals, from the producer to the consumer. That said, the Market State worldview is not about selling hot dogs or sneakers. It is not about simply advertising or "hawking" goods.

Marketing plays a role to be sure, but not in the simple sense of selling. The Market State worldview hinges on the idea, for example, that the past World Wars look nothing like the prolonged war on terror. However, World War II certainly serves as a key early indicator as the world shifted toward the postmillennial, 9/11 era. World War II began September 1, 1939, when Nazi Germany engaged in a campaign of war against Poland, and eventually all of Europe and Russia, based on the nation-state concepts of territory and ideology. However, Japan did not join World War II until more than two years later on December 7, 1941, for completely different reasons—Market State reasons. Japan joined World War II to protect its interest in trade routes and its access to Indonesian oil.

Today, ideologies and politics are traded across borders just like goods and services. With the understanding that these are key to winning the war on terror and have a direct impact on international aid and disaster response, mankind is now moving on a long road, away from stand-alone nation-states, to integrated Market States, in which there are huge stakes at play in planning to be a good neighbors, partners, and protectors of the people.

Consider what Phillip Bobbit, the author of *The Shield of Achilles*, has to say about the Market State: "[T]he simple difference between the two is that the nation-state derives its power through its promise to improve its citizens' material wellbeing, while the Market State is legitimized through its promise to maximize its citizens' opportunities. Or to put it another way, where the nation-state—be it fascist, communist, or democratic—is highly centralized, the Market State is fragmented and is run by outsourcing its powers to transnational, privatized organizations."[14] Bobbitt's definition of the Market State extends beyond terrorism to include natural disasters such as floods and earthquakes: "It's how governments respond that is important."[14]

Bobbit continues, "As the territorial membrane weakens, the distinction between law and strategy collapses. The threats we will soon be facing are not easily categorized as state aggressions. Indeed, for the first time since the birth of the state, a state structure is no longer necessary in order to organize violence on a devastating scale. And yet, this development makes the role of the state all the more crucial in achieving international peace and national security. This is because only a state can achieve a successful shift from retaliatory, threat-based strategies to defensive, vulnerability-based strategies. A market can never coordinate defensive tactics into a strategy; it requires a state, even if it is a Market State. In the new era, the state will be as indispensable to peace as it was in the past."[15]

As practitioners in the field, we must amplify the simple concept of being participants in achieving international peace, national security, and reestablishing the United States as the lamppost of democracy for the world. In the private and public workplace, we must elevate our practice, increase awareness, and combat apathy and bad news with action, responsibility, and pride. We will explore this notion later in this book.

Royal Dutch Shell, in its *2005 Global Business Scenario* report, put forth the concept that the Market State emerges from, "Two crises—in short, 9/11 and Enron—that have unfolded since 2001, affecting national security and trust in the marketplace. Both have highlighted the vulnerability of our globalized world. Western societies now expect the state to lead the restoration of physical security and market integrity. Middle Eastern, Asian, African, and Latin American societies have heightened expectations of peaceful solutions to wars and to persisting poverty. In addition to market incentives and community aspirations, these dual crises brings into sharper focus a third force, namely the power of the state to regulate and coerce."[10]

It is interesting to note that one of the "dual crises" cited by Royal Dutch Shell is the Enron debacle. The recent global recession, if nothing else, only amplified the Market State worldview and heightened an international sense of interconnectivity and shared risk. Emergency management practitioners who view their practice from a nationalist point-of-view, in which protecting the Homeland can occur without consideration for the Market State worldview, are naïve at best. Our ability to protect the Homeland from terror and natural disaster is fully dependent on the policy and politics of the Market State worldview, not to mention the globalized media.

The profession of emergency management is well positioned today to meet the expectations of emerging markets and their needs for solutions to persistent poverty and the lack of personal security given the history of our practice and its core skills. Given the number of U.S. companies sending their U.S. emergency managers into emerging markets to start BC/DR planning for those business units, we are the largest group of international ambassadors for security, democracy, and caring currently being deployed outside of U.S. aid groups and military.

The Market State and the Public Sector

In addition, the Market State worldview is very much at play in the United States, which is, after all, a *republic* of states. The DHS and FEMA rely on a state to declare a state of emergency before they take federal action toward providing relief. Because of a false sense of freedom to secede from the Union, many states are voicing their opinions about current policy and politics and threatening secession. It is interesting to note that among them is Arizona, which particularly takes issue with continuance of governance in a state bill titled HCR 2024: "If the President or any other federal entity attempts to institute martial law or its equivalent without an official declaration in one or more of the states without the consent of that State … individual members of the military return to their respective States and report to the Governor until a new President is elected."[16] In 2010, as many as nine states had similar bills under consideration, and while none of them have been passed into law, state governments are showing their reticence to yield to federal power, which has a vast, if not enormous, impact on emergency management. Consider too, that as of this writing, 26 states are challenging the federal government on the Health Care Reform Act, and other states contest the issue of federal influence on their sovereignty on issues ranging from immigration law to gun laws.

Behind these proposed state laws and the policy-makers that draft them, is the concept that the state is a consumer of federal goods and services. In a Market State world, certain security expectations in both the physical and market realm are brokered through state bills, policies, and political ploys. Emergency managers would be ill-advised to not sit up and take notice of the impact these dissenting political voices have on their field. They are a reflection of a populace that is wary of the federal government and which is wielding its influence strongly enough to gain the attention of governors and other policy-makers within their states.

The DHS and FEMA may meet resistance at instituting any control over a disaster or terror impacted state if that state chooses to leverage their Market State advantage. Their actions could subjugate its people to whatever harm such a catastrophe may bring simply to broker more power, funding, or influence at the national level. The reality of the U.S. landscape today is that Market State influences are shaping popular perceptions about our government. One needs to only look at recent lawsuits and state government claims that new health care regulations are illegal to begin to understand the dynamic of the Market State at play in the United States.

The FBI and DHS, as of this writing, are watching a group called the Guardians of the Free Republics for sending letters to governors that stated that they should leave office or they would be removed. The group wants to "restore America" by peacefully dismantling parts of the government, according to its Web site. FBI investigators did not see threats of violence in the group's message or the letters, but feared that the broad call for removal of top state officials could lead others to act out violently. Several states beefed up security in response.[17] Radical and extreme political worldviews in the United States are a symptom of the Market State era. They point to small groups bonding together as states, wielding power, and becoming contentious over resources.

At home and abroad, the emergency management field is now faced with a worldview that is extremely volatile and inclusive of many moving parts that simply were not recognized as in play prior to the new millennium. We ignore them at our own peril! Understanding that the Market State worldview can, and will, hamper or help in our ability to give aid and response to disasters and terror attacks for the coming years is a key to our effectiveness (see Figure 2.6). Changing this misguided perception about our field is an absolute necessity! The Market State world is a dangerous place, more dangerous and threatening than in previous eras; yet it holds out the promise that emergency management can master its skills, reposition its field, and engender trust, build security, and deliver the

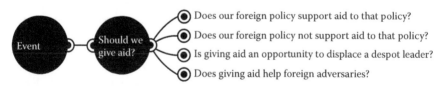

Figure 2.6 This decision-making tree illustrates the complexities at play when choosing to give aid to a foreign nation-state.

United States back to "the Land of the Free and Home of the Brave," even in the midst of discontent and fear that currently dominates our culture.

The Market State and the Private Sector

When first encountering the notion of a Market State world, we might assume it is purely a geopolitical view and merely impacts the work of emergency managers in the public sector. Certainly, our national stance on terrorism and disasters worldwide is impacted by this new development in geopolitical thinking; but the other influence is deep within private sector companies and has had a vast impact on how they conduct their emergency management programs.

Consider large multi-national companies that emergency managers might serve. The Market State environment encourages international trade and opens international markets. The term globalization is directly linked to the concept of the Market State. We are encountering more and more organizations, especially those in the Fortune 1000, which rely on foreign markets for the manufacture and sale of goods and services (see Figure 2.7). The term "emerging market" is often used to describe far-off consumer and business-to-business markets that were not previously within the scope of the private sector emergency manager's work—today they are.

Market State policies have been crafted to encourage trade and, therefore, increase the globalized supply and demand chain of companies

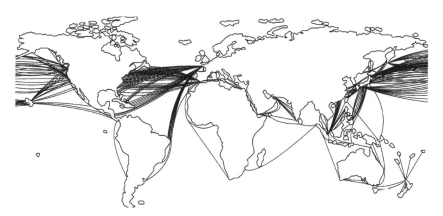

Figure 2.7 This illustration of global shipping lanes shows the interconnected nature of the Private Sector.

across multiple nation-states. Large enterprises often refer to markets in four geographic categories: the United States, EMEA, ASIA-PAC, and CANLA. EMEA is short for Europe, the Middle East, and Africa. ASIA-PAC usually stands for East Asia, Southeast Asia, and Oceana, although sometimes this area will also include Russia. Finally, CANLA is optional (as the United States can be replaced with the term The Americas), which includes Canada and Latin America. Many U.S.-based companies have interests in all of these market sectors and trade agreements come into play for each.

The North American Free Trade Agreement, or NAFTA, is an agreement the United States entered into with Canada and Mexico in the mid-1990s to increase trade in the Americas—continents connected by both landmass and similar political interests. While controversial from a public policy perspective, the Agreement has and will continue to create cross-border operations within this trade zone for U.S. companies that, prior to the Agreement, may have solely done all of their business in the United States. Today, U.S. firms operate many functions in Mexico and Canada, from manufacturing to management, and customer service operations.

A key provision of the Agreement to consider is called the "rules of origin," which dictates how much of a given object can be manufactured in Canada or Mexico before it is *not* considered to be "made in America." We might be surprised by the guideline. One such provision (from the Kyoto Convention) states that a product that has been produced in more than one country can be determined to have "origin" in the nation in which the last transformation took place. In other words, we might be working for a company in the private sector that has "Made in America" on every one of its products, only to learn that every piece of that product came into existence in Mexico or Canada and was finally assembled, or even partially assembled, in the United States and experienced its "last transformation" in the United States, thereby becoming "Made in America."

What NAFTA means to the emergency manager is that the private sector assets that need to be protected for their client may range from manufacturing plants in Mexico, to project management and customer service offices in Canada. From the supply chain to the distribution chain, the Market State effect of NAFTA is that very few companies can be wholly protected from risks that occur only in the United States, as they are dependent on international conditions to manufacture and sell their products.

Another similar economic and political policy is the European Union, or EU. The EU has created a single market that currently extends across 27 "member states" and is a hybrid system of import/export laws and monetary policy. Amongst other policy components, the EU focuses on social policy as well as economic cohesion. Much like NAFTA, it spreads the manufacturing, sales, and service of goods across multiple independent, yet networked nations. Nations that are party to NAFTA and EU trade agreements encourage through policy, taxation, import/export, and free trade among multiple nations. These practices have extended once U.S.-only companies to locations around the globe.

A similar driver, the interest in cost advantages and investment in "emerging markets" has caused many private sector companies to further fragment their businesses into India, Middle Europe, and China. What the Market State geopolitical environment has done for business has created a situation in which risk, along with the potential for reward, is now spread globally. What this means to the emergency management programs of these companies is that far-off risks can have very local impacts.

In the 1990s, many private sector emergency managers began standing up internal, headquarters-focused, U.S. programs for their clients. Today, these programs are being rolled out to supply-chain factories, component manufacturers, design departments, customer service centers, and other organizational assets worldwide. The Market State has changed the face of U.S. business in such a way that few emergency managers act independent of events around the globe, as they have the potential to impact the U.S. operation of an organization and the bottom line significantly. Increasingly, a sense of security, the hope of democracy and better living conditions, and care for employees abroad can only be good for business. Emergency managers working in globalized organizations should consider this as a top priority.

Realizing that the U.S.-based companies that employ us, and serve our needs as citizens, most likely have foreign assets and, therefore, foreign risk, significantly changes the role of the private sector emergency manager. Events half the world away can and will have an impact on the U.S. companies we serve, and designing programs for globalized companies here has a much broader scope than designing programs for "U.S.-only" companies.

The transnational agreements and arrangements that now extend enterprise around the world are the domain of wise emergency managers who are managing risk for U.S. companies. Distant events can have very real consequences locally, or here in the United States. In addition, the shape, scope, and approach to emergency management planning may be very different abroad than it is here in the United States.

The maturity of first response capabilities, the understanding of operating models and local law, and the legalities of protecting employees as well as computing and manufacturing hardware become highly nuanced and varied. The demands we face as emergency managers to generate appropriate levels of protection for our U.S.-based clients are quickly complicated by the Market State influence of globalization.

The history of preparedness, the Disaster Halo Effect, and the Market State have forced a change in how private sector organizations perceive preparedness. International law, local laws and customs, and the intertwined nature of business today, demand a global view and command over the practice of emergency management unlike any other time in the history of our discipline. Today's emergency manager is faced with global realities (Figure 2.8) and, as we will explore later in this text, the threats and opportunities that come with this new, much broader field.

2.9 CHAPTER SUMMARY

Looking back on this chapter, the relationship between the history of preparedness and large-scale threats is described. Emergency management

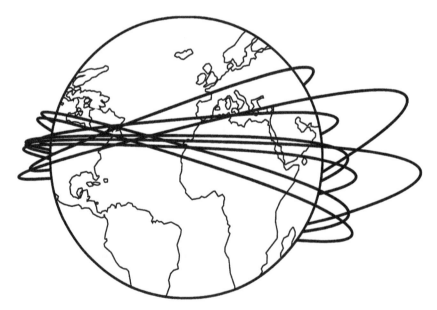

Figure 2.8 Our interconnected world.

has been moved to higher levels of practice and broader areas of awareness with every new event. Looking forward, we can see that the Disaster Halo Effect and the reality of the Market State are influencing emergency management today. The chapters that follow will explore what is now needed to better cultivate, design, develop, and operate emergency management and preparedness thinking under these conditions.

2.10 END OF CHAPTER QUESTIONS

1. How has the perception of new threats impacted the evolution of preparedness through history?
2. Describe the varied professional practices that have evolved in the field of emergency management and the broader interest that the layperson has in preparedness in the United States today. Explain the reasons for your answers.
3. What is the impact of the shifting geopolitical landscape and the difference in the way that the emergency manager should operate in the *Market State* as opposed to the *nation-state?*
4. Describe the meaning of the *Disaster Halo Effect* and the role of *emergence* in emergency management planning.
5. How does the Market State worldview impact U.S. effort in emergency management on a State and Federal level?

REFERENCES

1. Royal Dutch Shell Group. 2005. *Shell Global Scenarios to 2025, the Future Business Environment: Trends, Trade-offs, and Choices.* London: Royal Dutch Shell. Page IV.
2. 28 USC CHAPTER 33 - FEDERAL BUREAU OF INVESTIGATION Act, U.S. Code 28 (1966), sect.533.
3. Witt, James Lee. Leadership in Disaster Response. Speakers Notes. The University of Delaware. http://www.training.fema.gov/ (accessed October 6, 2011).
4. U.S. Department of Homeland Security. "One Team, One Mission, Securing Our Homeland." *U.S. Department of Homeland Security Strategic Plan Fiscal Years 2008–2013.* March 20, 2008. http://www.dhs.gov/xlibrary/assets/DHS_StratPlan_FINAL_spread.pdf (accessed February 8, 2011).
5. Latoff, Blair. *Secretary Tom Ridge to Chair U.S. Chamber's National Security Task Force.* January 26, 2011. http://www.chamberpost.com/2011/01/secretary-tom-ridge-to-chair-us-chambers-national-security-task-force/ (accessed July 4, 2011).

6. U.S. Department of Homeland Security. Remarks by Secretary of Homeland Security Tom Ridge at Miami-Dade Office of Emergency Management. July 30, 2004. http://www.dhs.gov/xnews/speeches/speech_0197.shtm (accessed October 10, 2011).

7. U.S. Department of Homeland Security. *Remarks by Homeland Security Secretary Michael Chertoff at the University of Pennsylvania Wharton School on Risk Management.* October 16, 2008. http://www.dhs.gov/xnews/speeches/sp_1224524493787.shtm (accessed March 17, 2010).

8. Corning, Peter A., PhD. "The re-emergence of 'embergence': A venerable concept in search of a theory." *Institute for the Study of Complex Systems.* July 6, 2002. http://www.complexsystems.org/publications/pdf/emergence3.pdf (accessed March 17, 2010).

9. Lewes, George H. *Problems of Life and Mind: The Foundations of a Creed.* Vol. 2. London: Trübner, 1875.

10. Royal Dutch Shell Group. "Executive Summary of the Shell Global Scenarios to 2025." *Shell.* November 5, 2005. http://www.static.shell.com/static/about-shell/downloads/our_strategy/shell_global_scenarios/exsum_23052005.pdf (accessed March 15, 2010).

11. Friedman, Thomas L. *The World is Flat: A Brief History of the Twenty-First Century.* New York: Picador/Farrar, Straus and Giroux, 2007.

12. Janicke, Kiraz. *Venezuela Steps Up Aid Effort to Haiti, Questions U.S. Military Deployment.* January 20, 2010. http://venezuelanalysis.com/news/5086 (accessed July 4, 2011).

13. Adelstein, Jake. Yakuza to the Rescue. *The Daily Beast*, March 18, 2011. http://www.thedailybeast.com/blogs-and-stories/2011-03-18/japanese-yakuza-aid-earthquake-relief-efforts/ (accessed March 30, 2011).

14. Crace, John. *All the presidents' man.* Interview: Philip Bobbitt, May 19, 2009. http://www.guardian.co.uk/education/2009/may/19/philip-bobbitt-kissinger-cuba (accessed March 20, 2010).

15. Bobbit, Philip C. "Marketing the Future of the State." The University of Texas at Austin: The School of Law. January 17, 2003. http://www.utexas.edu/law/faculty/pbobbitt/marketing.html (accessed March 18, 2010).

16. Arizona State Legislature. "HCR 2024." 2009. http://www.azleg.gov/legtext/49leg/1r/bills/hcr2024p.pdf (accessed March 20, 2010).

17. Winter, Michael. "Anti-government group tells governors to resign or be removed." April 2, 2010. http://content.usatoday.com/communities/ondeadline/post/2010/04/anti-government-group-tells-governors-to-resign-or-be-removed/1 (accessed March 18, 2011).

3

Scenario Planning, Strategy, and Risk Assessments for an Unknown Future

3.1 KEY TERMS

3.2 CHAPTER OBJECTIVES

After reading this chapter you will be able to:

- Describe the three main components that frame a sound emergency management program.
- Distinguish among various approaches to emergency management scenarios and strategies.
- Describe the most pragmatic approach for developing scenarios for emergency management and the four "must-haves" for scenarios given the new face of risk.
- Differentiate among scenarios, strategies, and tactics.
- Describe the meaning of the Zero Sum Scenario and why it is an important consideration in the practice of emergency management.

3.3 OVERVIEW: THE MARKET STATE INTRODUCES A NEW SET OF SCENARIOS

Chapter 2 introduced the concepts of the Disaster Halo Effect, emergence, and the worldview of the nation or enterprise operating in the geopolitical environment of the Market State. These concepts serve as the foundation of this text and were referred to in Chapter 2 as the new face of risk. In this chapter, we will lay the cornerstone of emergency management practices in this context. Here we will explore how emergence and the geopolitical conditions of the Market State "change the game" of emergency management from the start.

The first step of a sound emergency management program is the delivery of three key work products by emergency management planners. They are: scenarios, strategies, and, finally, risk assessments. In the field of emergency management, these three concepts constitute the initiation of emergency management planning, and should be reconsidered given the new face of risk as discussed in Chapter 2, specifically:

- The creation of First Event Scenarios, or probable and possible causes of disasters from which all meaningful impact considerations, planning, and testing of such plans are generated in emergency management
- The formulation of strategies, the broad-view constraints, and approaches to emergency management that a group of stakeholders agree will frame their overall attitude in planning for the possible First Event Scenarios
- The execution of Location-Based Risk Assessments, which determine the *likelihood* of First Event Scenarios that may become emergencies given the scenarios and strategies adopted by stakeholders in the emergency management process

Many texts and instructors in the emergency management field have devoted a considerable amount of time to discussing the need for practitioners to gain executive "buy-in" as the first step in emergency management program delivery. While we cannot dispute the need for some type of support (both budgetary and managerial) for any emergency management program, the simple truth is that if we are practicing in an environment that exhibits apathy—or a lack of commitment to emergency planning—then we should simply be looking for a new place to work! Organizations and enterprises that fail to recognize the potential disruption and harm that can come to them if they lack an emergency response capability *do so at their own peril*. Practitioners of emergency management who work in such environments will suffer in career limiting, thankless jobs. If the decision has not been made within the organization or enterprise to prosecute a sound approach to emergency management, move on!

The first steps of a sound emergency management program are framed by three distinct components:

1. First Event Scenarios
2. Strategies
3. Location-Based Risk Assessments

First Event Scenarios are rooted in one of five discrete risk assessment areas:

1. They have been peer-reviewed.
2. They have met a standard of measured likelihood.

3. They can be either remediated or mitigated.
4. They identify the First Event Scenario.
5. They presume that halo-effect events will be inclusive, and are not limited to likely events, but also include **Zero Sum Events**. Zero Sum Events are scenarios often taken off the table because stakeholders believe they are "end of the world" events that cannot be responded to such as war, solar flares, or large-scale earthquakes.

Strategies address the terms and conditions under which emergency planning and response should occur, but *are not operations or tactics*. They are predetermined approaches, methods, and guidelines used to remediate or mitigate possible First Event Scenarios. Strategies inform the tactical deployment of equipment, manpower, and planning time based on the desired outcome of the organization and the scenario type, but do not articulate specifics.

Location-Based Risk Assessments are uniform assessments of risk based on five core threat areas (addressed later in this chapter) that are applied on a location-by-location basis. Using this unified approach to determining the risk posture of each location is key in the Market State world, where assets and talent are deployed globally or nationally yet are subject to local risks, and the impacts may be felt globally.

These three components shape the emergency management program and inform decisions throughout the emergency management process. As understanding of the Disaster Halo Effect and emergence are becoming the norm, these steps are still misunderstood and poorly executed. To better conduct these cornerstone activities, we must clearly define and illustrate the meaning of each step and differentiate among past approaches and a refined view of these activities, including a focus on the impact of the Disaster Halo Effect on First Event Scenarios, strategy in the Market State context, and the need for Location-Based Risk Assessments (see Figure 3.1).

The key lessons of this chapter are that the Disaster Halo Effect, emergence, and Market State geopolitical forces are influencing the impact of disasters around the world and these foundations of emergency management must evolve. This chapter presents a definition of these core work products, as well as a forward view based on the new realities set forth in Chapter 2.

3.4 POOR SCENARIO PLANNING AS THE ROOT CAUSE OF POOR EMERGENCY RESPONSE

How we conduct our conversations around Emerging Risks and new scenarios is an important component of why information sharing is so

Figure 3.1   Key concepts in this chapter include First Event Scenarios, the planning and response strategy pyramid, and Location-Based Risk Assessments.

difficult. When confronted with new scenarios it is easy for naysayers to state, "We have never done it that way before," and to dismiss important information altogether. We will discuss the importance of strong communication skills and specific tactics for conducting meaningful, on-point, and driven conversations in a later chapter. For now, the age of dismissing ideas because "we haven't done it that way before" is over from a scenario, a strategy, and a risk assessment perspective if the field of emergency management is to stop being reactive and start being proactive as a result of our new understanding of emergence and the Market State. Consider the events of 9/11.

Osama bin Laden's Interest in the United States

One of the men impacted by the U.S. message of holy war was Osama bin Laden. While fighting in Afghanistan from 1979–1990, he was also involved in the globalization of Jihad (holy war) and the early al-Qaeda movement. **Globalization** is the act of spreading a network of nodes and connections around the world. These nodes and connections can be ideological, operational, or tactical.

When bin Laden returned to his home in Saudi Arabia as a hero of Jihad in 1990, one year after the Soviet withdrawal from Afghanistan, other events were taking place in the United States that were related to his ideologies. On November 8, 1990, the FBI raided the New Jersey apartment of El Sayyid Nosair, an associate of al-Qaeda operative Ali Mohamed and uncovered evidence of terror plots, including plans to blow up New York skyscrapers.[1]

That same year, the Iraqi invasion into Kuwait incensed bin Laden who believed that the invasion put Iraq too close to Saudi oil fields and

73

threatened Saudi sovereignty. He took his case to the Sultan, King Faud, and the Minister of Defense of Saudi Arabia and urged them not to allow non-Muslim troops into Saudi Arabia to protect the oil. He argued that his Mujahedeen (a person waging jihad) could push Saddam Hussein back to his border. He was harsh and critical of the Saudi monarchy during these meetings. Within a month of these conversations, the United States had troops in Saudi Arabia and the Saudis had exiled Osama bin Laden to Khartoum, Sudan.

Osama bin Laden openly denounced the Saudis for allowing U.S. troops on Saudi soil and viewed the U.S. troops as invaders, as he did the Soviets in Afghanistan. He also couched his argument against the U.S. troop presence as a religious affront, even betrayal. Having U.S. troops instead of Muslims defending Mecca and Medina, the two holiest sites in the Muslim world, enraged him. Up to his death on May 1, 2011, Osama bin Laden referred to the United States as "the betrayers."

The First Attack on the World Trade Center

Masterminded by Ramzi Yousef, the first attack on the World Trade Center (WTC) was carried out on February 26, 1993. A car bomb was detonated below the North Tower (Tower One) of the World Trade Center. The bomb, a 1,500-lb. (680-kg) urea, nitrate-hydrogen, gas-enhanced device was intended to knock Tower One into Tower Two, bringing both towers down and killing thousands of people. That did not happen, but the bombing did kill six people and injured 1,043.[2]

The ATF, FBI, and the NYPD quickly responded to the scene. Investigators surveyed the damage and looked for clues. While combing through the rubble in the underground parking area, a bomb technician located fragments from the vehicle that delivered the bomb. A vehicle identification number (VIN) found on an axle fragment gave investigators crucial information that led them to a Ryder truck rental outlet in Jersey City, New Jersey. Investigators determined that Mohammad Salameh, one of Yousef's co-conspirators, had rented the vehicle. Salameh had reported the van stolen, and upon returning to pick up his deposit on March 4, 1993, authorities arrested him.

Good detective work and interagency participation led to the rapid arrest of some of the key perpetrators of the WTC bombing. A cross-functional team of interagency experts did an excellent job of getting it done, and later applied the same techniques to the investigation of the Oklahoma City bombing. The reactive steps used to prosecute Timothy

McVeigh were a direct result of key lessons learned during the WTC episode.

Salameh's arrest led police to the apartment of Abdul Rahman Yasin in Jersey City, which Yasin was sharing with his mother. Yasin was taken to FBI headquarters in Newark, New Jersey, and later released. The next day he flew back to Iraq, via Amman, Jordan. In March 1994, Salameh, Nidal Ayyad, Mahmud Abouhalima, and Ahmad Ajaj were each convicted in the World Trade Center bombing. In May 1994, they were sentenced to life imprisonment. Yasin was later indicted for the bombing of the World Trade Center, and in 2001 he was placed on the initial list of the FBI's Most Wanted Terrorists, on which he remains today. He disappeared before the U.S. coalition invasion, Operation Iraqi Freedom, in 2003.

In 1994, the Saudis sent an emissary to Sudan demanding bin Laden's passport, and his family was persuaded to cut off his yearly stipend of roughly $7 million.[3] That same year the Sudanese government and the CIA both contemplated, but aborted attempts, to either capture bin Laden or expel him from the country.

Operation Bojinka

Operation Bojinka was a plan to plant bombs on 12 transoceanic flights between East Asia and the United States. All of the targeted flights had two legs and the plan involved placing bombs aboard the planes on the first leg, and then detonating them on their second leg. The planned series of terrorist attacks had initially been scheduled for January 1995.

That same month, Richard Clarke, head of counterterrorism at the National Security Council, discovered that Ramzi Yousef was located in Pakistan. Clarke tasked the FBI Counterterrorism Section in New York with his capture. An apartment fire in Manila on January 6, 1995, led police to discover evidence of the Bojinka Plot, and to the eventual arrest of Yousef. At that point, it was assumed that Operation Bojinka had been abandoned.

On February 7, 1995, U.S. agents raided the Su-Casa Guest House in Islamabad, Pakistan, and captured Yousef just before he could move to Peshawar. He was captured thanks to an informant, Istaique Parker—a man Yousef had tried to recruit. Parker was paid $2 million for the information leading to Yousef's capture. When he was discovered, Yousef (who was about to leave his hotel room that day) had chemical burns on his fingers. Agents found Delta Air Lines and United Airlines flight schedules in the small apartment.

They also found bomb components in children's toys and a detailed terrorist operation called "Bojinka." Bojinka implies explosion in many Arab dialects, but did not translate well for the agents investigating the case. Because of its varied uses, the word was easy to confuse, even if you were paying attention to Islamic extremist Web sites and communications. To foresee that Bojinka would result in the 9/11 attacks and would remain al-Qaeda's operational strategy through Christmas 2009 could hardly be foreseen given the state of our reactive approach to terror attacks.

Yousef was flown back to the United States and then flown by helicopter into Manhattan. In a bizarre and ironic twist, while flying by the World Trade Center Towers, he scoffed and told the FBI agents "with just a little more money, they would have come down, it is not yet finished."[4] He was sent to a prison in New York City and held there until his trial.

In court, Yousef said, "I am a terrorist, and I am proud of it as long as it is against the U.S. government."[4] On September 5, 1996, Yousef and two co-conspirators were convicted for their role in the Bojinka plot and were sentenced to life in prison without parole. U.S. District Court Judge Kevin Duffy referred to Yousef as "an apostle of evil" before recommending that the entire sentence be served in solitary confinement.[5]

The capture of Ramzi Yousef sparked something in FBI agent John O'Neill: an obsession with Yousef and the Islamic Extremist Movement— particularly the Mujahedeen. By November 1996, O'Neill was convinced that Islamic extremism was a major terror threat. In a speech at the Explosives Detection Symposium and Aviation Security Technology Conference in New Jersey,[5] O'Neill reportedly told the audience, "Interesting times lie ahead," as the main terrorist threat now came from transnational groups not backed by national governments. In short, O'Neill recognized that terrorism was working across borders in a Market State manner.

He also warned, "We see the intent is for a large number of casualties."[4] He was not alone; other experts who had briefed the FAA and Department of Transportation agreed, including Professor Stephen Gale, who said two days after the attack, "Even with the FAA ... they knew this was an option (a large-scale attack using commercial aircraft) ... They just discounted it and relegated it to the class of getting hit by a meteor."[6]

On September 11, 2001, that "meteor" struck and the horrible attacks of 9/11 were perpetrated against a United States that was unprepared. Had we viewed those events leading up to the attacks of 9/11 as part of a scenario planning exercise and a risk assessment for the World Trade Center, would there have been more concern, more alarm, or more preparedness?

Table 3.1 Key Events, 1977 to 2009

When	What
1977–1988	Soviet/Afghanistan Conflict: Radicalized into Holy War
1990	Osama bin Laden Returns to Sudan and is "Betrayed"
1990	Skyscraper Terror Plot Found in Ali Mohamed's Apartment
1990	United States Enters Saudi Arabia
1993	World Trade Center Bombing
1995	Operation Bojinka Plot Found in Manila Raid
1996	FAA and Aviation Security Conference Speakers Warn of Jumbo Jet Attacks
September 11, 2001	Planes Attack Twin Towers, the Pentagon, with Three Successful Strikes Out of Four
December 24, 2009	Christmas Day Airline Bombing Attempt

Table 3.1 allows us to see key events play out over a 32-year period.

The 9/11 Commission (formally known as the National Commission on Terrorist Attacks upon the United States) published its final report three years after the attacks. The Commission did not blame any one agency or administration for the attacks, but made it clear that many errors occurred prior to the event. The most important failure was "one of imagination." The final report said, "We don't believe the leaders understood the gravity of the threat."[7]

Considering the new face of risk we are covering, we can now recognize that *the threat of an asymmetric terror attack is a First Event Scenario.*

Most experts concur that the general principle of imagination *should* help ensure that future intelligence on terror attacks and the emergency response to them would work. An important question is at what phase in an emergency management program should imagination play a role? **Imagination** is the faculty or action of forming new ideas, or images or concepts of external objects not present to the senses. If imagination plays a role in emergency management, it is in the scenario-building phase. A more accurate description of the failure to build an appropriate response to 9/11 would be that there was a failure to imagine such a First Event Scenario. This most important finding of the Commission seems to have been swallowed up by the gaping administrative and logistic challenge of information sharing and interagency cooperation. The Commission did not recommend specifically how to implement "imagination" into the emergency management planning and response process. The quote from the Commission is often used to bolster some new plan of action or out-of-the-box program with little consideration for the creative process that is imagination at work in emergency management, specifically, First Event Scenario planning.

The term, "a failure of imagination" is actually a borrowed phrase from the field of epistemology studies on knowledge and human under-standing. It is generally used to explain a situation that is impossible to predict or foresee because it has never happened. This little bit of logic, known as **hindsight bias**, is the inclination humans have to see things that have already happened as more likely to happen again than those they have not. It suggests that people make the unforeseeable logical in hindsight by saying to themselves, "I never saw that before."

To say that the attacks of 9/11 were the result of a failure of imagi-nation is confusing because it implies we could not have foreseen what happened and, therefore, could not have stopped it, or responded to it properly. It is not very prescriptive. In fact, it is "post-scriptive." Very little prescriptive action can be gained from this sound bite. Of course, more information sharing and massive agency changes were undertaken as a result of the event, but what of foresight and imagination? Looking at the events leading up to 9/11, we can see the ramp up toward the final attacks clearly—*but that is in hindsight*. What about foresight? Expert sce-nario planning and an understanding of the First Event Scenario are what create foresight in our field. Without understanding these concepts, there is no imagination in risk management.

If emergency managers had plotted the intent of the WTC bomb-ing to bring down the Twin Towers as a viable First Event Scenario, and practiced scenario planning under those auspices, they would have con-sidered how the response would have been different if the bombings were a success, as they were on 9/11. In addition, they may have foreseen the long-range outcomes of 9/11 for first responders because they would have considered detailed scenarios such as the respiratory issues that would arise if responders were dealing with several floors of the build-ing on fire, let alone the whole building collapsing. By understanding the First Event Scenario, their improved scenario planning would have provided the much-needed "imagination" for our field. Look at the fol-lowing excerpt from the CDC regarding the respiratory impact of the 9/11 attacks:

> Although approximately 90% of FDNY rescue workers reported a new or worsening cough during the 48 hours after the attacks, only three FDNY

rescue workers required hospitalization for acute inhalation injury, and no FDNY rescue worker with chest pain had coronary artery disease. These findings are related to FDNY medical policy that does not allow firefighters to perform fire-fighting duties unless cardiopulmonary function is normal. During the 11 months after the WTC attacks, the number of medical leave incidents for respiratory illnesses increased, and approximately 500 FDNY firefighters might qualify for retirement disability benefits for new onset asthma and other reactive airway diseases. Increased bronchial responsiveness also has been found in firefighters with WTC-related cough. These findings might reflect delayed or progressive inflammation of the respiratory tract with or without repeated exposures and the synergistic inflammatory effects of sinusitis and/or gastro-esophageal reflux.

The high incidence of respiratory problems and related medical leave among FDNY rescue workers demonstrates the need for adequate respiratory protection. During the collapse, 52% of workers did not wear respirators, and 38% did not wear respirators for the rest of the first day. In addition, most of those reporting the use of a respirator during the first day used only a disposable paper dust mask that was neither NIOSH-certified nor fit-tested. However, despite widespread acknowledgment that rescue workers at future disasters be provided with respiratory protection as soon as possible, such plans will be successful only if barriers to use, such as supply, heat stress and discomfort, communications, training, compliance, and supervision, are resolved.

The increase in stress-related medical leave did not occur in large numbers until months after the attacks. Repeated exposures to toxins at the site and the increasing number of funerals and memorial services that firefighters attended during the next 11 months might have contributed to stress-related problems. In July 2002, new cases began to decline, but previous incidents of terrorism suggest that cases might increase after the one-year anniversary of the attacks. Especially for stress-related problems, these numbers do not reflect the full volume of health evaluations and treatment activity because many workers report symptoms and seek treatment while remaining on full duty. [8]

3.5 SCENARIO PLANNING AND THE FIRST EVENT

As discussed in the prior chapter, the roots of emergency management lay in the area of contingency and scenario planning. The trajectory of scenario planning is forever changed by the Disaster Halo Effect, emergence, and/or the influences of the Market State geopolitical condition. The 9/11 attacks are a testament to this fact. As you will recall, scenario planning and its close cousin, contingency planning, are preparing for the unforeseen and building strategies and plans based on those probable, or possible, futures. The challenge today is that the unforeseen is much more complex and convoluted in a Market State world. Local events can have national, and even global, consequences. In addition, they can have much greater impact, based on the Disaster Halo Effect, and as such, scenarios are taxed when presented with a myriad of halo effects that could be secondary to the First Event Scenario.

This is not to say that early practitioners of scenario and contingency planning did not consider outcomes and impacts other than those expected from a First Event Scenario, but that the scope of possible impacts was considerably less than it is in today's context of the Disaster Halo Effect, emergence, and the Market State. In fact, recent scenario planning could be said to be narrow in scope. Just look at how the effects of Hurricane Katrina were handled.

Hurricane Katrina

The likelihood that a hurricane of intense magnitude could make landfall over the densely populated area of New Orleans was a viable scenario. Additional scenario development may have included the possibility of hospital evacuations, elderly and animal care, the need for intense Federal assistance, and even the possibility of levee failure. The basic emerging qualities of "a hurricane hitting New Orleans" were most likely considered in that scenario. Like a movie script unfolding, with one causal event prompting the next, a broad scenario for Katrina most likely included some of the Disaster Halo Effects that could have been caused by the First Event Scenario.

However, given that the hurricane was the **Trigger Event** (when a First Event Scenario becomes a reality), one can safely say that the vast majority of Disaster Halo Effects went unplanned for (see Figure 3.2). Take for example such effects as looting and civil unrest, corruption by law enforcement, the delay in a Federal response due to legal matters, and the shooting of innocent evacuees at Danzinger Bridge, to name a few. A detailed review of Hurricane Katrina will be revisited later in this text, but for now, it is clear that all of the possible events of the First Event Scenario could not be accounted for and, therefore, were neither anticipated nor planned for. Remember that because of the Disaster Halo Effect and emergence, no matter how good the scenario is, it will be outstripped by the actual event, for which all possible impacts are nearly impossible to account for.

Figure 3.2 A trigger event is the start of a race. It can be any event that initiates a larger scale disaster.

We are often tasked with developing scenarios during the initiation phase of emergency management to frame what is probable, or during the testing phase of emergency management to establish that the response plans we have created can withstand the scenario-based test. What is problematic about scenarios is that from organization to organization, we are confronted with very different views of what a scenario is and the appropriate breadth or scope a scenario should entail.

Indeed, the scope of scenarios can be very wide. We have encountered enterprises who claim there are only two types of scenarios, and those that claim there are as many as 52. This broad scope of scenario possibilities is a signature symptom that indicates that modern emergency management practitioners have not reached a common ground to consider scenarios at all.

3.6 VARIOUS SCHOOLS OF THOUGHT FOR SCENARIO PLANNING

The Two Scenario School

In the Two Scenario School, a claim is made that there are only two types of disasters, the ones we cannot see coming, and the ones we can. They are often given as "9/11 and Katrina events." The concept is that 9/11 could not have been foreseen in terms of allowing for preparation of an emergency response because it happened without warning, and that Katrina somehow gave emergency managers time to move with the disaster at a more even pace as the event unfolded with predictability while the slowly moving hurricane approached land. This incredibly narrow view of scenarios is based on poor logic.

When originally presented with the concept of two types of scenarios it is tempting to imagine that some incredible shorthand has been created that limits the need for sound scenario planning to two kinds of possible emergency types, and that all forward emergency planning can proceed from this insight. After all, there is some basic truth to the concept that there are disasters that deliver warning, and those that do not. However, we would be wise not to move too fast down this path.

Having early warning of a potential event does little or nothing from a scenario point of view to illuminate all of the events caused by the Disaster Halo Effect that might occur after we slowly prepare for the hurricane to make landfall, or the tsunami to come ashore. Knowing that some events strike without warning and inflict massive damage does little to prepare us for the myriad of Disaster Halo Effects that, when taken in total, will constitute the disaster itself. In both cases, what the Two Scenario School does is flatly reject that the Disaster Halo Effect can be foreseen or not, and can strike with or without warning.

Another interesting flaw in the Two Scenario School is that while it appears that disasters we cannot see coming will be man-made, and that the ones we can see coming will be natural, this logic too, falls apart. There are many natural events that occur with no warning at all, and there are many man-made events, such as looting, imbedded within natural disasters. Finally, there are man-made disasters for which there are warnings: war, civil unrest, and famine and *to an extent*, terrorism.

There is no separation in the Two Scenario School for the source of the event—only that there are two types of scenarios that exhibit the prospect of being foreseeable or not, as far as the First Event Scenario is concerned, and that all downstream Disaster Halo Effects should be expected or discarded. This type of scenario casting does little to prepare emergency managers for the task of planning and responding to disasters, and leaves too much to interpretation and ad hoc scenario building.

The Only Reasonable and Likely Scenario School

Many enterprises and organizations task us with working with "reasonable and likely" scenarios. Presumably, these are scenarios based on probability, likelihood, and a sense of what is reasonable. Much of this approach is based on the regulatory language found in the guidelines presented to institutions that use the term "reasonable" to describe what regulated institutions should be prepared for. This approach to scenarios is also problematic.

Determining what is "probable" using mathematical probability is a highly disputed and questionable means of determining disaster scenarios. While some First Event Scenarios can be expressed as scientific probabilities, many cannot. While there are many methods of determining mathematical probability, for now, it is sufficient to note that emergency management practitioners are far from agreeing on any single mathematical formula for truly ascribing probability to a disaster scenario.

The term "likely" is also a slippery slope. From an emergency management perspective, "likely" is a completely subjective term. If something were indeed likely to occur, for instance a massive snowstorm that would halt all shipping operations, one would be better to take preventative action and relocate that aspect of an operation out of harm's way completely before the event ever happened. On the other hand, limiting emergency scenarios to only those things that are likely narrows the field of scenarios to only that which we have seen before because "likely" (for most of us) is that which has been previously observed. The problem with this thinking is that most disasters are revelations that have never been seen before, or at the minimum *occur in ways* never before witnessed.

Perhaps the most damaging thing about so-called "reasonable and likely" scenarios is that they limit the emergency management practice within these constraints to not preparing for the worst disasters of all—the disasters which are completely unthinkable and will require the most radical action and response to survive. For example, a bank that only prepares for "reasonable and likely" events may choose to completely ignore the possibility, however remote, of a new American Revolution. Such an institution would be ill-prepared to shift assets, protect property, and manage through such an event due to a lack of foresight forced into the scenario building process.

To sum it up, not planning for the unreasonable and the unlikely is a dangerous game. Disasters and acts of terrorism, current Market State driven events, and the highly interdependent nature of our economies and global natural resources leaves "reasonable and likely" scenario planning in a place that falls dramatically short of what mindful organizations should be considering in the emergency management realm.

The 52 Scenario School

The 52 Scenario School asks for every possible event or combination of events to be planned for based on 52 scenarios or more. These types of enterprises are often trying to micromanage all possible scenarios with the notion that each scenario will require a unique set of responses that can somehow be laid out and predestined for a specific response. We have encountered many organizations that have asked for an "if-then" type of relationship between scenarios and response activities. Herein lies the challenge; whether it is 52 or 520 possible scenarios, experience tells us it will be the 53rd or 521st scenario that will bring an organization to a halt. Furthermore, there are an infinite number of permutations of those scenarios based on the Disaster Halo Effect and emergence that would mutate the original event into a much larger and more multifaceted event than any of the original 52 scenarios might consider.

> All men can see these tactics whereby I conquer, but what none can see is the strategy out of which victory is evolved.
>
> —Sun Tzu, *The Art of War*, Sixth Century BCE

The First Event Scenario Approach

In the First Event Scenario approach, we propose an entirely new way to predict and manage risk. Generating a group of First Event Scenarios is the best approach we can take given Emerging Risk. First Event Scenarios consider all initial Trigger Events as equally threatening, with no particular eye toward the Disaster Halo Effect other than to acknowledge its existence, and to occasionally tweak the First Event Scenario for testing purposes. What the First Event Scenario approach premise holds forth is that there are four discrete measures of scenarios that render it workable for the emergency manager. These measures are:

1. The scenarios are firmly rooted in one of five discrete, Location-Based Risk Assessment areas (discussed later in this chapter).
2. The scenarios have been peer-reviewed and have met a standard of measured likelihood.
3. The scenarios can either be remediated or mitigated.
4. The scenarios are not limited to likely events but also include zero sum scenarios.

The third point is perhaps the most important: if any given emergency scenario cannot be remediated or mitigated, then the scenario cannot, and does not inform the strategy or improve the capacity of the emergency planning effort at all. **Remediation** means that the First Event Scenario has the potential to be stopped from becoming an event by means of applying a cure or solution to the risk. An example of a remediated scenario is a terrorist who is caught before he or she commits an act of terror. Another example is a flood that is diverted from a town by the creation of manmade causeways and run offs before it has the opportunity to become the First Event Scenario. **Mitigation** is the effort to reduce the severity of a Trigger Event; subsequent Disaster Halo Effects are reduced through prevention and include special measures and efforts which are often included in an emergency response plan—for rendering aid, assistance, and the recovery of areas impacted by a disaster. An example of mitigation would be to have a plan in place for providing security for international aid groups prior to the outbreak of civil unrest, or to have a plan in place for a secondary incident command center in the event that the primary incident command center is unavailable. The primary incident command center on 9/11 was in the Twin Towers, and there was not a mitigation plan in place for a secondary command center if the first was attacked. Rapidly choosing and setting up a wharf on the Hudson River as a new command location cost time and resources.

Mitigation is the stuff of recovery plans and response. Remediation is the stuff of prevention; it is one of the great challenges within the U.S. Department of Homeland Security. Terrorism is best remediated through intelligence and spy-craft, while disaster response is largely a mitigation and response-focused affair.

The four criteria in the First Event Scenario approach allow for intelligence to remediate risk and for planning to mitigate risk. This approach strikes a balance rarely reached in the public or private sector, and it is one with which we must come to terms within the emergency management community. While the third criteria requires that First Event Scenarios can either be remediated or mitigated, the fourth criteria allows for zero sum scenarios.

Zero sum scenarios are scenarios in which the First Event Scenario is so devastating that it appears there are no remediation or mitigation steps that will be viable for the organization. While the prospects of an Extinction Level Event (ELE) are certainly possible, and perhaps even probable given the historic record, it is important to note that many organizations shy away from cosmological or large scale events (such as the deployment of a suitcase nuclear device) simply because they are unimaginable. Comments such as, "then it wouldn't matter if we are in business anymore" are often voiced when these scenarios are discussed. Nonetheless, serious practitioners of emergency management cannot shy away from such large-scale events. If we are not planning for large scale, unexpected catastrophic events along with other emergencies, what is the true value of our practice?

The mass evacuation plan for a metropolitan area is an example of planning based on a zero sum scenario. The relocation of a business or the seat of a government is another such example. In the Market State world, many businesses fail to imagine a United States in which doing business is no longer possible, and that an exit plan to a more stable and safer nation may be necessary. However, during the Second World War, many banks and larger institutions successfully protected their assets by moving their organizations transnationally, e.g., to Switzerland.

While many enterprises discourage zero sum scenario planning, seasoned emergency managers will push for a range of scenarios that includes the possibility of a complete exit from the current location or position the enterprise holds, and the orderly and planned protection of people, processes, and assets in the event of a zero sum scenario. In short, zero sum scenarios cut our losses when the scenario is so damaging as to render any hope of response or recovery impossible. This is clearly the end point of the scenario planning spectrum and one that should optimally be reached for by any nation, state, or enterprise doing serious work in emergency management.

The key message in this section is that the "First Event Scenario" approach is best suited for managing Emerging Risk. It is rooted in a formalized risk assessment process, uses a peer-review process to establish likelihood, generates opportunities for remediation and mitigation, considers the Disaster Halo Effect, and includes the possibility of Zero Sum Events.

3.7 THE IMPORTANCE OF STRATEGY, LIMITATIONS, AND LATITUDES

A **strategy**, in the public or private sector, is a framework, or set of guidelines, on which to build emergency management programs. They are not operations or specific tactics. We should be wary of emergency managers who use the word "strategy" or "strategic" too often because a strategy is a framework that sits at a very high level within the planning pyramid and does not speak directly to methods, tactics, or operations specifically.

Strategies are derived from either national or corporate policies. From policy to strategy, the worldview of a subject as experienced by the nation, or enterprise, is passed down in the form of strategy into a stance toward a specific threat, or opportunity, based on that policy.

Policy and strategy only exist where two opposing forces are involved, require problem solving, and often are related to military thinking. **Policy** is the articulation of values and ethics under which nations and corporations conduct their business with others as well as internally. Strategy is how those values and ethics are conducted within varied conditions or scenarios. **Planning** is how specific values and ethics are cast against scenarios that are translated into actionable tactics. Finally, **operations** are how those tactics are carried out (see Figure 3.3).

While a discussion regarding policy and strategy may seem out of place for an emergency management practitioner, consider this: any emergency management planning that is conducted in absence of a direct connection to the policy and strategy of an organization is ill-informed and usually doomed to failure. National, state, and corporate policy is the vision statement behind any sound emergency management program. Likewise, broader national, state, and corporate strategies must be incorporated and complimentary to the creation of a supporting emergency management strategy.

The National Response Framework, published by the U.S. Department of Homeland Security in January 2008, provides a high-level view of the "who, what, and how" of emergency response as recommended by the

Figure 3.3 The Policy Pyramid places policy at the tip of the spear supported by Strategy, Plan, Tactic, and Operations.

DHS. According to this document, it is tied directly to a set of scenarios, which, "While not exhaustive, is representative of a broad range of terrorist attacks and natural disasters that would stretch the Nation's prevention and response capabilities. Collectively, they yield core prevention and response requirements that can help direct comprehensive planning efforts ..."[9]

It is interesting to note that the National Response Framework clearly identifies *Roles and Responsibilities* in its first chapter with an emphasis on the broad nature of the strategy itself and who it affects. Not unlike good corporate emergency planning strategies, the document does an excellent job of identifying stakeholders, describing what the national position is when responding to disasters, explaining how the nation is organized to implement response, places an emphasis on planning, and finally, provides additional resources for the reader.

The National Response Framework also notes that it is "Part of a Broader Strategy," which is the National Strategy for Homeland Security and that that strategy "reflects our increased understanding of the threats confronting the United States ..."[9] The National Strategy for Homeland Security exhibits succinct, direct, but general, guidelines that are clear and forward directives that can be informed by scenarios, acted upon by using tactics, and are supported by other operations. The strategy is boiled down into four key goals:

- Prevent and disrupt terrorist attacks.
- Protect the American people and our critical infrastructure and key resources.
- Respond to and recover from incidents that do occur.
- Continue to strengthen the foundation to ensure our long-term success.

The National Response Framework is similarly summarized with clear guidelines found in the Response Doctrine's Five Key Principles:

1. Engaged partnership
2. Tiered Response
3. Scalable, flexible, and adaptive operational capabilities
4. Unity of effort through unified command
5. Readiness to act

These examples from the National Strategy for Homeland Security and the National Response Framework are given to illustrate that strategy, when well-documented, provides guidance—not detailed planning or operational tactics. The recent revisions to these documents demonstrate that strategies must evolve. The National Response Framework is an evolution of the Federal Response Plan drafted in 1992, fifteen years prior to 9/11, and the National Strategy for Homeland Security was drafted in 2004 in response to the attacks of 9/11. These documents also illustrate that on a national level, the United States recognizes that an updated strategy is required given the new face of risk driven by emergence and the Market State—a strategy that ties to precise tactics.

In the private sector, there is also the need to tie policy, First Event Scenarios, and strategy into a concise vision for the emergency management program. When these elements are presented as the driving principles of a private sector emergency management plan, they are essentially the business case for the program. The business case in the private sector is a culmination of the driving principles of a program and presents the who, what, why, and general how of a program. When these three program elements of *policy*, *First Event Scenarios*, and *strategy* come together (see Figure 3.4), they accomplish three things:

- Location-Based Risk Assessments inform the strategy for emergency management.
- The First Event Scenarios paint a picture of the potential threats to the organization.
- The Strategy articulates the scope, stakeholders, and the configuration of committees and action items needed to remediate or mitigate the risk.

In the end, the organization relies more on operations and tactics.

Figure 3.4　The Strategy Pyramid shows how Location-Based Risk Assessments, First Event Scenarios, and Strategy frame our planning and response efforts.

> However beautiful the strategy, you should occasionally look at
> the results.
>
> **—Winston Churchill**

Delivering a strategy that is aligned to corporate policy and aligned to
First Event Scenarios will sell the program in the context of what the organization sees itself doing from a vision perspective, as well as what the
potential threats are and what the emergency management program pro-
poses, in broad strokes, to do about it. We have many organizations with
executive buy-in that lose their way in a two- to three-year period because
they lack these three essential program elements. To add depth to the
business case it is often recommended that a handful of key sites be visited in the first year of the program and Location-Based Risk Assessments
are completed.

3.8 THE LOCATION-BASED RISK ASSESSMENT

Now that we can define and understand the significance of First Event
Scenarios and the Disaster Halo Effect, and we have established that the
"First Event Scenario" approach is the preferred method for managing
risk because of its flexibility, we are now going to learn how to begin
implementing this approach by using a Location-Based Risk Assessment
(see Figure 3.5).

Risk to people, processes, and technologies protected by our emergency management programs are expressed as threats and vulnerabilities in the Location-Based Risk Assessment, and an emphasis is placed on
specific locations at which these assets reside. Rather than conducting a
global risk assessment, the Location-Based Risk Assessment considers the
threats and vulnerabilities at a very specific locale. This risk assessment
approach considers threats, vulnerabilities, and opportunities over a five-
year planning horizon across the following five-area spectrum:

1. Natural Hazards: Naturally-occurring hazards which present a
   regional threat to the location
2. Civil Unrest or Terrorism: Regional threats, based on geopolitical
   landscape or target of opportunity concerns that pose a threat to
   the region and, therefore, the location
3. Site Vulnerabilities: Location-specific vulnerabilities at the site
   that introduce risk

Figure 3.5 Location-Based Risk Assessments consider all the threats to a site from a Regional, Site, and Building perspective creating a view of the complete Risk Envelope.

4. Employee Safety: Vulnerabilities or mitigations that increase, or decrease, the threat to persons working onsite
5. Security Vulnerabilities: Threats that represent physical, security-related exposure at the location

The specific locations considered in the report should be based on a list of high-priority sites at which the organization does business and has critical infrastructure or key resources it wishes to protect. Understanding the dimensions of risks and their span of influence is an important component of Location-Based Risk Assessments. The **Risk Envelope** (the area in which risk manifests itself) for an enterprise is highly dependent on the location of the enterprise (or enterprise component). There are three fields in the Risk Envelope (see Figure 3.6):

1. The Regional Field: This field contains Natural Hazards and Civil Unrest/Terrorism risks to the location that have the potential to affect the usability, accessibility, and functionality of the site.
2. The Site Field: This field contains Site Vulnerabilities and Employee Safety vulnerabilities that are mutually exclusive from

Figure 3.6   The Risk Envelope consists of three concentric and expanding zones that move in or out from the Building Field (at the center of this diagram) to the Site Field and Regional Field. Like good security, good emergency management First Event Risk Assessments should include a minimum of three zones.

the building field, but influence the risk to the building and its occupants. For example, a secure building on an unsecured site is an invitation for disaster.

3. The Building Field: This field contains Security Vulnerabilities and represents the specific building(s) of concern (see Figure 3.6).

In the Regional Field there are five key questions regarding Natural Hazards that inform our view of the risk to the site:

1. Can events such as earthquakes, volcanoes, and landslides caused by mass movement of land originating from solid earth, pose a natural hazard risk to the region?

2. Could short-term events such as snow, ice/rain storms, tornadoes, hurricanes, tropical storms, or other weather-related anomalies

caused by atmospheric processes that occur in an annual cycle, cause a natural hazard risk to the region?

3. Might events caused by deviation in the normal water cycle and/ or overflow of bodies of water including flooding, mass movement and tsunami, cause a natural hazard risk to the region?
4. Could long-term events such as extreme temperatures, drought, and wildfires caused by long-lived, or macro scale (10-year cycle) atmospheric trends cause a natural hazard risk to the region?
5. Could events caused by exposure to toxic substances, including chemical exposures, cause a natural hazard to the region?

Also in the Regional Field, there are five key questions that inform our view of Civil Unrest and Terrorism for the site:

1. Are there indications from law enforcement or other sources that terrorists may target the site? Target density of key resources and critical infrastructure should also be factored into an overall regional risk score.
2. Might the site location, or line of business (financial or travel), make it a more likely target site for terrorism?
3. Does the site have such high organizational visibility (military base) that there could be a verified risk of terrorism and actions of civil unrest?
4. According to FEMA guidelines, are there materials or documentation on site that can be used in the manufacturing of weapons or that can cause environmental damage?
5. Does the site contain high-visibility employees or visitors (dignitaries) that may increase target threat potential?

In the Site Field, there are five key questions that inform our view of Site Vulnerability for the site:

1. Are there clearly stated, and readily accessible, Policies and Standards for protecting against a loss of power for indeterminate periods of time?
2. Could internal fires cause business disruption, and are there fire controls and suppression systems in place?
3. Are water sources such as fire suppression and water-based cooling systems regularly inspected to prevent unnecessary loss of manufacturing or IT operations due to leaks or breaks?
4. Do nearby operations such as manufacturing and chemical handling present a danger?

5. Do buildings sited in low-lying areas inhibit natural decontamination by prevailing winds and reduce the effectiveness of shelter in place activities?

Also in the Site Field, there are five key questions that inform our view of Security Vulnerabilities for the site:

1. Are there documented procedures in place for employees and visitors for requesting and approving access to the building and any sensitive areas of the business?
2. Are there passive perimeter controls, such as landscape and architecture, to reduce the threat of vehicular assault and accidental impact?
3. Are there methods and documentation in place for surveillance through Closed-Circuit Television (CCTV) and/or live monitoring to ensure building security?
4. Are there Policies and Standards in place for physical security of the Utility Main and Services to prevent unnecessary loss of power and access to data centers?
5. What perimeter controls are in place to protect high value assets based on security zoning, signage, and access privileges? Are they inspected and monitored to ensure functionality?

Finally, in the Building Field, there are five key questions that inform about Employee Safety:

1. Are there documented procedures for conducting safety training, triage, and employee safety concepts?
2. Are Policies and Standards for Hazardous Materials in place? Do standards exist for infectious disease (i.e., influenza) or other biological threats to reduce employee risk?
3. Are there documented procedures for hiring and firing, to ensure that quality, vetted employees work within the firm?
4. Are there documented procedures for building evacuations and personnel accounting to prevent unnecessary harm and loss in an evacuation emergency?
5. Is there a well-developed program in place for training employees in basic lifesaving techniques?

In all, there are five areas of concern in a Location-Based Risk Assessment that contain five unique questions apiece. This yields 25 points of First Event Scenarios to build from. In addition, the risk assessment identifies risks that might be remediated rather than mitigated, saving time and averting disaster. While there are many risk assessment approaches for varied fields, we have found this to be the most elegant and simplified approach to understanding risk based on location.

For now, this introduction to the Location-Based Risk Assessment will serve as a footing from which we can explore the means and methods under which risk data can be gathered, and the First Event Scenarios such data might imply.

3.9 CHAPTER SUMMARY

Looking back on this chapter, the relationship between First Event Scenarios and the Disaster Halo Effect is described. Emergency management technologies and experience has evolved to a level of complexity in which First Event Scenario events can be readily proposed while other Disaster Halo Effects should be expected, but rarely speculated.

In addition, the delivery of three key work-products—First Event Scenarios, strategy, and the need for Location-Based Risk Assessments—have been described as the first step of a sound emergency management program. This first step has, in turn, been explored with an eye toward identifying local risk in a global business and public government environment.

Looking forward, we can see that understanding the data that feeds First Event Scenario and Location-Based Risk Assessments will be hard to achieve in the global practice of emergency management (see Figure 3.7). The chapters that follow will explore what is needed to best gather data, articulate First Event Scenarios, and deploy sound emergency management programs considering the need for new, broader, and more global planning.

3.10 END OF CHAPTER QUESTIONS

1. How has the perception of new threats impacted the evolution of scenario planning and why do First Event Scenarios make the most sense in a globalized program?
2. Describe the varied professional practices that have evolved in the field of scenario construction and explain why they fall short when managing Emerging Risk.

Figure 3.7   The importance of emergency managers learning new methods for brainstorming, capturing, and organizing risk data is a key lesson in this text.

3. What is the impact of creating a business case based on the Strategy, First Event Scenario, and Location-Based Risk Assessment Triangle?
4. Describe the meaning of the Zero Sum Scenario and why it is an important consideration in the practice of emergency management.
5. Describe the most pragmatic approach for developing scenarios for emergency management and the four "must-haves" for scenarios given the new face of risk.

REFERENCES

1. Memorial Institute for the Prevention of Terrorism. http://www.mipt.org. (accessed July 7, 2011).
2. Mylroie, Laurie. *Study of Revenge: The First World Trade Center Attack and Saddam Hussein's War against America*. Washington D.C.: The AEI Press, 2001.
3. Wright, Lawrence. *The Looming Tower: Al-Qaeda and the Road to 9/11*. New York: Knopf, 2006; p. 91.
4. Kirk, Michael, director. "The Man Who Knew." *Frontline*. PBS. October 3, 2002. http://www.pbs.org/wgbh/pages/frontline/shows/knew/view/ (accessed July 4, 2011).
5. *The New York Times. Excerpts From Statements in Court*. January 9, 1998. http://www.nytimes.com/1998/01/09/nyregion/excerpts-from-statements-in-court.html (accessed June 17, 2010).

6. Schweiger, Tristan, and Josh Stanfield. *For Penn terrorism expert, attacks were only matter of time.* Comments on *Frontline*. September 13, 2001. http://www.pbs.org/wgbh/pages/frontline/shows/knew/view/ (accessed July 4, 2011).
7. Wright, Lawrence. *The Looming Tower: Al-Qaeda and the Road to 9/11.* New York: Knopf, 2006.
8. Centers for Disease Control and Prevention. *Injuries and Illnesses Among New York City Fire Department Rescue Workers After Responding to the World Trade Center Attacks.* September 9, 2002. http://www.cdc.gov/mmwr/preview/mmwrhtml/mm51SPa1.htm (accessed June 17, 2010).
9. U.S. Department of Homeland Security. *National Response Framework.* January 2008. http://www.fema.gov/pdf/emergency/nrf/nrf-core.pdf (accessed July 4, 2011).

4

Sources of Data for First Event Scenarios

4.1 KEY TERMS

99

4.2 CHAPTER OBJECTIVES

After reading this chapter you will be able to:

- Differentiate between data sources and data handling systems in the world of emergency management.
- Describe classified and unclassified data sources.
- Discuss the limitations of existing anti-terrorism and emergency management systems and modeling tools.
- Articulate how probability in and of itself may leave us short-sighted, and what the term possibility means when applied in anti-terrorism and emergency management.
- Understand User Bias and Power Users, and how these elements factor into our profession.

4.3 OVERVIEW: SOURCES FOR VALID FIRST EVENT SCENARIOS AND LOCATION-BASED RISK ASSESSMENTS

We have already stressed the importance of intelligence analysis that can draw on all relevant sources of information. The biggest impediment to all-source analysis—to a greater likelihood of connecting the dots—is the human or systemic resistance to sharing information.[1]

This contributed to a larger failure of analysis, a failure to connect the dots of intelligence that existed across our intelligence community and which together could have revealed that Abdul Mutallab was planning an attack[2]

The "failure to connect the dots" has been used as an explanation for the shortcomings of the counterintelligence and emergency management communities over and over again. In the case of 9/11, the inability to connect the dots was related to the intelligence community's unwillingness to share information. In the months leading to the attacks, abundant data was gathered by the different agencies on an unfolding plot to strike U.S. interests in a "near-term spectacular attack."[3] The organizational structure of our national intelligence was arranged "around the collection disciplines of home agencies, not the joint mission,"[3] thus impeding information and data sharing.

Prior to 9/11, the FBI was solely in charge of the homeland, and the CIA was in charge of collecting data and operating abroad; the Counterterrorism Security Group Director was not briefed on domestic threats and Customs and Border and Immigration Services worked on their own. Each agency had its own separate databases. All of these issues made preparation for the attacks of 9/11 and the construction of a response plan to an attack of this size impossible.

Eighty percent of the 1,330 victims of Hurricane Katrina were over 65 years of age and did not have the means to evacuate; no action was taken to ensure that they would receive the aid they would need even though this demographic data was available through the New Orleans Health and Human Services Department. The disaster in the Superdome was another example of a failure to meet the needs of the population.

The attempt to bomb Northwest Flight 253 on December 25, 2009, is the latest failure resulting from not connecting the dots. The White House Summary Report on the event identifies connecting the dots as one of the "failures and shortcomings" that made the event possible. Deficiencies in our ability to "identify, correlate, and fuse into a coherent story all the discrete pieces of intelligence held by the U.S. Government" are cited as an additional issue. Furthermore, on the operational level, this incident highlighted the lack of "rules and protocols to assign accountability and responsibilities" to follow the data stream on high priority threats, and to track and recompose it in a tactical, operational picture.[4]

In the previous chapters, we talked about the new face of risk in the Market State and how First Event Scenarios and the Disaster Halo Effect can help us think critically and systematically about current and future threats. Perhaps the most obvious changes that need to be to be considered are how we assess risks by utilizing risk assessment with an eye for First Event Scenarios and the Disaster Halo Effect, and how that thinking has an impact on our management of, and response to, risk. In this chapter, we will be looking at the data sources available that help us "connect the dots" when preparing First Event Scenarios and planning for risk.

In preparing First Event Scenarios, **data sources** are any agency or device that can provide original information. The first reason these must be established is that there are multiple data sources with varying levels of availability. Public Sector (government) data sources have security requirements that allow access only to those with specific security clearances. Private (owned by the general public) data sources are available to the greater public, but sometimes also have their own restrictions. However, no matter the data sources available, it is essential that all of the information be understood within its proper context and varying degrees of accuracy. To that end, it is important to note that the individual practitioner is the ultimate source of data—not the individual data sources standing on their own.

Ultimately, we will establish that the data you look at, in and of itself, is worthless without ensuring you gather all information available and use it to paint a bigger, more complete picture (Figure 4.1). We will be looking at several examples of how this applies and what it means to be a risk management professional by *becoming the data source*. Consider this: if the 25 First Event Scenarios we talked about in Chapter 2 are a starting point, the data we will be talking about in this chapter are the infamous "dots"—points of data that we can use to inform those First Event Scenarios. The data may seem static, stale, or even outdated. However, soon you will learn that because the dots can be informed by market thinking, they are actually much more complex.

Figure 4.1 Key concepts in this chapter include a failure to "connect the dots" as established by the 9/11 Commission, the downstream effects of disasters, and how marketing data is a sound benchmark of real-time situational awareness that could be used and emulated in emergency management.

4.4 THE NEW MADRID FAULT—A FIRST EVENT SCENARIO?

The New Madrid Fault Earthquakes

In Chapter 1, we described a scenario based on an earthquake along the New Madrid Fault line. Here are some additional facts about that possible event: The first recorded earthquakes in the United States were the New Madrid Fault Earthquakes that occurred between December 12, 1811, and February 7, 1812. The **New Madrid Fault Zone** is a 150-mile-long fault zone that passes through five states, beginning in Cairo, Illinois, and ending in Marked Tree, Arkansas. Within that short time, four quakes were felt in the area between St. Louis, Missouri, and Memphis, Tennessee. The earthquake of February 7 destroyed New Madrid and in "St. Louis, many houses were damaged severely." [5] All four quakes were of an estimated 7.3–8.0 magnitude, the largest ever recorded in the Continental United States. Only the sparse population present in the area during this time period limited the damages. The results would be catastrophic if the same type of quakes occurred today.

The quakes were felt across the United States with reports of bells ringing in Boston, Massachusetts, and Charleston, South Carolina. In Washington, D.C., windows and furniture were reported to be shaking. The oddest location-based account as a result of these quakes is that of the Mississippi River flowing upstream.

Even though these quakes occurred 200 years ago, their geological results are still visible. New lakes were created. The course of the Mississippi River was changed. The warping of the earth created uplifts and subsidence up to six feet. Finally, large sand blows, or sand volcanoes, were created by liquidized soil being ejected from the earth.

Modern Implications of the New Madrid Fault

The primary characteristic of this fault is that noticeable events are not as frequent as they are on the West Coast. The last major event of the New Madrid Fault occurred in 1895; 73 years later, "the next biggest quake was a 5.4-magnitude quake on November 9, 1968, near Dale, Illinois." [6]

This "dormant" status may explain why the New Madrid Fault has not received as much media attention as the San Andreas Fault, and why the efforts to retrofit buildings and prepare to respond to a catastrophic event in that location have been slow.

103

Knowing that a large earthquake along the New Madrid Fault is a perfect storm ready to happen, FEMA has attempted to accelerate response and planning activities around a New Madrid Scenario plan called the *NMSZ (New Madrid Seismic Zone) Catastrophic Earthquake Disaster Response Planning Initiative.*

Because of various geological factors, earthquakes in this area are potentially more lethal than in other parts of the country. The "physical properties of crust and geophysical properties of overlying superficial soils of the NMSZ"[7] area do not allow an easy dissipation of the seismic energy. In fact, the ground "shaking associated with"[8] the earthquake swarm of 1811–1812 was estimated to be 10 times larger than the 1906 San Francisco earthquake, and it was felt as far as 1,000 miles away, while the San Francisco quake was felt only 350 miles away. Another geotechnical feature that will amplify earthquake hazard and the potential catastrophic outcomes is the liquefaction susceptibility of the Mississippi River Basin. The effects of liquefaction on structure foundations, underground pipelines, and ducts are severe and prohibitively expensive to remediate.

The main differences between the 1811–12 events and a catastrophic event occurring now are the density of population and critical infrastructure present in the area. The corridor between St. Louis and Memphis is one of the most important gateways in this country (between the East and West) for interstate and regional ground transportation. FEMA, in collaboration with the Mid-America Earthquake Center and various universities, has developed a technical report on the impacts of a 7.7 earthquake along the New Madrid fault. According to the report,

> … damage to critical infrastructure (essential facilities, transportation, and utility lifelines) will be substantial in the 140 impacted counties near the rupture zone, including 3,500 damaged bridges and nearly 425,000 breaks and leaks to both local and interstate pipelines. Approximately 2.6 million households are without power after the earthquake. Nearly 86,000 injuries and fatalities result from damage.[9]

The impact on the buildings in St. Louis will be devastating because the adoption of mitigation policies has been very slow given the skewed (or distorted) perception of the likelihood of a catastrophic event.

Data that Supported the NMSZ Scenario

With the objective to develop a catastrophic, scenario-driven, earthquake response plan, this plan was modeled using the software packages

HAZUS-MH MR3[a] and MAEviz.[b] **HAZUS-MH** stands for *Hazardous U.S.-Multi-Hazard.* It estimates potential losses from floods, hurricanes, and earthquakes. It includes potential losses to physical damage, economic losses, and social impacts. **MAEviz** stands for Mid-America Earthquake Center. Using the consequence-based risk management methodology, and a visually based menu, its goal is to become the next generation of seismic risk assessment software by aggregating multiple data sources into one product.[10] As important as it is to develop a response plan, the question that must be asked is, "is there potential in this scenario of 'Garbage In-Garbage Out (GIGO)'"? To the point, the HAZUS-MH's outcome has not been validated against other types of consequence or estimation models/techniques or against empirical data regarding the current population of these areas.

The questions about these tools are, "are these software packages reliable?" How reliable is the input data? Is there potential in this scenario for "Garbage In-Garbage Out?"

We believe that the overconfidence in historical data, probabilistic deduction, and technology outcomes, conjunct with the lack of "creative foresight" and the impossibility to model novel events creates room for unexpected First Event Scenarios that will leave communities unprepared. Furthermore, it is not clear if, or how, these software models can account for the Disaster Halo Effect that would be caused by this First Event Scenario. Can a larger model be created that can account for the Disaster Halo Effect? You could ask if we are unable to see the forest for the trees. What are we losing when we rely on raw data alone and do not implement the tools of our instinct and creativity to develop a more complete view of the big picture? (See Figure 4.2.)

4.5 U.S. DATA SOURCES FOR FIRST EVENT SCENARIOS AND LOCATION-BASED RISK ASSESSMENTS

Take a moment to review how First Event Scenarios should be linked to location-based risk assessments. Recall that a location-based risk assessment model breaks down its findings and recommendations into five unique risk areas:

1. Natural Hazards
2. Civil Unrest or Terrorism
3. Site Vulnerabilities
4. Employee Safety
5. Security Vulnerabilities

Figure 4.2 Understanding the big picture includes everything within the Disaster Halo Effect, including even a single injured victim.

Each type of risk is set in a field:

1. Regional Field
2. Site Field
3. Building Field

It is helpful to think of the five risk areas and the risk fields as being ordered from the outside in, with broader risk (regional) moving closer toward more specific risk (location-based)—like a target.

All Risks are Local

In Chapters 2 and 3, we discussed the geopolitical worldview of the Market State and the emerging face of risk, and we broke down 25 First Event Scenarios in five key areas in Section 3.8. We might be tempted, from this point, to conduct remote risk assessments, using research tools and methods along with online questionnaires to assess the risk at any given site. In the next section, we are going to take a look at some of the databases and research tools that are used in the private and public sectors. However, before we haul off down the road of using so-called tools and research to "connect the dots," we want to be clear that we cannot accurately craft a risk assessment from the observations of others, and certainly not from the comfort of our cubical or armchair. *All risk is local* in this evolving, global risk model we are presenting. To understand this concept you have to physically go to a place to look and see.

Gengi Go Butsu (go look and see) is the Japanese management term used in *Kaizan*, or total quality management, for a method of reporting that simply makes sense. Generally, the rule is simple: do not bring to your supervisor's attention any problem you have not witnessed and tried to correct for yourself. In the Japanese auto culture of total quality, it is a recipe for handling disaster. The same applies to risk assessments. Of the 25 First Events for which we describe data sources, 20 of them require the assessor *to go look and see*. This is why sending out questionnaires takes the expert (you) out of the equation. It is like playing the game *Telephone* where one person passes a message to another, and so on until the last person tells the group what he thinks the original message is. There is room for misinterpretation, local color, and plain untruths to enter the equation. Nothing beats seeing for ourselves what the risks are.

You can Google anything and learn nothing in the process. Even the most reliable sources in the news media focus on local problem areas, while whole countries are relatively safe and tranquil. Consider this—are all business units in Mexico at risk today? Given today's headlines, our knee-jerk response is probably yes. The truth of the matter is there are many regions in Mexico that are often safer than our own cities.

All risks *being local*, if we want a *clear* picture of the world in which our enterprises or organizations are at risk, we have to go see them ourselves. Since we will be looking at sources of data, it is important to remember that no volume of data beats observation by a trained eye. There simply is no better tactic. The goal of this book is to inform our thinking and help develop the critical analysis skills needed in order to be keen observers of First Event Scenarios and the potential for Disaster Halo Effects. To do this, we must understand sources of data, but never forget that we are the best source of data there is. It simply cannot be emphasized enough.

Sources of Data for Various Types of Risk

While there are many sources of data that might inform a risk assessment, we are focused on the five core areas of a First Event Scenario; therefore, a great place to start is to read your County Level Emergency Management Office's *All Hazards Risk Assessment Report*. To find it, simply search online for "county or state name emergency management office."

Natural Hazards Risk Data
Geophysical Hazards
- Research the United States Geological Survey (USGS) and Federal Emergency Management Agency (FEMA) sites to gather information for the location of your business or organization.

Meteorological Hazards
- Research the National Oceanic and Atmospheric Administration (NOAA) and local FEMA Emergency Management Office Risk Assessments for information on weather patterns and risks.

Hydrological Hazards
- Research the FEMA record of County Declarations at http://fema. gov for information about risks in your area.

Climatological Hazards
- Research the Presidential Disaster Declarations found at http:// www.fema.gov/news/disasters.fema for long-term weather patterns and risks.

Industrial Hazards
- Research Geographic Information Systems (GIS) such as HAZUS-MH MR3 and also your local area to plot your own findings.

Civil Unrest and Terrorism Risk Data
The threat of civil unrest and terrorism presents itself in the regional field due to the high visibility of the site. Using methods from an Operational Security (OPSEC) threat assessment method, as well as methodologies from the U.S. Department of Homeland Security, you can determine the likelihood of an international or domestic terrorist-related event. Additional sources would include:

   a. Review the National Archive of Criminal Justice Data for historical civil unrest and general criminality of the county under consideration at: http://search.icpsr.umich.edu/NACJD/query.html? nh=50&rf=3&col=series&tx0=sda&fl0=&op0=%2B&ty0=w&col= abstract&tx1=NACJD&op1=%2B&fl1=archive%3A&ty1=w&&tx2= county-level&fl2=title%3A&op2=%2B&ty2=p&tx3=restricted&op3 =&fl3=availability%3A&ty3=w.

b. Assess the threat of terrorists attacking using Chemical, Biological, Nuclear, Radiological, and/or Explosives (CBNRE), or weapons of mass destruction (includes target data) at: http://www.rand.org/nsrd/terrpanel/terror.pdf.

c. Assess the threat of terror attacks based on target selection from the Office of Justice Programs, National Institute for Justice (includes rail, ground transportation, port operations, and critical infrastructure and key resources target reports from trusted sources, including the Rand Corporation): http://www.ojp.usdoj.gov/nij/topics/crime/terrorism/high-risk-targets.htm.

d. Review Crime Statistics from the Automated Regional Justice Information System available at the ARGIS portal: http://crimestats.arjis.org/.

In addition to those listed here, many sources of data regarding potential attacks are available to individuals who have appropriate security clearances. Included among them are closed-loop intelligence systems and open source data sets. The degree to which these systems interoperate and reveal motive, means of operation, and tactics is generally classified, and most are only accessible with clearance through Immigration and Customs Enforcement (ICE), the FBI, the CIA, or the National Security Agency (NSA). These include data gathered through traditional intelligence efforts.

Such intelligence efforts are generally referred to as follows:

• HUMINT: human intelligence gathered from ground personnel
• MASINT: intelligence based on measurements and signals
• SIGINT: intelligence based on signals interception
• OSINT: open source intelligence data gathering
• TECHINT: intelligence gathered from the analysis of equipment such as weapons
• FININT: intelligence gathered from financial transaction data mining

While these approaches to intelligence gathering are widely agreed to and used by many agencies including the U.S. Department of Homeland Security, all of them are classified and the systems that support them, or integrate them, are not a matter of public record. For example, the NSA is rumored to use a system called TEMPEST for eavesdropping on potential terrorists and criminals. However, the capabilities and *even* the acronyms of the NSA's systems are highly classified, which leaves some practitioners with data sources only available in the private sector.

- Researching data from HAZMUS
  - Gathering local FEMA Emergency Management Office Risk Assessments
  - Researching current events and reliable news sources

Site Target Risk

- Research if there are known, specific threats reported by law enforcement, or general threats based on the site being identified as a target of opportunity. These should be measured and evaluated by discussing the site with local law enforcement agencies and security personnel.

Public Visibility Risk

- Research should be based on public opinion, current political or cultural movements and values, and/or the tenor of the site's business. Researching current and reliable news media and staying vigilant with regards to public perception of the site is critical to staying on top of the risk.

Organizational Visibility Risk

- Assess risk by knowing the organization's visibility and functionality. Is it highly visible in the public eye (like a military base) that hosts mission-critical personnel or capability? Determine the risk by researching the verified risk of terrorism and actions of civil unrest for the area. Discuss with operations and facilities personnel how the organization is seen in the public eye, and what security measures are in place.

Hazardous Materials Risk

- Assess the storage of any materials classified as "Hazardous Materials" which are viewed by the U.S. Department of Homeland Security as being targets of opportunity. Research this risk through an onsite evaluation and discussions with facilities or operations personnel regarding the storage of materials classified as such.

High Profile Operations Risk

- Research the frequency of entertaining, or publicly hosting, high-profile persons on a regular basis. Also determine security controls, or lack thereof, during high-profile visits as well as predominant signage and flashy public relations events. Overall, risk is determined by the level of marketing, public relations, and discussions with the site owners regarding how such high-profile operations are managed.

Site Vulnerability Risk Data
Power Risk
- The power infrastructure supporting the site and the potential loss of electrical power need to be calculated by meeting with site owners or facilities personnel to determine if there is sufficient upstream power (power generated by power companies) to provide for redundant power sources.
- Through an onsite investigation with facilities and IT personnel, backup power via Uninterrupted Power Supplies (UPS) and a generator with fuel or a fuel contract needs to be determined. Measuring backup power is expressed in number of days and the type of fuel agreement.

Internal Fire Risk
- Research current fire notification and suppression systems to prevent the unnecessary risk of internal fire doing damage to persons and/or equipment as appropriate.
- Fire risk is calculated in the U.S. by meeting with site owners or facilities personnel to determine fire monitoring, alarm systems readiness, and type of fire suppression system used.

Water Damage
- Water sources such as sprinklers, cooling systems, and water pipes need to be inspected regularly to find and prevent leaks in order to limit preventable water damage to facilities and IT equipment.
- Conduct a thorough site evaluation and have discussions with facilities personnel or operations personnel.

Proximity Risk
- Research, through a site evaluation and discussions with facilities or operations personnel, the proximity of hazardous nearby operations such as manufacturing and chemical handling. Losses to hazardous sites within the proximity can result in losses at your site. Be prepared by knowing what they are and countering the risks they present.

Low-Lying Terrain Risk
- Campuses or buildings sited in valleys or low-lying areas are prone to flooding and the settling of heavier airborne hazardous materials. Research, through a site evaluation and discussions with facilities or operations personnel, their risks and how to best counter and/or reduce such damage.

Employee Safety Risk Data
Physical Security
- Conduct a physical inspection of documented procedures for conducting safety training, triage, and employee safety concepts.

On Site Hazardous Materials Response
- Conduct a physical inspection of documented procedures for responding to hazardous materials as indicated by FEMA, the Occupational Safety and Health Administration (OSHA), and other agencies. Include consideration for single-site command and control of incident.

Employee and Vendor Background Checks
- Conduct a physical inspection of documented procedures for hiring and firing of employees and contractors. Well-defined hiring and firing processes ensure that quality, vetted employees work within the firm. They also ensure that when an employee leaves there is a methodical approach to removing access to physical and intellectual property.

Building Security and Egress Standards
- Physically inspect the site for documented procedures for building evacuations and personnel accounting. Well-mapped, designed, signaled, and tested employee evacuation routes lower employee loss vulnerability. A current listing of employees who are on site should be maintained at all times.

Employee Safety Awareness and Participation
- Conduct a physical inspection for documentation that determines Policies and Standards for Employee Safety Designations. Shelter-in-place training lowers employee vulnerability to external events. A well-developed program for training in basic life-saving techniques is vital. At each site, identify who is responsible, for what area, and what level of command they possess.

Security Vulnerability Data

Security Vulnerability data is broken down into five key areas in the location-based risk assessment model, for which there are many data sources. Utilizing U.S. Department of Homeland Security (DHS), Crime Prevention through Environmental Design (CPTED), and Physical Controls, this analysis determines the likelihood of a physical security breach resulting in building damage, building closure, or other disruptive events due to ease of target identification, lack of building security, and the site profile hazards that are identified.

Site Perimeter Controls
- There should be documented procedures for requesting and approving access, periodically revalidating, and removing physical access rights. Channeling employee, vendor, and visitor traffic through distinct access points is mandatory. Signage for public areas is preferable, while signage indicating sensitive areas is not.
- Conduct a physical inspection of the facility, including site perimeter controls such as fencing, guard gates, and patrols.

Passive Hardening
- Inspect the site for the presence of passive objects such as walls, bollards, street furniture, sculpture, and landscaping. These passive objects serve as physical deterrents, or assets, to a physical attack. Knowing their location determines possible benefits or disadvantages for risk.
- Conduct a physical inspection of the facility. Be sure to inspect passive perimeter controls such as landscape elements, architecture, and visibility for internal occupants.

Site Surveillance
- Conduct a physical inspection of the facility including surveillance controls, record and retention time, and blind spots. Closed-Circuit Television (CCTV) monitoring, or the lack thereof, affects site vulnerability.

Utility and Main Service Protection
- To prevent the loss of power and operational capacity, conduct a physical inspection of the facility for the location of utility mains and services.

113

High Value Asset Protection

- Conduct a physical inspection of the site, including perimeter controls, badge readers, locks, and mantraps. Also inspect for documentation of Policies and Standards for the security of high value assets based on security zoning, signage, and access privileges.
- Research the presence of documented procedures for requesting and approving access, along with a current list of employees and third parties with physical access to high value assets.
- Inspect to confirm that the physical location of High Value Assets is at the center of the building, distant from exterior walls and public areas.

Summary

Even given a mammoth understanding of these disparate systems, the blind spots of why and how, and the lack of understanding regarding real-time impacts to persons on the ground is clear. We do not have command over these "dots." The conclusions that can be drawn from the consideration of known operative systems in the emergency management world are that first, to be effective, we would have to have unfettered and complete clearance to access all of the data that was just reviewed in order to perform what the White House refers to as "all-source analysis." Second, the data itself must be of the highest quality and cannot be manipulated or malformed based on any bias. Third, this data cannot be outdated or static. Finally, one would have to read, interpret, and access an infinite number of systems to gain any insight into a pending attack. In short, we would not only need to be omnipresent, but omniscient.

Considering that the White House is concerned that emergency managers are failing "to correlate, and fuse into a coherent story all the discrete pieces of intelligence"[10] the reader might ask if there are sufficient plot elements or data available at all to tell such a story. If there were, who might have access to all of the data and be analyzing it in such a way as to reveal possible outcomes—including means, motives, and tactics? In truth, the problems with the "dots" (beside their obvious lack of integration and transparency) is that they are not well positioned to enable the telling of a story at all; they are being affected by User Bias, and some are highly classified. In the end, this leaves very little to work with when calculating risk or **probability** with a high degree of confidence.

This is not to cast disparagement on any agency or department within our government. However, all the data sources available speak for themselves when they declare that all computational systems have limitations. These systems are not a stand-alone solution to making correct estimates and goals for emergency planning; they are a tool, that when combined with the first-hand observation of the trained eye, allows us, the expert, to become the best source for data.

4.6 WHAT COMPUTERS CAN, AND CANNOT, TELL US

Any view of the role of the computer and computational systems in predicting and mitigating risk has to be confronted with limitations. No matter how much data they have to offer us, the expectation that stories might be based on the data that originates in these systems must be part of a "reality check." Within this ideological frame, the voices of Ray Kurzweil and Ervin Laslo haunt our present reality. Kurzweil claims that an age of "spiritual machines" is near and assures us that we will reach a state of **Artificial Intelligence** (AI) in which human intervention is of little need. Artificial Intelligence, coined by John McCarthy, is "the science and engineering of making intelligent machines."[11] Ervin Laslo lays claim to an interconnected world in which poverty, disasters, and terrorism are "leveled" by a rush to global Internet connectivity. It seems that the original notion of the computer as the ultimate solving machine, embedded in the birthing of computers themselves, is perhaps not so grounded in reality.

Modern researchers in the area of AI are finding that the most challenging aspect of rich data systems is that they do not know how to make inferences or identify what we want to know. In short, if we do not ask the question, they do not give the answer. In fact, the biggest problem facing the development of AI today is relaying to applications and systems what we want and what our "gut," or intuition, is leading us to do next. What we are pointing out here is that, lacking human agency, these systems are limited in their application. In fact, there is a large body of work in the area of what a human actor might "do" next in computer sciences, but it is more often applied in marketing and rarely applied in emergency management. For the moment, we will focus on the limitations of computing systems used in our field. Then we will have a discussion about computers in marketing.

Today in emergency management, computers cannot tell us what we do not ask, or know how to ask. This is precisely why there continues to be a failure in "connecting the dots." We do not ask the right questions. One system or a group of systems may have every dot, but not the equation to marshal

115

those dots into a meaningful threat picture, much less a story. We may not even know what to ask a computer to look for if codes are being used, or if data is being passed that seems irrelevant to what we think we are looking for. Computer assisted emergency response is an important area of growth in the profession; but to be clear, the computer is assisted by expertise and intuition only afforded by human agency at this stage of development.

However, in marketing, data collection about human behavior and decision-making is a contact sport. What if the data we were working with impacted every dollar our client earned and every vote our constituents made? While it might be acceptable in emergency management to work with questionable data when crafting First Event Scenarios, such an approach would never fly in marketing or politics. In these fields, data gathered and properly analyzed is dollars earned and votes won. There is very little margin for error. Because of this need for accuracy there have been developed advanced analytical tools to consider all of the possible things you might "do" and identify that which you are *most likely to do next*. Marketing systems that study human behavior are extremely deft at telling us about the "why" and "who" of consumer behavior (see Figure 4.3).

Some may argue that this is simply influence marketing, but the rich sets of data, the analysis applied to them, and the lateral relationships embedded in the programming look a lot more like intuition than anything we have seen in emergency management computer science. Consumer

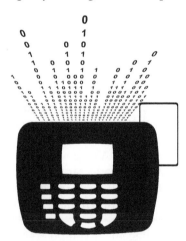

Figure 4.3 Every credit card transaction (as depicted by the device above) tracks a consumer's real-time preferences for stores, brands, travel arrangements, and other data used by marketing professionals to predict consumer behavior.

science is in fact brilliant when we look at the data. For instance, it was recently discovered that every location where an iPhone or GPS enabled iPad has ever been kept is stored in a system log file, and sent remotely to Apple headquarters. Google conducts a similar practice with its Android phones and tablets. Imagine the telling insights from this type of data that can be used by the manufacturer when they have information for *every user on the planet*. Face it—businesses compete on analysis of customer data. That is, they bet big dollars on knowing what you will do next and telling stories to you about it. We will talk more about marketing intelligence later in this chapter.

4.7 USER BIAS AND POWER USERS

Garbage In-Garbage Out is a common concept in the computer science and information technology fields. The concept highlights the fact that computers and software are tools made to process input of any data (accurate or erroneous) and produce outputs. What you get out of the system is only as good as the data that is entered. It is self-evident that the products or outputs deriving from this incorrect, not pertinent, or simply wrong data have the very same characteristics: they are incorrect, not pertinent, or simply wrong, and therefore, are not usable.

The real issue is that those in our profession, on a daily basis, use these faulty, incomplete, or imprecise outputs in the decision-making process. "Garbage In-Gospel Out" is the latest permutation of the acronym GIGO. It is used to define the ironic tendency to put excessive trust in "computerized" output data, and on the propensity for both laypeople and experts to blindly accept computerized outputs as "Gospel." **User Bias** is exactly this uncritical propensity to believe the computer models of future events regardless of other evidence, or the incompleteness or doubtful pertinence of the data used to populate these models. User Bias is the type of misuse that is likely to happen in emergency management. This is a critical point to all of us in our profession; we need to keep it in mind, constantly reminding ourselves that we cannot take this information at face value, but always question it and look at it in the context of the entire risk assessment being conducted.

In December 2006, Goldman Sachs' indicators and risk models began suggesting discrepancies among models, profit, and perception of the market. After a 10-day period in which Goldman's mortgage business lost a considerable amount of money, "a meeting of about 15 people, including several risk managers and the senior people" was called to take a harder look at the situation. To the top executives, the situation, "felt like it was going to get worse before it got better...so we made a decision: let's get closer to home" (reining in the risk).[11]

The top executives ditched the data and acted on their gut feelings and started looking at the real profit and losses—which leads us to the introduction of Power Users. A **Power User** is anyone who knows a system so thoroughly that they are able to use it to its full capacity, beyond what most people are capable of doing, sometimes even beyond its intended purpose, but still accomplishing the required task. Given that the Value-at-Risk (VaR) computer model was the standard by which traders and institutions could rationalize all manner of risk choices, the real Power Users who invented the VaR model used it based on their prior knowledge. In fact, the real Power Users were *out of the market* well before it went south. They were the guys who understood that the VaR models included fringe investment instruments that were responsible for those fat tails (an unlikely distribution of odds)

Writer Michael Lewis is the author of several books that deal with diverse subjects, from investing strategy to personal journeys in discovery. The reader may know him from his book *The Blind Side*, which was released as a major motion picture in 2009 starring Sandra Bullock. However, his book *The Big Short* is an excellent study of the financial meltdown of 2008-2009.[12] All of his titles share a common theme: extraordinary people who do extraordinary things in extraordinary times. *The Big Short* studies the other side of the financial meltdown—the Power Users that won big during the disaster.

According to Lewis,[12] as early as 2003 and continuing through 2005, a small group of hedge fund managers saw the impending catastrophe of the VaR model and, specifically, the instruments hidden within the VaR data—subprime mortgages. By 2005, this small group of individuals who actually saw the risk started taking bets that what the VaR was saying was highly unlikely, something hidden in the 1%–5% risk margin. They started betting that subprime mortgage bundles being sold by Goldman Sachs and others would fail. The only way to bet on that idea was to buy insurance for those mortgage bonds (you cannot buy a short stock on a derivative inter-bank bond). This instrument is known as a credit default swap.

One of these small hedge funds started buying up high-risk instruments with $100,000 of investment capital. Quickly, as strange things started happening, their $100,000 investment became valued at $15 million. Betting on the fat tails, the unlikely, they started cashing in.

They literally went looking, essentially, to make bets on unlikely things happening. They would buy options to buy stocks far, far away from where the stocks were currently trading. They did it with currencies. They did it with commodities. They scoured the world, essentially looking to make best on extreme things happening.[13]

Each of their investments was small and exposed very little of their fund to risk because the events they were betting on were very unlikely to happen. Most of the time they were wrong, but when they were right, their investments paid off—and in multiples. By late 2006, the original investment of $100,000 was worth $15 million. This is where subprime mortgages really came to their attention and they saw that this was the type of bet that had been doing well for them. They saw that they could buy insurance on these pools of subprime mortgages, and they started to study the subprime market very carefully.

Once they understood the social implications of what they were learning, "they start[ed] screaming at the top of their lungs that there is fraud in the system."[12] But very few people listened, including the FCC. In the meantime, their $15 million investment became $120 million by late 2008 to early 2009. Here is the point about the Power Users we are discussing: they understood the flaws in the VaR model, looked at the edges of the data, and saw an opportunity to manage risk in an aggressive way. The initial results spoke for themselves—$100,000 became $120 million in a period of less than five years.

What made these individuals in Lewis's work Power Users? First, they understood the VaR and the fat tails and dug deeper to understand the assumptions that may or may not have been correct in the data—they looked for error. Second, they understood that incremental, small "experiments" with the data would yield results with low risk. Third, they mastered the nuances of the model to gain a competitive, proactive edge. Essentially, they were Power Users because they owned the data, they owned the systems, and they took the model assumptions and variances very, very seriously. So much so, that they were tremendously successful.

Lewis has a bit more to add here that is very relevant to this text. A Power User is more than just a person who is close to the data and the assumptions within the model. A Power User is someone who is not afraid to consider the data in terms of the story it tells. He says, "The thing that was, to me, so interesting about them was all these people who were in a handful who saw the disaster happening before it happened, they all had something about them that enabled (them) to see it." [12] Lewis goes on to explain what he thinks that something might be.

"I mean, this is a story about human perception as much as it is anything else … It was peculiar to be running around the world just looking for unlikely things that might happen (and) that the markets were underestimating." [12] In other words, the perception that the data in the VaR showed upside and proactive wins was counter to what the system and data was meant to do, which was, to show potential losses. This difference in perception, this Power User Bias, allowed these fund managers to do something very few investors could do—take into account the real likelihood of risk and act on it. "It told you that there weren't enough people thinking this way. There weren't enough people taking into account the real likelihood of extreme change in the world, and they were." says Lewis.[12]

As demonstrated by the Power Users, data and its sources are either an asset or liability. Humans make a habit of relying on the past to determine the future. When you factor in computers that can consume vast amounts of data, calculate it, and spit out a statistical photograph more detailed and enigmatical than an MC Escher drawing, we have a propensity to trust that information as the gospel truth. That said, the information presented is only as good as what was entered, and without being able to understand the raw data, the "solutions" presented are not worth the paper they are printed on. To be successful we must be able to critically evaluate the raw data, and place it in the bigger picture of our risk environment. But remember that we said in Section 4.4 that even raw data in and of itself is useless if we do not learn how to interpret that and get back to using our "guts" and intuition to determine risks and solutions. Ultimately, *we are the supercomputer* that is analyzing data and determining risk. And we are better than a supercomputer because we have an imagination—we can use unknown information deduced from what is known, and take risks in our thinking to determine risks that the data does not foresee. *We are the supercomputer,* and we have been there!

4.8 CLASSIFIED MEANS NOT ACTIONABLE IF INFORMATION IS NOT SHARED AMONG THE RIGHT AGENCIES

It is important to point out that over 80% of the data and systems sets we reviewed in 4.5 (these inform Natural Hazards, Civil Unrest and Terrorism, Site Vulnerability, Employee Safety, and Security Vulnerability) are not available at all to those of us in the private sector, and 50% or more may not even be available to all levels of local, state, and even federal emergency management roles. The small pool of talent who has access to such data hampers determining who the Power Users are and who is most likely to connect the dots and do an all-source analysis.

An important component of the discussion about data in the realm of emergency management is that information sharing and classification of data makes it impossible for many of us in the private sector to study, aggregate, and leverage the data we have—even if we are responsible for **Critical Infrastructure and Key Resources (CI/KR)**. Critical Infrastructure and Key Resources are organizations that are identified as delivering goods or services that are fundamental to running a society. The public sector does not have it much easier as their challenges still hinge on interagency cooperation and the rough terrain of information sharing across multiple sources. Power Users in either the private or public sector of emergency management will be hard pressed to "connect the dots" when many of the dots are obfuscated by the nature of their classified status. Core to this challenge is the balance between public safety and national security.

Simply put, classified data is not available to all practitioners, and therefore, is not actionable between agencies or industries. Later in the text we will explore meaningful workarounds and approaches to gather intelligence outside the classified realm and how to make informed decisions based on that data. But for now, the point has been made that we have few dots, the dots are subject to error, and there are few Power Users that actually have enough command over the dots to render a coherent risk or threat picture—let alone, tell a compelling story about risk.

The end game today is to connect the dots and present risk, threat, and probability models. Stories have not yet been fully embraced by the emergency management community, and probability models are the dominant factor in predicting risk potentials. Given the statements from the White House and other political actors, tomorrow's endgame may be considerably different for us. In later chapters, we will be discussing the power of stories and narratives to better illustrate First Event Scenarios and to communicate appropriate response measures.

4.9 PROBABILITY, POSSIBILITY, AND RISK

According to the definition adopted in this book, **risk** is an exposure to the *possibility* of injury or loss. It can be represented by the answers to three questions: What can happen, how often or how likely it can happen, and if the event has happened what are the consequences? Risk is also an exposure to the chance of injury or loss. It always has a negative connotation because "it refers to avoiding a negative outcome" and it is "bound to the idea of controlling the future."[14]

It seems that there are more risks today than ever before in human history. It can certainly be said we are more informed of risk than ever before because of media and globalization. It seems that our awareness of risk itself drives fear (and sometimes terror, higher and higher) in a self-perpetrating cycle. Anxiety has become a household word, even an unfathomable part of the human condition. Even as we have become more aware of risk, or risk keeps increasing, a widely agreed upon definition of risk still keeps eluding us. In our opinion a risk can be described by answering three questions: What can happen (possibility), how likely it is (probability), and if the event has happened (risk).

Risk has become such a central fixture in our daily and psychological life that we are not even capable of dreaming of our demise. For example, you have probably dreamt of falling, but you have probably never dreamed of impact and the end of your life. You awoke startled, but safe, just before the moment of impact. However, this built-in risk aversion psychologically handicaps us from the start when it comes to understanding the full range of risk at the personal level. We "systematically violate the principles of rational decision-making when judging probabilities, making predictions or otherwise attempting to cope with probabilistic tasks."[15] When facing uncertainties we rely on experienced-based problem-solving (heuristics) to help in the decision-making process, and our judgment is often biased.

Understanding risk is fundamental to emergency management professionals. As experts, it is obvious that we have to prepare for threats and hazards that have been documented and on which we have historical data to determine probability. As experts we are also expected to prepare for the threat of tomorrow—the perfect storm, the event we never see coming.

Probability can be determined by using Bayes' Theorem. This approach interprets the concept of probability as "a measure of state of knowledge"[16] and it is considered an "evidence-based approach."[17] Answering the three questions of risk, Bayes' Theorem determines probability with a) scenario: what can happen—possibility, b) likelihood: how often or likely it can happen—probability, and c) consequences: the results of a First Event Scenario—risk. The Bayesian probability and Bayesian statistical inference models are the most commonly adopted approach to determining probability.

122

The latest theories on probability and statistics (such as Possibility Theory) are extensions of what is known as "fuzzy logic" or Possibility Modeling. Whereas probability estimates use one measure to calculate risk (probability), possibility theory (or fuzzy logic) uses two measures: possibility and necessity. Both measures range from 0 to 1, where a 0 value of **possibility** means an event is impossible and a "1" value means *the event is totally possible.* In "necessity," a "0" value means an event is not necessary and a "1" value means an event is necessary. Necessary, as used here, refers to those conditions within the Universe that may be a natural and required outcome, while not previously observed in history.

Going back to our field, the standard practice of risk assessments in emergency management is to analyze multiple risk factors as deemed important and to assess those risk factors based on probability. The confusion in this system stems from as many as dozens of varied means of risk and threat analysis with little consideration for the method of probability assessment used. Depending on how much weight is placed on each criterion, two emergency mangers could easily arrive at different, and what appear to be arbitrary, conclusions based on the same assessment. This challenge in the profession makes it very difficult to quantify the value and accuracy of probability-based risk modeling.

Emergency management students and practitioners need to understand that these analyses create an exponential curve that skyrockets the likelihood of occurrence from an "if" it will happen to a "when" it will happen. What has changed in the discipline of emergency management is that risk has become mobile, networked, and much more difficult to predict. The classical probability models of the past are of little use in the face of such massive change and new models. Ideas and thinking need to be revised in order to effectively measure, communicate, and militate against Emerging Risks. As practitioners in the field of emergency management, we face risks today that are much different than they were even five years ago.

Globalization, just-in-time supply chains, and real-time communication have become both goods to be protected and risks to be dealt with. Certainly, few could argue that the risk of today is the same as it was five years ago. Yet we are consistently tasked with speaking to probability or likelihood as if it gives "scientific" reason to our projections. Nothing could be further from the truth, *given the wide range of variables at play that make all things possible. We need to consistently understand probability is largely based on our subjective confidence* (see Figure 4.4).

123

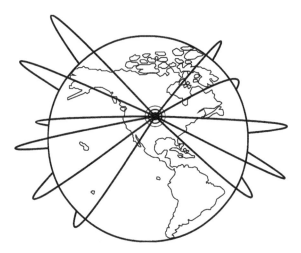

Figure 4.4 While the organizations we work for may be based in the United States, many of them are dependent on a globalized supply chain and events that happen around the world— forcing us to reconsider the scope of probable scenarios.

The U.S. Department of Homeland Security and other agencies (including the Department of Energy, the Army, Air Force, and NATO) have recently started holding sessions with a team called Sigma. They come together at meetings with names like the 2009 Homeland Security Science and Technology Stakeholder Conference. The stakeholders at these meeting discuss the new face of risk and the possible future solutions that might be used to respond to them or mitigate them. Interestingly, the stakeholders are a mix of public and private sector industry leaders, and the staff at Sigma—who are science fiction writers! Clearly, though. leaders are looking toward the future to understand the risk of our new world.

4.10 ALL SOURCE ANALYSIS AND STORYTELLING

As discussed earlier, even the most mature data and data sets are weak in the who, what, and why of victim behavior and understanding the nuances of local, on the ground reactions to an event. Often, the risks associated with on the ground realities catch us off guard.

Sourcing data from the cultural and marketing landscape and positing that data in a format that is accessible to stakeholders is what

124

differentiates many of the scenarios in this book from the standard, stoic scenarios so common to our practice. The scenarios in this book are lateral in their thinking and presentation, but they are, none-the-less, believable and informative. The reason for this is that scenarios based on cultural attractors and actors are stories of the novelty of human experience and the experience of encountering the human agency of innovation. This is the power of moving toward a more informed risk modeling capability that is inclusive of imagination and the unexpected (often human-driven) outcomes.

Cultural and marketing-sourced data is highly believable because it resonates with our own experiences as humans and goes beyond the realm of data and into the realm of story. Stories and narratives are incredibly powerful; the tradition of narrative (or stories) informing decisions and morals goes all the way back to the great philosophers of Greece. Rich cultural histories of a peoples' risk and their indicators are part of oral traditions as exhibited by the indigenous people of Indonesia during the Boxing Day Tsunami. For instance, recent research about the oral tradition of "storytellers" saving lives when tsunamis strike is emerging in our field with overwhelming and positive results. In small village cultures, the Lapuns, or "storytellers" are responsible for handing down traditional archeological and human evidence to the tribe so that they can understand the evidence of a tsunami before it strikes. (See Simon Day's excellent presentation on this topic from the University College London.[18])

Treated as force-multipliers, cultural and marketing data sets can capture the essence, mood, and tempo of events in a predictive and proscriptive manner when the tools of marketing and cultural studies are applied to the potentials for disasters and terrorist innovation.

Where does cultural and marketing data come into play in the data sources listed here? What are the sources for this type of data in the field of emergency management? Much cultural and trending data can be found in the open source data sets listed later in this chapter and, more specifically, the U.S. Department of Homeland Security's open-source monitoring programs. In other agencies, Open Source Intelligence (OSINT) and Human Intelligence (HUMINT) are the domains in which market intelligence and cultural theme tracking would fall. The degree to which we can use these systems to prepare is debatable, as is our ability to share our findings across agencies.

What is not debatable is that very few professionals in our field have a background in understanding cultural or marketing trends, or insight

125

into other open source data sets from which to gather such intelligence. We will be exploring this further in later chapters.

Some of the data systems used by U.S. corporations to understand market trends and cultural moods are listed here. Be mindful that professionals are interpreting the data and using their expertise to create informed decisions based on the data found in these systems. Typically, these Power Users are very successful at understanding the impact of the data they collect and the audience they serve.

The *Worth Global Style Network* (WGSN) provides a two-year-forward fashion and architecture forecast to designers. *Style Sight* provides culture trends, behavioral data, and vision boards of fashion, interiors, and product design along with key phrases and stories of how these data become likely lifestyles.

Boing Boing (http://boingboing.net), a daily blog, provides an ongoing dialogue regarding subcultural trends and global technology trends. *Strange Closets* (http://www.strangeclosets.com), another blog, tracks an admixture of product, interior design, and government affairs by telling stories about the data they are gathering from the field. *The Satorialist* blog (http://www.thesartorialist.com) tracks street styles around the world with daily updates and short stories about field data they collect. *Nue Black* (http://www.neublack.com) tracks new products, new social trends, and new design trends in real-time and tells stories about where they think this data will take us. *Cool Hunting New York* (http://www.coolhunting.com) has crowd-sourced the effort to track this data and tells stories about new products, new styles, and lifestyle attitudes from many voices and perceptions around the world.

While these examples relate specifically to fashion and design, you can choose any area of interest from architecture, cars, technology, and even food to see examples of trending and marketing from consumer hotspots anywhere in the world (see Figure 4.5). It is important to note that these same trending and marketing techniques are occurring with jihad, pipe bombs, hacking, and other forms of terrorist activity as well as natural disasters.

To better understand how we might use marketing information to probe predictive and prescriptive decision-making, we will need to look at units of measure and the modes cultural themes take within the sphere of marketing business practices and then apply them to emergency management. Understanding what Coolhunters, Early Adopters, and designers are considering when looking at trends, and how they take cultural ideas and carve them into measurable units is the next step. What we are

126

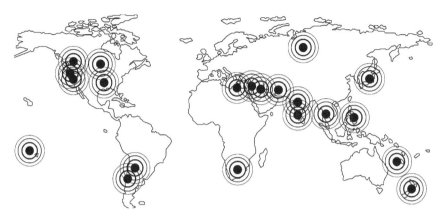

Figure 4.5 Consumer data from global hotspots are tracked by multi-national corporations to better understand ever-changing marketing trends.

after is a unit of measure that is used to aggregate varied data into stories and trends. This unit is the ever-popular and ever-changing meme.

4.11 END OF CHAPTER QUESTIONS

1. What are the different data sources and data handling systems available to us to help us determine and manage risk?
2. What are the classified and unclassified data sources? What are their advantages and disadvantages?
3. After learning about all of the existing anti-terrorism and emergency management systems available to us, what are their limitations? How do those limitations impact us in the ability to perform our work with professionalism and expertise?
4. Considering the way probability has been used in this book, how can probability put blinders on us in the execution of our job? How do we need to view possibility when it is applied to anti-terrorism and emergency management?
5. In this chapter we learned that there are not many "dots" for us to connect. Considering the data sources available and the problems that are inherent in them, what is the biggest threat to our profession when using them as tools? What is the best way to avoid this threat and even implement it into our assessments?

NOTES

a. HAZUS MR3 is a software modeling tool that analyzes potential losses from floods, hurricane winds, and earthquakes based on population and economic loss from buildings and infrastructure.
b. MAEviz is a tool that integrates spatial information, data, and visual information into an environment for performing seismic loss assessment and analysis.

REFERENCES

1. National Commission on Terrorist Attacks Upon the United States. "The 9/11 Commission Report." *GPO Access.* July 22, 2004. http://www.gpoaccess.gov/911/index.html (accessed March 23, 2011).
2. Obama, President Barack. *Obama outlines security review of terrorist attempt.* January 7, 2010. http://projects.washingtonpost.com/obama-speeches/speech/162/ (accessed March 24, 2011).
3. National Commission on Terrorist Attacks Upon the United States. "The 9/11 Commission Report." *GPO Access.* July 22, 2004. http://www.gpoaccess.gov/911/index.html (accessed March 23, 2011).
4. The White House. "White House Review Summary Regarding 12/25/2009 Attempted Terrorist Attack." January 7, 2010. http://www.whitehouse.gov/the-press-office/white-house-review-summary-regarding-12252009-attempted-terrorist-attack (accessed July 5, 2011).
5. United States Geological Survey. *Historic Earthquakes: New Madrid Earthquakes 1811–1812.* http://earthquake.usgs.gov/earthquakes/states/events/1811-1812.php/1811-1812.php (accessed February 11, 2010).
6. The USGS, Historical Earthquakes. New Madrid 1811-1812 Earthquakes. Earthquake Summary. http://earthquake.usgs.gov/earthquakes/states/events/1811-1812.php.
7 Rogers, J. David. "Consequences Resulting from a Major Earthquake in the Central U.S." *Missouri University of Science and Technology.* August 13, 2008. http://web.mst.edu/~rogersda/nmsz/Consequences-NewMadrid%20EQ-Aug2008-USGS.pdf (accessed February 8, 2010).
8. United States Geological Survey. *Historic Earthquakes: New Madrid Earthquakes 1811–1812.* http://earthquake.usgs.gov/earthquakes/states/events/1811-1812.php/1811-1812.php (accessed February 11, 2010).
9. Elnashai, Amr S., Lisa J. Cleveland, Theresa Jefferson, and John Harrald. "Impact of New Madrid Seismic Zone Earthquakes on the Central USA, Vol. 1 and 2." *Illinois Digital Environment for Access to Learning and Scholarship.* January 14, 2010. http://www.ideals.illinois.edu/handle/2142/14810 (accessed February 12, 2010).

10. Mid-America Earthquake Center. *MAEviz Software*. 2006. http://mae.cee.uiuc.edu/software_and_tools/maeviz.html.

11. McCarthy, John. *What is Artificial Intelligence: Basic Questions*. November 12, 2007. http://www-formal.stanford.edu/jmc/whatisai/node1.html (accessed February 11, 2010).

12. Lewis, Michael. *The Big Short: Inside the Doomsday Machine*. New York: W.W. Norton & Company, Inc., 2010.

13. National Public Radio. *How A Few Made Millions Betting Against The Market*. March 16, 2010. http://www.npr.org/templates/story/story.php?storyId=124690424 (accessed March 23, 2010).

14. Giddens, Anthony. "Risk and Responsibility." *The Modern Law Review* 62, no. 1 (January 1999): 1–10.

15. Slovic, Paul. *The Perception of Risk (The Earthscan Risk in Society Series)*. Oxford: Earthscan Publications Ltd, 2000.

16. Annis, Charles. *Bayesian Thinking*. August 10, 2010. http://www.statisticalengineering.com/bayes_thinking.htm (accessed July 4, 2011).

17. Kimura, Claudine. *Case Based Pediatrics For Medical Students and Residents: Chapter XXII.2. Evidence-Based Medicine*. March 2003. http://www.hawaii.edu/medicine/pediatrics/pedtext/s22c02.html (accessed July 4, 2011).

18. Day, Simon. "Traditional Knowledge of Tsunamis Saves Lives." Aon Benfield UCL Hazard Research Centre. http://www.abuhrc.org/Documents/Simon%20Day%20-%2012th%20October%2009%20-%20part%202.pdf (accessed February 13, 2010).

5

Memes Make Meaning:
Introduction to Memes and Clusters

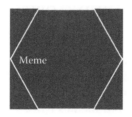

5.1 KEY TERMS

5.2 LEARNING OBJECTIVES

After reading this chapter, you should be able to describe:

- How memes aggregate ideas and concepts
- The four potentials of memes and how they can be used to understand how they might adapt
- What we can learn from memes if we start using them to create meme clusters
- Why most disasters have memes at play, and how memes can be used to better understand and communicate the dynamics of a situation
- What the cutting-edge application of meme clustering means to the fields of anti-terrorism and emergency management

5.3 CHAPTER INTRODUCTION

We have been building a view around risk that starts with the premise that we are now operating in a Market State and that the dynamics of risk have changed as a result. Further, in Chapter 2, we discussed the Disaster Halo Effect, wherein First Event Scenarios are a grounding concept for crafting reasonable scenarios that are inclusive of other events that accompany disasters and terror attacks. In Chapter 4, we discussed the "dots," or data sources, that inform First Event Scenarios and how that data may be old, stale, and static. We also established that the practitioner of emergency management is the best source for close-in analysis of the data.

At first glance, the task of "connecting the dots" appears to be overwhelming. It may seem that there are as many potential dots as there are stars in the sky. To an extent they *can be* categorized by size, shape, location, growth rate, and their potential for emergence. However, simple categorization is not all there is to connecting the dots—there is more to it! In this chapter, we will be exploring the anatomy of risks and response in terms of cultural and marketing phenomena. We will also look at how data is collected and disseminated in the competitive world of marketing.

We will see how elements of risk and marketing are interpreted, used, and formalized within the emergency management domain, and the issues they pose when creating First Event Scenarios that fit well within the context of the Market State and its dynamics. The key reason for this is that the most informative data for First Event Scenarios is a meme. In short, a **meme** is a cultural interpretation of the events around us (see Figure 5.1). The one thing that makes a meme unique—this unit of data *morphs.*

This chapter takes the data we discussed in Chapter 4 and adds a human element by proposing that politics, ideas, and values can be added to data and present the notion of a meme. It illustrates how memes can be used to understand social trending and how those social trends are likely to evolve with time. In addition, we consider why most disasters have memes in play and how the emergency manager might work with them.

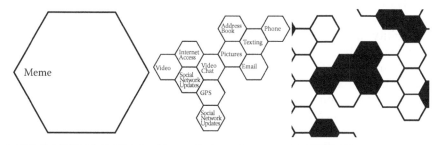

Figure 5.1 Key concepts in this chapter include the meme as a cultural or trend identifier, the memeplex as a grouping of cultural or trend ideas, and that memeplexes can be used to capture emergency management data (black hexagons at right).

Further, we will illustrate how memes enable deeper narrative and story-telling for the emergency manager so that multiple threats, hazards, or rogue outcomes can be viewed holistically. We will also discuss how memes can be used to better diversify and manage messaging based on memetics when such data is available to emergency managers. Finally, we offer a definitive means for considering memes and measuring their potential as risks and their potential for creating solutions.

A First Event Scenario can be changed radically by the memes at work when the event happens. Understanding the probability and possibility of a First Event Scenario do little to inform you about the Disaster Halo Effect as influenced by a memeplex surrounding the event. For instance, an earthquake is a clear First Event Scenario. The data we would source outside of marketing and cultural data would shape a response appropriate to such an event. We might even include all downward events in the stream such as fires, water shortages, and evacuees. Now enters the memeplex Narco-Jihad. The First Event Scenario is radically altered. Like the meme itself, it virally infects the First Event Scenario rendering all response political, dangerous, and even opportunistic.

Memes politicize and polarize. They mutate everything they touch. Is our fear of an earthquake in Mexico City larger than our fear of harm during a response? Is the will of the Narco Kings such that they might leverage the event in their favor? Perhaps this is the most dangerous concept of the meme in emergency management: how long until a patient enemy uses a natural disaster to "kick an enemy that is already down?" Why not wait for a First Event Scenario involving a major snowstorm prior to attacking the Twin Towers, or a tsunami prior to bombing intelligence offices throughout Micronesia?

The question is not *if* memes will be leveraged to the advantage of an enemy and disadvantage of first responders. The question is *when*. Even our ability to respond to natural disasters changes First Event Scenarios by changing the underlying cultural data.

Clearly, while First Event Scenarios are easy to understand using the static data we have, it is critical to remember that this data does not move, and is based on poor probability mathematics to boot. The memes that surround us radically change natural disasters from random, natural events, into disasters that have political meaning. In many ways, terrorism is an act of human agency and is expected to contain the twists, turns, strategy, and surprises that come with a planned attack. With that said, we do not want to lose sight of the fact that *we should expect to see the same twists, turns, and surprises imbedded in natural disasters.* In the Market State, natural disasters have become political and socio-economic, opportunities for marketing ideologies that may not be in line with those of first responders, and therefore, will be vastly more complex.

For emphasis, while we deal with many issues in this text relating to terrorist activities, we need to see emergency management moving toward a practice in which even natural disaster First Event Scenarios are considered to be morphological in nature and under the influence of memetics. Nothing is exempt from this law. This is the very nature of Emerging Risk and the Market State.

5.4 WHAT IS A MEME?

A meme is a simple concept that is pregnant with depth and meaning. It is very important to understand a meme and its function because it is a powerful idea to reckon with if you want to connect the "dots" of data we just discussed in the previous chapter. In a meme, we can identify the way a society understands the events it has experienced or foresees; it continually changes to keep those events meaningful and relevant to the each generation. A meme is cultural data, or a social trend, that is more reliable than the data covered in Chapter 4—and it is *real-time* data. There is nothing speculative about it; it *is* really happening. A meme is always going to be a reliable source of information when it is applied to a First Event Scenario and the resulting Disaster Halo Effects.

More technically, a **meme** is a postulated unit of cultural or marketing ideas that can also take the form of products, practices, or ideologies (see Figure 5.2). Scientist Richard Dawkins first used the term in his book, *The Selfish Gene.*[1] A meme, like a gene, takes a host (a person, media position, cultural talking point) and then it spreads through the means of speech, gestures, advertising, and other media. While many theorists resist the notion that ideas evolve like genes (because ideas do not follow biological

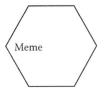

Figure 5.2 A meme, like a virus, takes a host and then it spreads through the system by means of speech, gestures, advertising, and other media.

rules), the term meme has been used principally by social sciences rather than by hard science and is highly applicable to our field.

A meme is a discrete building block made up of many ideas and realities that result in a single position, product, or tactic. It has sociological appeal that makes it contagious, or *sticky*. **Sticky** means that a concept easily clings to our thoughts and becomes a part of our daily life. While "memes lack philosophical appeal,"[1] because they are not all inclusive or do not seem to allow for multiple influences, the notion of a unit of measure for an idea or novel concept as the atom at the center of a movement or trend in movements is a very powerful tool. The meme allows us to look at a position, a trend, an idea, or ideology, and an outcome or a possibility in the realm of many other memes and their influence.

By studying memes we learn three things that allow us to make the most of the information they do, or will, represent. First, memes can be manipulated, malformed, reverse engineered, or reengineered altogether. **Reverse engineering** is the process of understanding how a product works, or is designed, and then using it in a manner for which it was not originally intended. In short, memes can take what appears to be obvious and make it vastly more complex. Second, memes aggregate data. Finally, memes can be adapted, meaning they can be taken out of context, taken into new contexts, or morphed to fit one's needs.

The notion that a meme has a certain inherent viral quality to it makes it possible for tracking a group of ideas or outcomes. **Viral** is the adjective that defines the diffusion of ideas, trends, and fashion via media, word-of-mouth, texting, the Internet, and other social networks. For example, rather than list all of the varied components of social media we simply call it social networking. **Social Networking** is a social structure of individuals, or organizations, of nodes. Social networking becomes a multi-dimensional shortcut, a meme, which lets us shorthand all of the technical, sociological, and potentially threatening or beneficial outcomes imbedded in a slew of technologies and ideas that make up social media.

The meme also allows for the clustering and solar mapping of larger ideas and helps us understand broader geopolitical, response, and other emergency management concepts. **Clustering** is when two or more nodes are mutually associated with one another and grouped together to create a large node. **Solar Mapping** is a method of visualizing data around a primary object of interest. Using memes to trend ideas and innovations allows for the discrete identification of a set of concepts or ideas, creating a constellation of "dots." Coolhunters hunt memes, as we will see in

Chapter 6, and then they place these multi-dimensional objects on the continuum of the innovation adoption, as we will explore in Chapter 8.

One way of thinking about memes is that we can use them to understand the replication and duplication of ideas as well as their evolution, once they are identified. This can yield valuable insights into how a broader cultural theme can evolve. We can also inspect the meme itself to see how it might evolve. Whether a meme is harmful (or "maladaptive"), or helpful and well adapted, is part of what we need to comprehend as emergency managers. Memes as units and as pools, and how a meme can aggregate data, are all aspects we need to consider as we incorporate cultural and marketing theories into our practice. This deeper dive on marketing theory will inform a marketing approach to emergency management that will allow us to look at various cultural phenomena from a new angle in the social science context to see how they affect risks, threats, and our field—both positively and negatively.

Here is an example that applies to the field of criminal justice. Short Message System (SMS) was invented at the beginning of the 1990s "primarily to be used by the hearing impaired."[2] By 2000, Short Message System became known as "texting" and had already reached the "tipping point" to become one of the most-used means of communication between cell phone users. The texting meme became highly popular among teens and young people to the point that it replaced traditional phone conversations as the choice method of communication for large swaths of these groups. This trend, as a testimony of the richness of this meme, has created a new jargon with specific grammar and spelling, and even new literary genres such as cell-phone romance novels for teenage girls.[3] In our field, texting has been adopted as a "static"[a] tool to enhance the emergency notification systems capabilities. We say static here because current SMS capabilities used by emergency management notification systems do not leverage all the capabilities of smartphone technology including location based data, video, motion, and a myriad of other means of communication, measurement, and correlation embedded in these mobile phone systems.

Nonetheless, by 2005, the texting meme had mutated and maladapted into **sexting**.[4] When cell phones began featuring small, low-resolution cameras and began sending those images through SMS, now called Multimedia Messaging Service (MMS), minors, especially young girls, began sending nude photos of themselves through the cell phones. As the trend developed, state and federal laws[5] were passed that stated minors caught sexting can be prosecuted and risk becoming registered sex offenders. This is regardless of whether they exchanged pictures between "sweethearts," or spread their photos with malicious intent.

The inclusion of video cameras[6] in the latest generations of cell phones has again morphed this meme, as we now have the ability to transmit HD quality video over wireless cell phone networks. This is where *pattern recognition* and *trend spotting*, concepts that we will discuss further in the following chapter, become invaluable for emergency managers. We need to understand that memes are social and cultural building blocks that can be plotted, tracked, and accounted for in our domain (see Figure 5.3). When applying this approach to using memes as building blocks, we create a clear picture of socio-cultural evolution. As marketing theory is applied in our practice, it provides much deeper insight into what emerging threats look like and how best to respond to them. We can imagine the valuable information and foresight that can be achieved by tracking the different mutations of relevant memes before they can be exploited to generate disturbances in society.

Beyond technology and the application of memes to the world of popular culture, memes can be political, ideological, or even tactical.

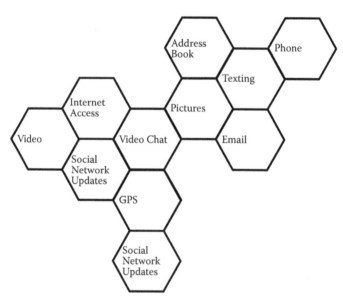

Figure 5.3 Given the advanced capabilities of modern smartphones as captured on the left of this memeplex, one can observe the social and cultural building blocks that indicate an evolution in cell phone design.

For instance, consider a meme that posits that mandatory inoculation during a viral outbreak is a conspiracy designed by the government for mass eugenics. This "conspiracy theory" is already viral and has been widely distributed in U.S. society through alternative radio channels, blogs, and YouTube videos. As we have seen in reality, such scenarios are not far-fetched and the public opinion can be shaped or conditioned. The implication for emergency managers is that there is the potential that they will not be trusted during an event; and worse, first responders might be met with threats and actual violence during their response efforts.

One question is whether or not cause and effect simplify the meme of sexting. For example, simply boiling it down to "one thing leading to the other" without any chance of free will or randomness playing a role suggests that all outcomes are expected outcomes. While there are many varieties of deterministic thought that prevail in probability event calculations and thinking, the notion that event A leads to event B, which logically leads to event C, is the type of potentially dangerous causality that we are bringing to the forefront in this discussion. Having moved beyond probability, we are now focused on possibility.

To diversify the "causal chain" approach, emergency managers should pay close attention to the lines of evolution and maturity of relevant memes and set hard trigger points along these lines that can generate certain response actions. For example, the negative public response to the H1N1 flu vaccination is a concrete example of the "evil government plot" meme at play and showed its destabilizing potential. In the fall of 2010, during the response to the swine flu threat, this meme had gained traction in the public opinion. It had clustered with the anti-government meme and the anti-vaccine meme that had already gone viral and "dominated the attention"[7] of public opinion at the same time. The public outrage reached a climax when some jurisdictions issued statements that mandated the vaccination for their employees.

At the U.S. Department of Homeland Security, U.S. Department of Health and Human Services, and the Centers for Disease Control, all the groups responsible for the vaccination campaign and the response to the flu pandemic, were "genuinely baffled"[8] by the public reaction, especially when compared with the acceptance of the general flu vaccine in the previous years. The reader can understand how establishing these trigger mechanisms and trigger points on the trajectory of the "evil government plot," the anti-government, and anti-vaccine memes, could have helped emergency managers break free from the expected chain of events and from the proscriptive response to the H1N1 flu, and may have provided them with the foresight necessary to understand how the general public would have reacted. And, thus, how to modify messaging to counteract these various anti-vaccine sentiments.

It is important to focus on how we apply our view of expected outcomes in understanding the causal chain of disasters and terror attacks, and how we use different strategies to exhaust the search of possible outcomes in the chain of events. This search of possible outcomes should not exclude random outliers of the chain "A" and "B" that might create "F" (a rogue outcome), or "a black swan,"[9] because "F" is deemed as impossible or improbable.

How we respond to events is the outcome of this constant work of searching for new solutions to new challenges. **Game theory** (competition measured in terms of gains and losses) is often used to test response capabilities. Often, it is the A, B, C expected order of the game programming itself that causes response efforts to come unhinged during mock exercises and drills.

Even in the most basic games, in which chance has nothing to do with the outcome—such as Chess or Go—random moves can radically alter the outcome of game play and change the board. All moves and counter-moves cannot be known; therefore, any act of randomness will change the game. Too often, it is the game changer that emergency managers find themselves responding to.

Because there are so many events that do not fit within the deterministic "A leads to B, leads to C" construct, some philosophers argue that all events are "in-deterministic" (that all events alternate between chance and necessity), where the first cause is change and the second maintains the unchanged, or static. This leads to many situations in which rogue outcomes are unavoidable. This logic accounts for things that seem to happen by chance or without any order at all.

While the methods used in this book take many random, or chance based events, and illustrate their relative likelihood, we must still maintain the footing that there are events that are purely random and novel. An interesting portion of the argument around how things are naturally random is the notion that the preservation of a thing is due to necessity and novelty; therefore, it is not the result of chance, but evolutionarily forces. In other words, people, ideas, and memes, not unlike viruses, must adopt randomly in order to evolve and survive.

Cultural and market studies in this area see the idea of "random chance" as the sparks of innovation—that new ideas become the fires of products and are preserved within the market by necessity. Thus, moving the novel to the mundane as a meme starts out as a new cluster of ideas and then moves across time and culture into the area of old and tiered. The idea of chance, or randomness, allows for free will and the ongoing repercussions from those first causes to *persevere*. Those ideas also allow for randomness and outliers much more readily than formal cause and effect propositions. How novel events are tracked—and their progress is measured, will be further explored in later chapters; but for now we will be discussing what a meme is and how they tend to grow and stick.

By understanding memes, emergency managers and counter-terrorism professionals can group ideas together in meaningful ways, communicate them as a singular unit, and then see how these groups of ideas might interact or evolve into expected or unexpected outcomes. By grouping ideas into memes, we give data meaning and are able to connect larger groups of ideas together to better understand them. In short, memes give meaning and structure to random ideas. It is important for us to understand and begin implementing these principles because terrorists and criminals are already using these tactics all the time.

5.5 MEMES IN ACTION: THE BESLAN MASSACRE

When the Soviet Union collapsed in 1991, the different Republics that made up the former union (Armenia, Azerbaijan, Belarus, Estonia, Georgia, Kazakhstan, Kyrgyzstan, Latvia, Lithuania, Moldova, Tajikistan, Turkmenistan, Uzbekistan, and the Ukraine) were virtually bombarded with Western ideas, ideologies, and products. In short, the countries that emerged as post-Soviet states were immersed in Western memes. Even Russia herself was introduced to radical new ideas, ideologies, and products that were not allowed under formal Communism.

From 1991, and increasing dramatically through 2001, international companies and other interests began inflecting popular culture, marketing techniques, and new products into this virgin frontier. In the past few years, access to satellite TVs, cell phones, and the Internet has caused a boom in entertainment and popular culture marketing. Of course, some of the post-Soviet states, like the Ukraine, "Westernized" more readily due to their historical and cultural links to Western Europe. Other former Soviet Republics, both in the Caucasus and in Central Asia, did not participate in this process, but rather leaned toward their Muslim traditions.

Far away on the Southern border of greater Russia, the state of North Ossetia and the town of Beslan held on to many of their old ways and traditions in spite of television, cell phones, and other western products and ideas creeping into their daily lives. One of those traditions is known as "The Day of Knowledge", or the "First of September."[b]

The "First of September" has a deep cultural significance for Russians and former Soviet Union states. It is a festive and important day, and even holds a theme in children's rhymes. It is a very important day for first-graders who usually celebrate the day with schoolmates, their parents, and other adults who gather together to celebrate the end of summer and the beginning of the school year. Adults and children wear suits and formal dresses. Balloons are released. Everyone shows up to see their children begin their education with pride. It is a school event in Russia every bit as well attended as the end of the year's other festivities.

Many of the memes discussed in this chapter were at play on September 1, 2004, when "First of September" festivities were underway at Beslan School Number One. A police van and a military truck, known as a GAZ-66, pulled up to the main gymnasium of the school. Approximately 1,200 people were gathered inside, a majority of them children. People outside of the school thought nothing of these vehicles, according to some of the witnesses. They imagined that a training exercise was underway, or that the vehicles were part of the festivities.

What happened next, and during the three-day siege that followed, is much disputed as media reports and various investigative and government inquiries contradict one another. First, there was the unusually large crowd. Second, there was the very soft target of the school. (A **soft target** is a military term that refers to undefended targets populated by civilians.) Third, there were the official-looking vehicles used in the initial attack. Fourth, there was the use of suicide bombers and automatic weapons by the attackers on innocent children. Finally, there was the utter chaos in Command and Control that resulted from the attacks. In fact, this horrible attack is very similar to the Rave Massacre Scenario found in Chapter 1.

The terrorists that poured out of those official-looking vehicles wore suicide bomber vests, took over the school, rigged it with explosives, and killed the strongest of the young boys and men at the school on the first day. By the end of the three-day siege at least 396 people, mostly hostages, were killed. A final assault on the school by Russian counter-terrorism teams ended the bloodletting. A report by the United Nations states that more than 1,200 people were killed or injured in the attacks.[10]

Much of the confusion around this event is the result of the memes deployed and exploited, the radical nature of the attack itself, and the resulting loss of Command and Control over the situation that resulted in the final gun battle during the hostage crisis. Even handled with an eye toward objectivity, complete accountability for the incident would have to lay the blame for the event at the feet of the terrorists themselves who used automatic weapons, IEDs, and body vest bombs to wantonly murder innocent men, women, and children. The Russian counter-terrorist teams on sight those three days were the best teams in the Nation, and while they have received much criticism about the final assault on the school, it is clear that the terrorists inside were the first event and had to be dealt with.

As professional emergency managers, we should study closely the tactics employed by the Chechen rebels that perpetrated this, and other attacks, in Russia. Chechen rebels are linked both to al-Qaeda and the mafia. Using these diverse connections, they have the ability to strike viciously—and mix at their advantage Western memes with terrorist-related memes to attack with impunity anywhere within Russia. One needs to only look at the Dubrovka Moscow Theater Attack of 2002, the Beslan School Siege of 2004, or the Bali Nightclub Bombing of 2002 to see memes at play in the strategies and tactics employed to conceive, plan, perpetrate, and carry out these past attacks.

A quote from one of the children who survived the Beslan School Siege should stick in our minds, "There is no God. Only force… military force."[11] By updating our methods of managing and predicting risk we will be offering much more than military force. We will be offering prevention. And the good news is, this *is* an attainable goal.

5.6 COMPLEX SYSTEMS: WHY RICH DATA SETS AND NOVELTY REQUIRE TRENDING AND MEMES

Why should emergency managers care about memes? There are two reasons: first, an understanding of cultural evolution provides critical insight into the process of change and communication around how an event may occur, and how to best tell that story. Second, a better awareness of how ideas can be grouped in our minds allows us to become better masters of memes. If the reader masters memes, he or she can better understand and manage change and the unexpected or unforeseen—which is critical to successfully managing Emerging Risk.

Emergency management and the entire group of roles attendant to its practice compose a complex system. A **complex system** is a multi-node, highly clustered network. We can tell that work in the field is complex just by the nature of the data and systems reviewed in Chapter 4. However, to justify the need for a shift in thinking and mastering memes, the reader has to understand that emergency management is a complex system because it has all of the hallmarks of complexity theory associated with it.

At the highest level, emergency management can, and often does, discuss complex processes in very simple terms. As emergencies happen, emergency managers respond, deploy resources, and manage the event through to recovery and a state of stability. However, just stepping in a bit closer, we can see that emergency managers deal with more choices than that.

At the next level, an emergency happens and emergency managers respond with a multi-disciplinary group of other responders; establish command and control; assess damage to various individuals, infrastructure, key resources and facilities; triage varied impacts; create new supply chains to replace those lost during the event; manage medical, fire, and security resources; restore public confidence; and manage through to recovery as secondary, tertiary, and even rogue outcomes manifest themselves. Still, we have to go one level deeper in order to meet the standard of a *complex system*.

One level deeper, we see the hallmarks of a complex system become apparent. There are four general, but key, hallmarks of **complex systems**:

1. A state of constant and ongoing novelty and innovation
2. Complexity in decision-making based on many specialized and varied inputs from multiple disciplines
3. Complexity in span of control based on multiple shareholders in which the components can stand alone or be dependent on one another, yet share the same goals and outcomes
4. Emergence of unexpected outcomes

Looking at emergency management more closely, we can say that emergency managers start with scenarios and probabilities that are nearly always based in novel and innovative events—in much the same way that emergency room doctors start with a patient that walks in the front door exhibiting a new condition or injury. Next, many complex decisions must be made by the emergency manager based on specialized and varied inputs from sources such as GIS data, USGS data, impact assessments, and the victims' reaction to the event—in much the same way that that ER doctor must perform screening tests (blood work, EKG data, and X-rays) to arrive at a diagnosis. Then, depending on the initial diagnosis, the opinions of other experts and specialists, law enforcement, search and rescue, evacuation control, and affected population are considered before moving forward with decision-making—in the same way as ER doctors must consult with other specialists and experts, including the members of the victim's families. Finally, emergency managers must be prepared to deal with secondary, tertiary, and random outcomes as they initiate recovery, just as the emergency room doctor must be prepared for the first cause diagnosis to lead to discoveries of other injuries or underlying conditions.

Emergency management is a complex system. The emergency management stakeholders self-organize (another hallmark of complexity) around an event, make decisions with multiple decision nodes across a vast domain of knowledge, do not have time to wait until "all of the evidence is in" to move, and often must accept incomplete solutions when full solutions are unrealistic due to time constraints. Algorithmic decision-making trees are useless in emergency management. There is simply too much subtlety and data to handle all possible events. Looking at the "80/20 Rule," much of our emergency management field has focused on the 80% of the events that might be managed by such stringent controls, while the other 20% has been missed time and again.

In reality, the "80/20 Rule" is more likely the "50/50 Rule" given that we believe many events have been shoehorned into the 80% rule set, but are actually highly novel and complex events. While you will have to judge for yourself, we feel it is fair to say that there is at least a 20%-plus range of events in which the current hierarchal and algorithmic approach fails.

Mastering memes allows us to organize complex systems, dominated by rich data sets and radical novelty. Being better organized, we are able to inform a broader range of events and responses without deteriorating the whole field into chaos. Sound emergency management operations must be optimized from the start to live at the edge of chaos, to handle a multitude of different problems simultaneously, and be resilient no matter how complex or novel the First Event Scenario is. An elastic and scalable capability must be introduced to assist in planning and preparing as well as responding appropriately.

5.7 MASTERING MEMES

A meme is like a virus because it replicates, mutates, and adapts, except that it is not biological; it is more like a thought or idea grouping that evolves with time and new events. Memes allow us to group ideas and ideologies into compact communication nuggets that are easy to communicate, catch on to, and manipulate. Consider this example: what encapsulates narcotics trafficking, cartels, radical Islam, and Jihad then rolls all of these ideas into a single concept and delivers it in two very clear and easy to understand words? Narco-Jihad.

ICS is a meme. As an acronym, it stands for **Incident Command System** and it is a management framework developed in the early '70s with the purpose to create a consistent approach to manage incidents despite their scale, or the number of organizations involved. It also makes up a whole school of ideas that spread out beneath the surface of the meme including the chain of command, communication, recovery priorities, reporting, roles and responsibilities, and other key components of a strong ICS system. The ICS meme is now used to rapidly share or replicate a grouping of ideas about command and control. However, we do not think often enough about memes and ideas related to cultures and domains outside of the ones with which we are familiar. This insular attitude is in large part responsible for why data is not distinguished and categorized often enough, or well enough, for us to have rich conversations and to tell the stories we need to relay in order *to get in front of risk*.

Recall the dots we spoke of earlier, and that they do not mean anything in and of themselves. The output is only as useful as the input, and we need to be able to consider the data as is, assemble it, and intuit risk if we want to get ahead of the game. We do that by paying attention to memes as new sources for information and organization. The memes we spend time learning about *are the dots* we need to be looking for and connecting. Memes enable us to be the best at creating distinctions and categorizing things to connect the dots. Grouping things on the fly and creating meaning from dots is what memetics is all about. Our sexting example at the beginning of this chapter is a meme. So are flash mobs, raves, and reverse engineering. They are groupings of multi-dimensional ideas that help us understand a broad picture of multiple, complex data points. A **flash mob** is a large gathering of people that happens suddenly and unexpectedly in a public place. A **rave** is an underground, yet highly organized, party involving music and dancing.

Using the broad picture, we can connect dots as groups to see how to better plan and respond to events. In Chapter 1's Rave Scenario, a combination of memes came together in not an unlikely fashion and wreaked havoc on a city. Looking at the dot of Jimmy's MySpace page might not have prepared the city for what was to come. However, looking at the broader memes surrounding the event might have been a start (see Figure 5.4).

Using memes is a way to see the forest through the trees. A mastery of memes allows for conversations to be meaningful, quick, and deep. The chaos created by the scenario just mentioned was simply a failure to identify memes as *meaningful* dots in order to see the potential of where those dots were and where they were heading. This failure to connect the dots did not occur with dots that are not there. It happened with data that, in reality, was there, but was not being looked for.

Flash mobs, raves, texting, social networks, reverse engineering, unregulated soft targets, and sleeper cells are all memes at play right now, and in your own city. The rave scenario that was presented simply leveraged these eight memes and brought them together in the same place. You may be asking yourself, why would anyone do that?

5.8 TERRORISTS AND MEMES: COMPLEX SYSTEMS AND THE 15% RULE

According to Gary Ackerman and Jeremy Tamsett's[12] book, *Jihadists and Weapons of Mass Destruction*, modernity has left radical Jihadists with no upper hand in conventional warfare.

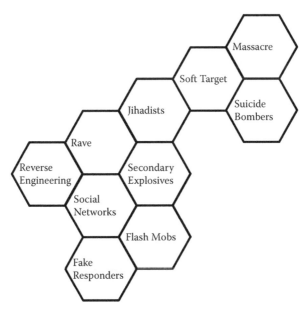

Figure 5.4 Memeplex of the rave massacre scenario.

This leaves those with grandiose visions little choice other than to pursue their aims asymmetrically, which usually translates into applying what little force they have against civilians and other "soft" targets. It also means leveraging the new opportunities provided by the information revolution for disseminating their message, both to potential converts and conspirators and to a worldwide audience through alternative media outlets.[12]

Jihadists started using the Internet as a recruiting tool in the mid-1990s; certain U.S. agencies did not enter the space of online recruiting with a strong effort until 2009. What does that imply? It implies that we could learn from our enemy here, or we could learn from the best meme collectors on the planet—marketing companies. Either way, we must learn.

Remember the basic characteristics of memes: they can be manipulated, malformed, reverse engineered, or reengineered altogether (or **translated**). Marketing theory has mastered these same performance characteristics and has used them with great success in different facets of product development and market penetration. A great example is a dance called Tecktonik. This dance craze looked like a spontaneous trend, but was actually a manipulated meme.

Tecktonik started in a nightclub located in a suburb of Paris called Metropolis. The owners of the club, Alexandre Barouzdin, a former Merrill Lynch investment banker, and Cyril Blanc, a ballet dancer, in 2006, began organizing what they called *Tecktonik Killer Nights*. These all-night dances brought in up to 8,000 dancers at a time. There they introduced the dance style that had been percolating in Northern Europe for some time—a mix of break dancing, pop locking, light sticking, and vogueing.

The dance moves put much more emphasis on upper body and leg movements than break dancing or other contemporary styles. This movement is popular with house music, techno music, and electronic music fans. A distinctive Tecktonik look grew with the dance scene; skinny jeans, fluorescent T-shirts, and flashy neon accessories were requisites.

By 2007, Barouzdin and Blanc had organized 120 parties worldwide and the partners realized that the merchandise rights that came with the marketing of Tecktonik represented an opportunity to cash in. In July 2007, when Tecktonik was starting to really take off in France, they signed a derivative product development deal with TF1 Licensing, a subsidiary of France's biggest TV channel, and took the commercialization of their brand to a new level. They *translated* (a marketing term) an existing street trend, the Tecktonik meme in this case, and used it for a marketable business advantage.

TF1 created Tecktonik T-shirts, energy drinks, magazines, and all sorts of merchandise controlling not just the brand name, but its image too. Switch on the television and you will see kids dancing Tecktonik in advertising for mobile phones. Go to the supermarket in any European town and you will find Tecktonik PlayStation games and Tecktonik school bags. The Tecktonik Company and TF1 have, rather cleverly, co-opted many of the first and best dancers by putting them on their books and booking them as their "talent." When work in TV ads or music videos comes along, they push for their dancers to get the parts. Tecktonik will most likely move out of the test market of Europe soon and into the mainstream of the United States.

Barouzdin and Blanc followed the three steps to mastering a meme. First, they manipulated an existing data set—the dance movement in Northern Europe, so that it would appear to be their own invention in Paris. Second, they aggregated other memes, such as street fashion, video games, music videos, and a talent agency into their meme. Finally, they stand poised to adapt it once it burns out in Europe for a larger market— the Americas.

5.9 FUSION CENTERS DO NOT MAKE MEMES: FUSION PEOPLE DO

In the *9/11 Commission Report*, Thomas Keene famously stated that the U.S. intelligence community suffered from "a failure of imagination,"[13] in anticipating, preparing for, and mitigating the risk of an asymmetrical terrorist attack on U.S. soil. The statement made for a great sound bite in the wake of 9/11. Further study into the problem revealed that traditional means of information sharing across public safety, intelligence, and emergency management communities was no longer effective in the modern threat environment. Thus, the concept of the **fusion center** was born.

Fusion centers consolidate, analyze, and distribute (share) information through many organizations—or silos within an organization—in order to enhance the ability to foresee and hopefully to forestall acts of terror, natural disasters, and other Emerging Risk. There are approximately 80 fusion centers in operation at the federal and state level today. Many of them are connected to the Homeland Security Data Network (HSDN) and have access to the National Counterterrorism Center (NCTC). There are also three metropolitan fusion centers operating in New York, Los

Angeles, and Dallas.[14] This adoption leads one to believe that the potential of a logical step into the private area is feasible. There is demonstrated growth in concept and understanding of public and private fusion centers nationwide and an overall trend toward adoption.

> Officials cited a variety of reasons why their state or local jurisdiction established a fusion center. To improve information sharing—related to homeland security, terrorism, and law enforcement—among federal, state, and local entities and to prevent terrorism or threats after the attacks of September 11 were the most frequently cited reasons.[15]

The U.S. Department of Homeland Security (DHS) and the Federal Emergency Management Agency (FEMA) have been seeking the assistance of the private sector in identifying, preparing for, and responding to risk for some time. Former DHS Secretary Michael Chertoff has stated, "September 11, 2001, taught us the importance of strong public–private partnerships and information sharing."[16] Eight years later as H1N1 became a very real threat to the United States, FEMA Director Janet Napolitano told the media: "So—individual, family, private sector, government, everybody has a shared responsibility and a role to play in this effort."[17]

How does the public/private partnership take form and deliver intelligence and response capabilities in a cost effective, secure, and constitutionally ethical manner? The private sector could follow the public sector's lead and create private fusion centers that integrate threat intelligence, planning, and mitigation while communicating their findings with public fusion centers. Many of the challenges faced by the public sector are not found in the private sector. It may be that private fusion centers are a component of the public and private partnership equation because they are fairly effective. State and Local Program Office, Office of Intelligence and Analysis Director Robert Riegle testified before Congress, "Fusion centers are force multipliers. They leverage financial resources and the expertise of numerous public safety partners to increase information awareness."[18] Based on his testimony, public fusion centers have curried much political and funding traction in the past five years.

The DHS, through the Office of Intelligence and Analysis, provides personnel with operational and intelligence skills to the fusion centers. This support is tailored to the unique needs of the locality and serves to:

- Direct the flow of classified and unclassified information
- Provide expertise
- Coordinate with local law enforcement[19]

DHS' approach seems to be working; yet the implementation of public fusion centers is not without its own challenges.

The utility of fusion centers in the public/private partnership is centered on the performance of public fusion centers and their challenges. Addressing issues found in the implementation and operation of public fusion centers will speed the creation of private fusion centers. At issue are the long-term sustainability of public fusion centers and the near-term integration of intelligence with state and national command and control capabilities.

In a review focused on issues and challenges encountered at the state and local level, the Government Accountability Office (GAO) conducted an in-depth review of the current status of operational public fusion centers. There are 43 centers reviewed in the report and the "top-of-mind" concern for those public servants interviewed for the report was the long-term viability of public fusion centers.

> Officials in 43 of the 58 fusion centers contacted reported facing challenges related to obtaining personnel, and officials in 54 fusion centers reported challenges with funding, some of which affected these centers' sustainability. The officials said that these issues made it difficult to plan for the future and created concerns about the fusion centers' ability to sustain their capability for the long-term.[15]

Nearly all public fusion centers have DHS and FBI personnel assigned to them. Cross-agency representation and intelligence data flow by and between varied agencies appears to be robust. The Department of Justice (DOJ) seems to be slow to integrate; however, DHS and the Department of Defense (DOD) are working to solve this challenge. The GAO recommends that more be done in the area of long-range mission planning and resource review to ensure sustainability of the fusion centers. Specifically, the "GAO is recommending that the federal government determine and articulate its long-term fusion center role and whether it expects to provide resources to help ensure their sustainability.... The DHS and PMISE (Program Manager, Information Sharing Environment) reviewed a report draft and agreed with our recommendation."[15]

As ongoing efforts are made to address the long-term sustainability of public fusion centers, the near-term reality of a public fusion center lack of response looms. While the patriots who currently work within public fusion centers are doing everything within their means to share information, another catastrophic event not responded to effectively could lead to immediate and fatal results. U.S. temperament around disaster response is on a tight trigger, and failure to participate in response activities could be a real blow to the public fusion center program. A Katrina-like event, without deeper integration and role-playing beyond intelligence sharing by national fusion centers, could become a major policy and funding issue.

Citizens and policy-makers must see public fusion centers as playing a direct role in the response to disasters as well as in intelligence gathering. They cannot remain in the intelligence-sharing role only and not take some of the spotlight when their good work prevents or lessens the impact of the next U.S. disaster. One might consider how the National Infrastructure Protection Plan (NIPP) might be more deeply integrated into the public fusion center model to avoid such a calamity.

NIPP is a key piece of policy that

> Provides the coordinated approach that will be used to establish national priorities, goals, and requirements for critical infrastructure/key resources protection so that federal funding and resources are applied in the most effective manner to reduce vulnerability, deter threats, and minimize the consequences of attacks and other incidents.[19]

NIPP ties directly to DHS's guidance to the private sector for areas assessed as Critical Infrastructure and Key Resources (CI/KR), among them privately held hospitals, banking systems, and utility companies.

The DHS has identified CI/KR in the private sector. They have issued guidance on how private businesses can monitor, gather intelligence on, and have a response strategy in place for possible or probable attacks. Yet, the Federal Sector Specific Agencies (SSAs) involved in the day-to-day operations of public fusion centers have not been reviewed to determine the utility, potential, and reality of their individual proactive response capabilities. In short, SSAs do not provide a sound point of reference for private fusion centers.

Federal Sector Specific Agencies are regulated by a key piece of legislation, the **Posse Comitatus Act**. Posse Comitatus is Latin for "power of the county" and is a federal law enacted June 18, 1878, to prevent the Federal Government from using military forces for purposes of law enforcement. This Act presents a unique challenge in enabling fusion centers to play a key role in response efforts, even though they are fully functional, high-tech information centers for threat recognition and analysis. Again, public fusion centers lack a reference guideline for private fusion centers because they have not addressed this issue. For public fusion centers, Posse Comitatus is the core challenge; not providing clear guidance to the private sector on how it affects them deters from private fusion center creation.

While some radical anti-Federalist movements may argue that recent Army operations and scope of control statements made by United States Northern Command (NORTHCOM) bypass the need for Posse Comitatus, it should be clearly noted that any statement by the U.S. Army neither constitutes law, nor does it effectively augment or change Posse Comitatus. Specifically, the announcement that the Third Infantry Division's First Brigade Combat Team (CBT) will be under the command of NORTHCOM and may be "called upon to help with civil unrest and crowd control or to deal with potentially horrific scenarios such as massive poisoning and chaos in response to a chemical, biological, radiological, nuclear, or high-yield explosive (CBRNE) attack,"[20] does not change the Posse Comitatus Act.

The act of deploying U.S. Military personnel and resources in intelligence gathering, disaster response, or for other reasons on U.S. soil is widely regarded as a "no-no" by some Americans. According to the American Civil Liberties Union (ACLU), "We're setting up essentially a domestic intelligence agency, and we're doing it without having a full debate about the risks to privacy and civil liberties."[21]

The Posse Comitatus Act is possibly one of our most important U.S. legal treasures, and is viewed as being adjunct to the Constitution. It clearly outlines the role of U.S. troops, intelligence, and the Federal reach within the bounds of statehood. In addition, SSAs at the federal level determine state and local level boundaries that present rough legal ground when responding to a national level disaster or terror attack. The ability for public fusion centers to extend themselves into command centers is core to our national protection; however, issues in policy, law, and the practice of common sense remain as long-term challenges.

To exacerbate the challenge, the future of Federal and State funding is unclear and hard to negotiate. If overall federal funding levels for homeland security decrease, it is possible that there will be some level of decrease in the Homeland Security Grant Program (which) is comprised of five interconnected grant programs:

1. State Homeland Security Program
2. Urban Area Security Initiative (UASI)
3. Law Enforcement Terrorism Prevention Program (LETPP)
4. Metropolitan Medical Response System (MMRS)
5. Citizens Corps Program (CCP)

The issues impacting the long-term sustainability of public fusion centers are important to contemplate as DHS seeks to use the fusion center concept in the public/private arsenal. Core among these are the underlying philosophy, civil liberties concerns, and the timing and funding of private fusion centers. Concern around the federal role of fusion centers is a key challenge as presented under Posse Comitatus. The statement by Masse and Rollins,[22] "the concern is to what extent, if at all, First Amendment protected activities may be jeopardized by fusion center activities" highlights this key issue. Fortunately, the need to be respectful to civil liberties and privacy as a result of 28 CFR Part 23 guidelines and recommendations by other "think tanks" take further action to assure that public fusion centers are not put at risk as a result of abuse or infringement of civil liberties. The amended 28 CFR Part 23 is a guideline for law enforcement agencies as recommended by Executive Order to increase in data sharing and intelligence operations. "28 CFR Part 23" is a federal regulation that was issued by the U.S. Department of Justice in 1980, revised in 1993, and clarified in 1998 to address circumstances that evolved with changing technologies and law enforcement needs. 28 CFR Part 23 is applicable to criminal intelligence systems, offering guidance on the collection, storage, and dissemination of criminal intelligence information.[22] This is the key non-legislative and yet binding federal guidance that enables Fusion Centers to exist and operate.

It is possible that without the redressing of these outstanding policy issues public fusion centers, command centers, incident commanders, and first responders will likely muddle through, as we have in the past, unless the threat of ill-conceived policy is taken as a clarion call to better integrate command and control with intelligence. Dr. Miriam Mosser states it clearly when she says that we must "share criminal information and intelligence analysis to create a broader emergency management mitigation."[23]

By addressing core issues and policy concerns surrounding public fusion centers, DHS can create a model of ease of use and integration for the private sector that includes information sharing and community response capability in a manner that respects both federal and state law, including privacy issues facing the private corporation such as the Health Care Information Personal Protection Act (HIPPA) and Personal Credit Information Data Security Standards.

Today, private fusion center guidelines are the same as they are for public sector fusion centers and have the following limitations:

1. They are voluntary.
2. The philosophy outlined in them is generic and does not translate theory into practice.
3. They are oriented toward the mechanics of fusion center establishment. [23]

Lack of funding, logistics capabilities, legal concerns, and apathy are serious problems impacting the effective creation of private-public information sharing and response to terrorism and other catastrophes. With few exceptions, corporations, privately held small businesses, and an array of private organizations in the areas of Critical Infrastructure and Key Resources as identified by DHS and FEMA, have simply not stepped up to engage with these agencies. Determining the means—including financial, logistic, and legal—needed to affect the creation of private sector fusion centers is the key to enhancing public safety.

So while the basic issues surrounding public fusion centers loom, let alone the notion of private fusion centers that might add to the depth of information and capability around the protection of private enterprise within the Critical Infrastructure and Key Resources (CI/KR), it seems we are still asking the wrong question. It is not an issue of whether or not a fusion center can bring data into the same room on a state-by-state level. It is a question of how and who is best outfitted to do an "all-source data analysis" of those "dots" that lead us to First Event Scenarios as they come into the fusion center.

As important as consolidating and sharing information between the private and public sector, we suggest that mastering memes will enable specialists within fusion centers to perform all-source data analysis by meaningfully grasping data sets, aggregating them, and enabling the telling of meaningful stories about them. The meme has proven to be a powerful tool in the context of competitive businesses, and we feel strongly that it will be even more effective in the context of emergency and risk management. The data shared at these fusion centers will be more thoroughly analyzed and understood because it will be in the context of a society.

5.10 MASTERING MEMES: A METHOD FOR ALL-SOURCE ANALYSIS

Applying memes to the emergency management domain allows for the use of innovative means to connect the data we work with every day. It also allows us to build new solutions in our response and communication capabilities. This results in an improved ability to foresee and prepare for events. A great example is what Science Applications International Corporation (SAIC)[c] is doing with social media to increase information sharing. The meme they started with is called *Virtual Worlds*, which is similar to *Second Life*. *Second Life* is an online **virtual world** that allows the player to assume an alter ego and interact with other people as avatars (a digital icon representing a real person). As an avatar in *Second Life,* people share information, trade, and visit places in a virtual environment.

SAIC has acquired from Forterra System Inc.[d] their On-Line Interactive Virtual Environment (OLIVE), which is a closed, virtual-world platform, for national security organizations. This platform employs virtual reality to transform processes, advance collaboration, data sharing, training, simulation, and planning.

The Department of Defense and the Air Force have adopted a similar virtual environment called *MyBase.* The way in which Emergency Management has adopted Virtual Worlds resembles the way we have seen other memes mastered in previous examples. First, an existing data set is taken in and manipulated: *Virtual Worlds.* Second, data is aggregated to create a new meme: *MyBase* or other Federal virtual world. Finally, there is adaptation: the add-ons and security protocols that will make these virtual worlds hack-proof and secure for military operations and applications within DHS and FEMA.

Mastering memes moves us from looking at a data point and data sets in a mono-directional way to looking at them as aggregated classifications of multi-dimensional groupings of data. Memes allow us to manipulate, aggregate, and adapt data sets as needed. Using memes, we are able to leverage data sets that help us achieve our tactical and strategic goals, and also understand what types of memes (types of multi-dimensional data) are at play during an actual event. To broaden our understanding of memes it is worthwhile to dig a little deeper into how they might be organized.

5.11 GROUPING IDEAS, TACTICS, AND IDEOLOGIES: CATEGORIZING MEMES TO TELL THE STORY

In order for us to use memes to our advantage, it is a good idea to understand that memes can be categorized into potentials. Let us consider four key types of potentials you should be looking for when considering a meme:

1. Is there a proximity to memes, or a similarity in memes that makes them likely to combine, and/or morph, into one another?
2. Is there a tactical advantage to one or more memes being leveraged that would not otherwise be there if the meme was left to stand on its own?

3. Is there popularity to a meme that makes it attractive for would-be terrorists, nation-state actors, or even first responders that, if morphed, could yield a result?
4. Would the proximity, popularity, or tactical advantage embedded in the meme result in an adaptation that could yield positive or negative results?

Using these four questions, we begin inspecting memes to better understand their positive and negative potentials. Going back to our texting example, is there a proximity meme or a similarity to other memes that makes them likely to combine and morph into one another? Yes—if we can add a picture to a text message then we can show what is happening as opposed to typing what is happening. Is there a tactical advantage to one or more memes being leveraged that would not otherwise be there if the meme was left to stand by itself? Yes—reporting to an Emergency Operation Center (EOC) with pictures of damage assessments using cell phones and text messages is a faster and more efficient way of incident reporting—even more so than we currently have in place. The new meme could be called "Social Response Messaging" (SRM).

Is there popularity to the meme that makes it more attractive to first responders? Yes—it is a portable and reliable way to get messages from point A to point B; but we would have to adapt the network to make it secure.

Finally, do the proximity, popularity, and tactical advantages embedded in the meme provide positive or negative results? In the case of **Social Response Messaging**, or SRM, it delivers positive results. Many companies and agencies have made this leap. Going mobile with information sharing is working across a broad range of emergency response and anti-terrorism efforts. It is important to notice that we do not view it as a meme, but it is. It is a meme because it is a collection of ideas that follows all of the rules of memetics that are outlined in this chapter. Look at the reasoning:

First, the idea of SRM is replicated from texting. Second, it aggregates ideas about emergency management, such as the risk assessment, into the mix and enlarges the meme. Third, it adapts to be more secure and applicable in our professional environment. Finally, the meme has been inspected from four key vantage points: proximity, popularity, tactical advantage, and the end result.

It is this grouping of ideas, ideologies, or tactics as memes that allows for rapid decision-making and good or bad outcomes. Using a similar approach, we can use memes to build scenarios, and identify intelligence operations and workload based on potentials. It would be good if we could see the same potential targets as clearly as our adversaries do. However, there is no silver bullet to be one step ahead of terrorists or Mother Nature. That said, memes have been used to do just that.

5.12 GROUPING WITH VISUALIZATION

Unlike a social network diagram that identifies the relationships between one bad guy and another, a meme cluster allows for the mapping of ideas and helps us map their relationships and potentials for adaptation. A **social network diagram** is the topological arrangement that visually maps the elements and the configuration of physical and/or logical connections between the nodes of a network. A **meme cluster** is a co-adapted stable set of memes that is very stable and tends to be difficult to invade by new memes (see Figure 5.5). Social networks have two fundamental units or *topoi*: nodes and links. **Nodes** are individuals in a social network, and a **link** is interdependency between nodes. In a network diagram, a terror cell for example, the cell leader and his associates are all considered nodes. The links are lines that connect members to each other, and to the leader; they give us some insight on the structure of the network we are facing. If nodes are uniformly connected, the network is structurally cohesive. If

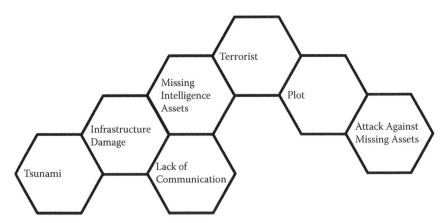

Figure 5.5 This co-adapted set of memes illustrates a scenario in which terrorists leverage a natural disaster to their advantage. Once a stable set of memes are introduced in a memeplex, it is a difficult task to invade the memeplex with new ideas.

the network is hierarchically connected, it gives us a good understanding of its center—or leadership—but a poor understanding of its edges where the links are sparser. **Edges** are the topological extent, or end of the visualization of the exterior parts of a social network. Subgroups, or regions, of the diagram with higher connectivity between nodes highlight the presence of *cliques* or *clusters*.

A particular type of network visualization, called a solar map, has a recognized center, but the links between nodes are less formalized. Social network diagrams can give us a great deal of information on the topology and the static relationships between the nodes and on the different parts of the network. An advantage is that they are a good means of portraying relationships. A disadvantage is that they do not fully illustrate ideas, intentions, or potential tactics and dynamic relationships. An example of this is if there is more than one kind of relationship. For instance, if we have a line connecting Saddam Hussein[24] to his son, should we say the line represents his *son,* or his *enforcer?*

These diagrams are typically drawn out using software that allows for any two nodes to be connected by a single line. Some programs are working to create more than just bidirectional connections between nodes, such as "father and son" but also to add depth to indicate multidimensional relationships between the nodes (such as "father, son, enforcer, sold guns to, met with…").[12] This depth of relationship between the nodes is an important step forward in social network diagrams, but the nodes themselves still seem flat. A person's name is not enough for us to fully understand who they are, what they are doing, and what they represent. Even though a multidimensional view of the relationships between nodes is an improvement, it will still only shed a dim light into the social network being analyzed.

Some academics in the field of terrorism are dismissive of social network maps altogether. Their reasoning is that the connections between operatives within terror cells change very rapidly, and the nuances of how people are really connected cannot be afforded with a simple social network map. In fact, lately, the term blob has been used more than the term network within intelligence circles to describe al-Qaeda because of the lack of a rigid structure that al-Qaeda and other terror cells exhibit.

This is where a meme cluster becomes a much more powerful tool. As mentioned, memes are expected to do at least three things—replicate, aggregate, and adapt. In addition, memes can be people, places, things, ideas, tactics, or even mixtures of all of those things. Finally, memes are expected to cluster, collide, and commingle. An example of a meme cluster is a richer view of the operations of a terror cell; the operations of an emergency response team during an event would be a meme cluster.

First, the nodes in a meme cluster are more like onions than a bidimensional solar system. A meme node has many layers of ideas, individuals, and tactics inside it—the node itself is richer. In fact, a node in a meme cluster can even be a **meta-meme**, or a grouping of memes into one node. Second, memes do not only have relationship lines that connect them to other memes, they also have overlap and potential adaptations that can be illustrated as lines of adaptation of strings of additions. Finally, because memes can be illustrated in a meme cluster as deep nodes—with many means of relationships including overlap, adaptation potential, and aggregation—as a meme evolves, the meme cluster not only illustrates what is, but what may be.

Meme clusters lend themselves more readily to mapping all of the factors at play during intelligence gathering, briefings, planning, and communicating. They give us depth, motive, means, and relationships. They deal with the blob much better than social network maps do.

Using the methods just described to assemble data into meaningful memes to create predictive and reasonable advanced notice through intelligence, or using them to build better tools for information sharing is just the tip of the iceberg.

5.13 CHAPTER SUMMARY

In thinking about the emergency management domain, we realize that social study disciplines and marketing can offer important contributions to our field in terms of critical/strategic thinking and tactical tools. In this chapter, we have described how the data and dots collected in Chapter 4 can be manipulated, aggregated, and expected to adapt (again and again) when they are treated as memes.

Memes allow us to group ideas, tactics, ideologies, and other concepts into meaningful units of measure. We can then replicate and adapt them into useful analytical and operational tools using the four potential metrics of a meme we have identified: the proximity and similarity to other memes, the tactical advantage of a meme, the popularity of the meme, and finally, whether an adaptation of the meme would yield positive or negative outcomes for emergency managers.

Understanding that memes can be utilized in a deterministic fashion, or evolve in a random way, was discussed early in the chapter. We have reviewed how memes have the potential to create new tools such as virtual worlds and better real-time assessment tools. We have also illustrated the outcomes of memes when they are reverse engineered that lead to terrible Trigger Events such as the Siege at Beslan.

Near the end of the chapter, we discussed how meme clustering compares to social network diagramming and leads us to deeper nodes, better relationship visualizations, and an allowance for mutation, adaptation, and transformation. Going forward (Figure 5.6), we will look at what marketing theories can tell us about trend spotting in Chapter 6, and how trends and memes can be tracked in Chapter 8.

5.13 END OF CHAPTER QUESTIONS

1. Take the idea of Unified Communications: what is embodied in the term and how would you illustrate it as a meme?
2. Using a current scenario in your workplace, can you identify the meme(s)? Is there more than one?
3. Reflect on your personal experience—have you spotted a cultural meme that has an impact on the field of emergency management or anti-terrorism? How could this meme be beneficial and/or harmful?

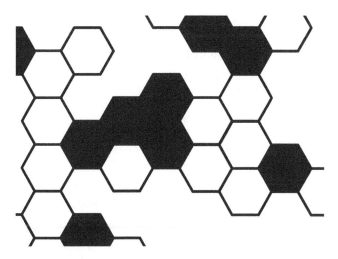

Figure 5.6 The meme and meme clusters are an important building blocks as we move forward into Chapter 6.

4. Looking at the various stakeholders in your work group, are there individuals who are more likely to think about scenarios in terms of the memes that constitute their makeup? What makes some people more apt to think in terms of blobs of data (memes) versus charts and graphs with limited detail?
5. Consider meme clustering. Write a two-page proposal on a new approach to emergency response planning that utilizes meme clustering to identify and track a current scenario or potential event.

NOTES

a. We mean static because SMS Emergency Notifi cation systems use only the technological component of this powerful meme, leaving unexploited all the other dimensions that could give a richer situational awareness. This is a typical example of the engineering driven and postdictive approach to emergency management.
b. North Ossetia is located in the Caucasus. It borders internally within Russia with Kabardino-Balkar Republic, the Stavropol Krai, Chechen Republic, and Republic of Ingushetia, and internationally with Georgia and South Ossetia.
c. Science Applications International Corporation (SAIC) security and consulting conglomerate in the United States: http://www.saic.com.
d. Forterra System, Inc. is a technology innovation firm. http://www.forterrainc.com.

REFERENCES

1. Dawkins, Richard. *The Selfish Gene*. New York: Oxford University Press, 1989.
2. Urmann, David H. *The History of Text Messaging*. August 30, 2009. http://www.articlesbase.com/computers-articles/the-history-of-text-messaging-1177228.html (accessed September 3, 2009).
3. Onishi, Norimitsu. "Thumbs Race as Japan's Best Sellers Go Cellular." *Herald Tribune*. January 20, 2008. http://www.heraldtribune.com/article/20080120/ZNYT05/801200832/1283/BUSINESS10 (accessed August 15, 2009).
4. Barbieri, Annalisa. "You don't know what sexting is?" *The Guardian*. August 7, 2009. http://www.guardian.co.uk/lifeandstyle/2009/aug/07/sexting-teenagers-mobile-phones (accessed August 16, 2009).
5. National Center for Missing and Exploited Children. "Child Pornogrophy Fact Sheet." http://www.missingkids.com/missingkids/servlet/PageServlet?LanguageCountry=en_US&PageId=2451 (accessed August 15, 2009).

6. Galanos, Mike. "Commentary: Is 'sexting' child pornography?" *CNN*. April 8, 2009. http://edition.cnn.com/2009/CRIME/04/08/galanos.sexting/index.html (accessed August 16, 2009).
7. Dawkins, Richard. *The Selfish Gene*. New York: Oxford University Press, 1989.
8. Whitelaw, Kevin. "Flu, Me? Public Remains Wary Of H1N1 Vaccine." *National Public Radio*. October 17, 2009. http://www.npr.org/templates/story/story.php?storyId=113873021 (accessed October 23, 2009).
9. Taleb, Nassim Nicholas. *The Black Swan: The Impact of the Highly Improbable*. New York: Random House, 2007.
10. Griffiths, Emma. Transcript: PM, UN Warns of Violent Reprisals for Beslan School Siege. October 15, 2004. http://www.abc.net.au/pm/content/2004/s1220346.htm (accessed October 6, 2011).
11. *Children of Beslan*. (59 min.) Directed by Leslie Woodhead and Ewa Ewart. BBC and HBO Documentary Films, 2005.
12. Ackerman, Gary, and Jeremy Tamsett. *Jihadists and Weapons of Mass Destruction*. Boca Raton: CRC Press, 2009.
13. Cooper, Anderson. "Transcripts." CNN.com. July 22, 2004. http://transcripts.cnn.com/TRANSCRIPTS/0407/22/acd.00.html (accessed July 11, 2011).
14. Biddick, Michael. *IT Fusion Centers*. June 4, 2009. http://www.informationweek.com/blog/main/archives/2009/06/it_fusion_cente.html (accessed August 16, 2009).
15. U.S. Government Accountability Office. *Homeland Security: Federal Efforts Are Helping to Alleviate Some Challenges Encountered by State and Local Information Fusion Centers*. October 2007. http://www.gao.gov/new.items/d0835.pdf (accessed August 16, 2009).
16. Biesecker, Calvin. "DHS Releases National Infrastructure Protection Plan." *Defense Daily* 230, no. 65 (July 2006): 4-4.
17. Napolitano, Janet. "Remarks by Secretary Napolitano at Today's Media Briefing on the H1N1 Flu Outbreak." *U.S. Department of Homeland Security*. May 4, 2009. http://www.dhs.gov/ynews/releases/pr_1241530553980.shtm (accessed May 18, 2010).
18. U.S. Department of Homeland Security. "Testimony of Director Robert Riegle, State and Local Program Office, Office of Intelligence and Analysis, before the Committee on Homeland Security, Subcommittee on Intelligence, Information Sharing, and Terrorism Risk Assessment, "The Future of Fusion Centers: Potential Promise and Dangers." April 1, 2009. http://www.dhs.gov/ynews/testimony/testimony_1238597287040.shtm (accessed August 16, 2009).
19. U.S. Department of Homeland Security. "National Infrastructure Protection Plan." *The Official Website of the Commonwealth of Massachusetts*. http://www.mass.gov/Eeops/docs/mema/emd_advisory_committee/appendix_b/national_infrastructure_protection_plan/NIPP%20Plan%20-%20Full%20Document.pdf (accessed May 17, 2010).

163

20. Cavallaro, Gina. "Brigade homeland tours start Oct. 1." *Army Times*. September 30, 2008. http://www.armytimes.com/news/2008/09/army_homeland_090708w/ (accessed May 17, 2010).
21. Masse, Todd, and John Rollins. "A Summary of Fusion Centers: Core Issues and Options for Congress: RL34177." *Federation of American Scientists*. September 19, 2007. http://www.fas.org/sgp/crs/intel/RL34177.pdf (accessed August 16, 2009).
22. Institute for Intergovernmental Research. *Frequently Asked Questions*. http://www.iir.com/Justice_Training/28cfr/FAQ.aspx?AspxAutoDetectCookieSupport=1#q1 (accessed July 11, 2011).
23. Mosser, Miriam. "Intelligence Has No Value." Speech Given at George Washington University. 2009. (accessed August 14, 2009).
24. Wilson, Chris. "Searching for Saddam: A five-part series on how the U.S. military used social networking to capture the Iraqi dictator." *Slate*. February 22, 2010. http://www.slate.com/id/2245228/ (accessed May 18, 2010).

6

Coolhunters and Pattern Recognition

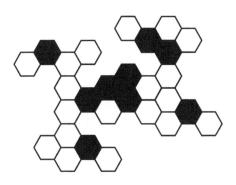

6.1 KEY TERMS

165

6.2 LEARNING OBJECTIVES:

After reading this chapter, you should be able to describe:

- How Coolhunters identify memes and apply them to their field
- The role that Coolhunting and Pattern Recognition can play in emergency management and preparedness
- How early adoption is the fundamental quality of meaningful narratives and leads to change in complex systems and data
- Why the strongest Pattern Recognition Specialist should be recognized as an All-Source Data Specialist and should be responsible to create a forward view story.

6.3 CHAPTER INTRODUCTION

In Chapter 4, we looked at data—the "dots" of data points and systems that we ponder while designing responses to possible events. In Chapter 5, we looked at how data creates memes and meme clusters to aggregate the dots into meaningful groupings of ideas and thinking that help us articulate the possibility of future events. In this chapter, we will look at the skills required to recognize patterns and generate meaningful narratives from data, trends, memes, and their clusters (see Figure 6.1).

Coolhunting, a term coined in the early 1990s, refers to a new breed of marketing professionals with an ability to search out, and spot, early adopters and emerging trends. Technology's ubiquitous presence has

Figure 6.1 Memes can be tracked as they are chosen by early adopters, recognized by coolhunters, and finally translated and commodified by pattern recognition specialists.

created the platform and need for a much more sophisticated Coolhunter that goes beyond fashion and trend spotting. Today's Coolhunters range across the technology, architecture, fashion, and food industries. They have an eye for what is next. They are expert "data detectives" living in a world with "too much information" and are able to separate signal from noise, then narrow that noise down to the next technology, housing, fashion, or food trend. They have a laser-like ability to recognize patterns and early adopters. They can see, or even feel, the next big thing before it happens.

They are the curators of cool, a genetic amplifier in the Market State that hypes the best of the best to position it for brand success or, if used for nefarious purposes, failure. Coolhunters are capable of looking at the wants and needs we have today and projecting them into the tomorrow of our lifestyle.

On the flip side of Coolhunting, these heavily influencing curators can also cause anti-movements, anti-fashions, and full-out assaults on brands, ideologies, and movements. Any emergency manager who underestimates the power of keeping a Coolhunter happy is one who is asking for trouble. These are our most vocal cheerleaders and critics. Public relations will be part of any future First Event Scenario for emergency managers who know their stuff. These individuals will position us to become more than emergency managers—the influence of a Coolhunter on our field can reposition the role of emergency managers into that of *business accelerators*.

In the corporate United States, Coolhunting and trend spotting have not yet been reverse engineered to mislead. But abroad, top marketing firms are using counter-Coolhunting techniques to prepare markets and ensure the success of new product launches. Consider this example: word of mouth marketing, particularly to 21- to 25-year-old males by strong, classy women in clubs to influence the market for Brand X Jeans. The counter-Coolhunters send in sponsored influencers (paid drinks, front-of-line privileges) to virally spread bad news about Brand X: It is out of style. It is too tight, or it is too baggy. Brand X hurts small animals in their manufacturing processes.

Meanwhile, Brand Y Jeans are on the real Coolhunter path. They have the right fit, the right logo, and they are nice to animals.

Under these business pressures, Coolhunters are becoming widely utilized in large corporations and industries in which design and advertising plays a significant role in creating the bottom line. They are brought in to understand the emergent memes in the markets. Using focus groups, open source data, and word-of-mouth, they understand patterns and

167

trends within a target demographic or culture, and the objective of the Coolhunter is to appropriate this data into a strategic meme and predict the next "big thing."

Coolhunters seek out individuals from their target demographic who are regarded as trendsetters or early adopters. Rogers[1] defined the term **early adopter** as a customer/user of a given product, company, or technology. In politics, fashion, art, and other fields, they are usually called a trendsetter, or as someone who takes on a new idea much earlier than the mass market. It is important to understand that the early adopter is a person who is ahead of the curve, on the bubble. Coolhunters often use these individuals to go "undercover" and gather information secretly amongst their peers, and then report their findings back to the Coolhunter. This is a popular method of Coolhunting because it gives the Coolhunter insight into the target market from within the early adopter's natural environment. In addition, Coolhunters look at their conversations with people who exhibit early affinity with new memes. It is the Coolhunter's job to make an observation and predict changes in new or existing cultural memes.

How is this relevant for us? Given the multiple sources of complex data and systems pointed out in the previous chapters, we need to prepare not only for the probable, but also for the possible. To do this, we need to apply Coolhunting techniques to our field and master the skill of all-source data analysis. Coolhunters have had commercial success creating meaningful narratives from analyzing data, meme hunting, and recognizing patterns. By doing the same thing, we can have professional success hunting for the possible and the probable.

It is evident that the notion of Coolhunting is also applicable to other social trends, such as politics, revolution, and finally terrorism. When applied to these other domains, the meme "cool" loses its aesthetic and positive connotations but retains others, such as originality, innovation, attractiveness, impressiveness, cutting-edginess, unconventionality, and even rebel-like appeal. In this volume, we will continue using the Coolhunter meme for its capacity to convey all these connotations.

Best of breed Coolhunters practice lateral thinking,[a] generating ideas that are designed to break current thinking or behavioral patterns, spotting trends intuitively, and eliciting novel ones. **Lateral thinking**[2] refers to a method of problem solving that is not immediately obvious and results in outcomes and ideas that could not be achieved by traditional deductive reasoning. It also refers to solving problems and reasoning through an indirect and creative approach. With very little data, this type of Coolhunter, a **Pattern Recognition** Specialist, can identify a trend based on his or her inherent ability and knowledge. The term Pattern Recognition is associated with gaming, Coolhunting, battle planning, and combat training. It is important to understand from this that this skill is not used only by the marketing industry; these highly skilled, highly educated Coolhunters have a great deal of informed intuition about a group or product range. Much like our best intelligence agents and emergency managers that use a mix of "local knowledge" and hard-won experience, Coolhunters use Pattern Recognition to move along the tenuous thresholds among gut, trend, and rumor to achieve tremendous results. When applied to anti-terrorism or emergency response, Pattern Recognition allows creative foresight and local knowledge to generate fast, insightful results. However, these skills are often met with skepticism because of our need for "evidence" before action.

General David Petraeus in the Army/Marine Corps Counterinsurgency Field Manual writes, "… pattern analysis tools assist in developing event and doctrinal templates to depict enemy tactics."[3] General Petraeus was tasked, between 2004 and 2006, as Commanding General of the Command and General Staff College, to oversee the publication of Field Manual 3-24, *Counterinsurgency*. This manual reviews twenty years of Army and Marine Corps counterinsurgency doctrine as it had become clear, during the Iraq War, that the tactics and strategies employed by our men and women in uniform were not as effective as they could have been in modern era urban warfare. The Department of Defense (DOD) and the Defense Advanced Research Projects Agency (DARPA) are working diligently to enable operations that are agile and adaptive. This means that looking at memes and meme clusters using Pattern Recognition Specialists and Coolhunters is core in developing more agile, creative, and adaptive policies, doctrines, strategies, and tactics for emergency management.

6.4 FROM DOTS AND PATTERNS
TO BELIEVABLE STORIES

One of the most important concepts to convey is that in order for emergency managers to succeed, they have to become "all-source data analysts" and they have to master the art of creating *narratives*. Narratives are meta-memes that incorporate data/dots, memes, patterns, trends, and the complexity of the real world into believable stories. While the reality, the world, is the objective field of our analysis—"our object of inquiry"[4] from which we draw our data—we construct our knowledge of the world through narratives and categories that are socially or intellectually created. And, to a certain extent, these narratives and categories should be "evaluated according their internal coherence rather than their correspondence to some *preconceived* reality."[5]

> Constructive formats such as written (poetry, prose, essays, etc.), oral (speeches, storytelling, etc.), picture performances (song, movies, theater, or dance), and multimedia ones (video games, computer generated models, Web casts, etc.) describe and order these different sequences of data sets, ideas, memes, and memes clusters. This cognitive approach is instrumental to fully discover all the possibilities that the objective reality can produce—not only the probable ones or the convenient ones.
>
> Those who wish to do us harm only need to succeed once, while those involved in the homeland security arena need to get it right every single time, 100 percent of the time.[5]

The cautionary tale of "getting it right 100 percent of the time" is one of the most widespread bits of commonsense in our domain; and, like most good urban legends, it enforces the idea of conformity.[b] On the other end, this is a reductive, or defective, approach. It focuses our attention on the need to find the only one "right" scenario, instead of looking to the whole set of possible scenarios that will most likely include the one that will manifest itself as a real event in the end.

Here is a real world example. The last car exiting the last ferry of the day from Victoria Island, Canada, to Port Angeles, Washington, "was a green, rental Chrysler 300 with British Columbia plates."[6] Customs inspector Diana Dean asked a few routine questions of all drivers coming out from the ferry. When she stopped the last car, the driver struck her as "fidgeting, jittery, and sweating. His hands disappeared from sight as he began rummaging around the car's console."[6] His answers, in broken English, did not add up. He seemed to be on a business trip to Seattle, but he was entering the United States through Victoria Island. This is a quite unlikely route for a businessperson; it is a typical tourist one, as you need to take three ferries to reach Seattle. To give her time to make a decision about what to do with him, she gave him a customs declaration to complete to keep him busy.

By the time the driver completed the declaration, "Dean observed, he was acting 'hinky.'"[6] At this point, she asked the driver to step outside the vehicle and open the trunk. Other inspectors came over to back her up, and she told them she believed that this was a "load vehicle"—a code for cars used for smuggling drugs. In the spare tire compartment, they found "several green bags that appeared to be filled with white powder, as well as four black boxes, two pill bottles, and two jars of brown liquid."[6] Dean and the other inspectors were quite sure that they had stopped a drug dealer. They soon discovered the person they stopped was a 32-year-old Algerian al-Qaeda operative by the name of Ahmed Ressam. They had disrupted the plot to detonate two bombs at the Los Angeles International Airport; the second bomb was to be detonated as rescuers rushed to the scene after the first explosion. A second bomb, designed to kill first responders—much like the secondary attack meme used in the Narco Jihad Scenario in found in Chapter 1—is not often contemplated or even considered by emergency managers.

Customs inspector Diana Dean was able to recognize and analyze the data: Ressam's strange trip itinerary and his "fidgeting, jittery, sweating" clues. She was able to recognize the patterns: the single driver and suspicious behavior. She was able to turn all of these different elements into a believable story: the driver of the green, rental Chrysler was a Hispanic drug trafficker trying to smuggle narcotics into the United States. Even though she was not 100 percent correct, the narrative she created was one of the possible narratives compatible with the situation she was dealing with and she acted accordingly.

What are the characteristics of a narrative, and what makes stories (narratives) believable? Every story has a beginning—a "once upon a time." This once upon a time has to be based on what is possible. It must be based on facts or data that substantiate the assumption of the story.

In Chapter 3, we looked closely at the data sources available to emergency managers today and discussed alternative data sources that should be employed to become an "all-source data analyst." In constructing narratives that could encompass the potential threat and risk that we face, data operates as a tool to create the "suspension of disbelief" necessary to allow us to look to all the possibilities without bias. For example, even in the presence of intelligence that could lead one to consider that terrorists may use "Hijacking and even use planes as missiles,"[7] as the 9/11 report stated, intelligence officials and we, as the emergency management community, suffered from "a failure of imagination" and did not "suspend our disbelief"[7] regarding such a possibility.

Once the data is deemed credible, we can take an unbiased look at the situation at hand. What are we going to find? The Coolhunter will see all of the potential trigger events inherent to the particular market he is scouting for the next "big thing." Likewise, the "all-source data analyst" will see all of the potential disasters or attacks that can arise. The credible data by themselves do not create a story; they only highlight the trigger event.

A good story needs a middle in which the trigger event develops into secondary, tertiary, and even quaternary events. The outcomes of these events are naturally linked to the emergent meme clusters that are at play in any particular situation. To become a credible story or narrative in its entirety, the emergent memes have to cluster themselves following the four potential characteristics of the memes that we discussed in the previous chapter: Proximity or similarity potential, tactical potential, popularity potential, and risk or reward potential. The ability to recognize these patterns of aggregation is what defines Coolhunters, Pattern Recognition Specialists, and Trend Spotters.

Looking back at 9/11, we can now see how the mechanics of the failure of connecting the dots and creating a believable narrative played out. The data was there, but the elected officials and the emergency management community did not use it to create the "suspension of disbelief." Neither were they able to develop a trigger event (hijacking of planes), which would have led to the development of secondary (using planes as missiles) and tertiary events (taking on the U.S. government by attacking the Pentagon or the White House).

In Chapter 4, we looked at a successful example of connecting the dots and creating a believable narrative: the dance craze called Tecktonik. Alexander Barouzdin and Cyril Blanc were able to analyze the data, highlight trigger events, and recognize potential patterns of aggregation of the memes at play. First, they elicited data sets: the North European techno music scene and the early 1980s revival in fashion. Second, they used the proximity potential to cluster the memes. They exploited the not-so-obvious connection between these data sets: German groups like Kraftwerk and Einstürzende Neubauten started the techno movement and were instrumental to the propagation of the early 1980s European street fashion. They aggregated these memes with other fashions and dance memes/trends of the same period that developed in the United States, such as break dancing and African American hip-hop street fashion. They exploited the tactical potential. They took two other groundbreaking "inventions" of the early 1980s—music videos and videogames—and tactically used and adapted them to the Internet age. They exploited YouTube/MySpace and the online gaming phenomenon.

What is absolutely genius about Barouzdin and Blanc's operation is their ability to create a narrative—a credible story that could spin off and be converted in a successful engineered product that was perceived as a "spontaneous" trend.

This takes us to the last step: every good story has an end. This end in our cognitive construction, to be believable and useful, should reveal the course of action. In the Tecktonik example and generally, in the marketing sphere, the "end of the narrative" gives the Trend Spotter a reasonable approach to creating a successful product or advertisement campaign. In the Emergency Management field, the "end of the narration" gives us a workable and possible approach to mitigate or prevent the possible scenario on which our cognitive effort has focused.

Throughout this section, we have highlighted several times the importance of what makes this cognitive process, the creation of narrative, believable: How the "stories" created must be based on convincing data, patterns, and implementation strategies. The success of the strategies that stem from the narratives we create as Emergency Managers relies also on our ability to transmit and assimilate these strategies, and on our ability to listen and communicate effectively.

In Chapter 4, we talked about the power users from *The Big Short* and how they won big during the disaster by betting against the market. All of the characters presented in Lewis's account, on one or more occasions, tried to warn the SEC or other market players of the looming disaster. Harry Markopolos, the Madoff whistle-blower, did the same thing. In neither of these cases did the SEC or other authorities intervene. It seemed as though the financial market was so corrupt and numb that it was unreceptive to any attempt to illuminate excessively risky business practices.

The narratives Markopolos put forward were based on credible data sets—the same ones that other analysts were seeing. Their narratives were not believable for the large majority of the financial community. They failed to create that "suspension of disbelief" that allows one to look at the situation at hand with fresh eyes, and they failed to convince the financial community that their motivations were unbiased and disinterested. In short, they did not create a meaningful story about the pending financial disaster that was believable.

Unlike Barouzdin and Blanc, who mastered the "reward potential" of meme clustering and creating a trend perceived as spontaneous, Markopolos and several other whistle-blowers were not able to make their motivation believable: they did not portray themselves either as speculators or as heroes.[8] Our field does not base decisions on profit or expected value, but on a more difficult to quantify set of parameters. Different, or conflicting, priorities and needs, risk attitudes, and psychological constructs such as biases, heuristics, and bounded rationalities make the decision-making process less transparent than the maximization of profit. The implication of this complexity is that, in order for narratives to be accepted, they have to have a higher degree of "believability" that could overcome all divergent forces.

Communication is a two-way street: it implies the ability to transmit narratives and information, and to assimilate them when you are on the receiving end of the communication stream.

Crisis communication, as it is devised today, is only one aspect of the narrative's transmission and assimilation. We need to be able to deploy the whole cadre of the "constructive formats" in the same way that Barouzdin and Blanc did with Tecktonik. Understanding that we need to create stories using data and memes as a basis for a complete narrative that has a beginning, middle, and end, we will move on and return to the challenge of creating meaningful communication in future chapters.

6.5 COOLHUNTERS AND EARLY ADOPTERS[1]

Coolhunters and Pattern Recognition professionals are experts in seeing what is needed next. In fashion and consumer trends, Pattern Recognition detects these shifts or opportunities *before* they happen. People who are good at Pattern Recognition use micro-trends and the insight provided by early adopters with the goal to capture and to capitalize on the trend before it goes mainstream. They are highly paid for their professional skills and developed intuition. Together, Coolhunters and Pattern Recognition professionals could be called Trend Spotters. However, to spot trends, one must understand where they originate, with whom, and how they will be adopted and diffused. This requires insight into the influence and behaviors of early adopters.

Early adopters use a blend of social monitoring, internal metrics, and gut instinct to make choices. Their behaviors and attitudes (which are their tactics and purchases) are based on cutting-edge influences and creative foresight. It is a do-it-yourself proposition from the start. An early adopter is not necessarily a consumer, they can also be a do-it-yourself maker—a creative individual who applies foresight and imagination to make something that later becomes a major trend. In politics, fashion, art, and other fields, they are usually called trendsetters. Whatever you call them, they usually get there first.

A typical early adopter is a consumer that will, in addition to using a vendor's product or technology, also provide considerable data and intelligence to the manufacturer/vendor to help him identify further development, future product releases, or marketing messages. Since the early adopter takes the risk of embracing the next new thing and often is exposed to problems, risks, and annoyances that are common to early stage product testing or deployment, their experiences can lead the Coolhunter to gain meaningful insights about what works and what does not in a market segment.

Sometimes the early adopter is likely to not have enough money to buy the things that they would like to have in the first place, or the patience to wait until they come out at a lower price and have been modified. Therefore, they tend to do as they please and to build things out of the box. In other instances, early adopters have access to money, can buy things early, at a higher purchase price, and can afford to set the pace. Since they can have anything they want, they tend to be fickle and easily displeased, but if they DO like something they have purchased, they recommend the product to others.

As it turns out, teens and preteens represent huge groups of early adopters. This is why al-Qaeda is reaching out to them now. They adapt to new ideas more readily than adults and are less leery of failure or standing out. Scientists have studied the phenomena and many link it to an underdeveloped frontal cortex in young people that leaves them with lower inhibitions. Add to this the pressures of having no jobs or prospects for income and the heavy influence of religion as a marketing tool, and it is easier to understand a young terrorist's beginnings and motivations. Marketing professionals look for these adopters to help shape (commoditize) the development of products targeted at young adults and adult audiences.

Because kids are often early adopters and less afraid of change, they often see outcomes well before adults do and need fewer than two dots to make a connection. They infer outcomes from very little information and the early adopters use creative foresight and intuition to place them well ahead of the curve in fashion, technology, and life. They can spot what is *now* in a heartbeat and look at it with some disdain, as they are constantly moving toward what is *next* (see Figure 6.2). The kinds of creative play and "coloring outside the lines" projects used to promote innovation strategies in adults are based on the premise that the uninhibited "child within" can link into the creative adult within and demonstrate better innovation and foresight. Strategically speaking, thinking like a child is good for business. It simplifies things down to what we know based on very little information and a solid dose of gut. This may also be true for emergency management.

175

Figure 6.2 Young people are less afraid of change and are often early adopters, spotting new trends and incorporating them into their lifestyle.

Thinkers like Tom Peter and Bill Rawlston have espoused this strategic approach to foresight and planning for years. Business executives view it is something akin to a "retreat" in which they learn the "voodoo" of seeing into a possible future. It often informs their thinking; it often misguides them. Whichever, they are seldom unprepared for what might come next.

In Coolhunting and Pattern Recognition, one only needs to see a tactic or trend work once and hold it up against other data to know it will happen repeatedly until it will ultimately go mainstream. The best intelligence agents do this all the time, but are often dismissed because they use their "guts" in situations where only strong evidence is traditionally used. Emergency managers who "get that bad feeling" are often not able to act because their judgment is scrutinized, rather than being trusted based on their experience and past performance. Kids, on the other hand, do not take "no" for an answer when they believe something is true based on knowledge, intuition, and gut.

6.6 PATTERN RECOGNITION—THE PROS IN ACTION

Malcolm Nance, in the *Terrorist Recognition Handbook*, uses the term pattern analysis to imply the same type of foresight that can be gained when professionals apply analysis to pattern recognition. He says,

> Pattern and frequency analysis is the study of certain characteristic patterns that can be identified and predicted. If a tactic is being used again and again and as a group gains experience, a pattern is established, and the group may move on to a different tactic.[9]

176

On the next page, he encourages his reader to reach deeper than "certain characteristics," writing, "Common sense is the most disregarded intelligence analysis tool in our arsenal."[9]

Pattern Recognition is what the great military writer John H. Poole is talking about when he uses the term "that sixth sense" in *The Tiger's Way*.[9] He quotes Dr. Masaaki Hatsumi,

> It is of the utmost importance to immerse and enjoy oneself in the world of nothingness. In this world of nothingness, one must see through to the essence of common sense, or knowledge, or divine consciousness, make a decision, and translate it into action.[10]

As much as "the world of nothingness" sounds like some type of ESP baloney, the idea that we have knowledge and common sense to take in what is around us and make a decision, then to translate that into action is nothing like ESP—*it is sound reasoning*. Very similar to what Nance stated, sound reasoning is something we seem to have lost in the hubris of evidence and paperwork that makes for good investigative work and emergency management.

Pattern Recognition is routine in military operations. An example of this is told in Dan Baum's "Battle Lesson: What the Generals Don't Know."[11]

> A small unit of American soldiers was walking along a street in Najaf [en route to a meeting with a religious leader] when hundreds of Iraqis poured out of the buildings on either side. Fists waving, throats taut, they pressed in on the Americans, who glanced at one another in terror... The Iraqis were shrieking, frantic with rage.... [It appeared that a shot would] come from somewhere, the Americans [would] open fire, and the world [would] witness the My Lai massacre of the Iraq war. At that moment, an American officer stepped through the crowd holding his rifle high over his head with the barrel pointed to the ground. Against the backdrop of the seething crowd, it was a striking gesture.... "Take a knee," the officer yelled.... The soldiers looked at him as if he were crazy. Then, one after another, swaying in their bulky body armor and gear, they knelt before the boiling crowd and pointed their guns at the ground. The Iraqis fell silent, and their anger subsided. The officer ordered his men to withdraw [and continue on their patrol].

Had it not been for the officer's recognition of the situation, and his intuitive response and action, it would have ended disastrously.

Coolhunters and Pattern Recognition Professionals are experts in the flow of data and the subtle mashups it takes to move them from one place in the cultural landscape to another. (A **mashup** is a combination of existing data with new information to make a new thing altogether. It is prevalent in digital media, but is seen even in programming and text-books. See Figure 6.3.) They cut, paste, and synchronize real property into unreal property from street fashion, to the catwalk, and finally to the store hanger. These manufacturing companies, their designers, and the early adopters they study have no compunctions of "science" in their field. No, they embrace the fact that their work is an act of creative foresight and that they are indeed, artists.

As previously stated, with Coolhunting and Pattern Recognition, we only have to see a tactic or trend work *once* and hold it up against other data to know it will happen again and again, ultimately going main-stream. If an early adopter grabs onto that idea and Coolhunters are spot-ting the same idea before it starts to take off, then a Pattern Recognition Professional would latch on quickly.

This type of low-investment, high-yield strategy for managing prod-ucts is applicable in terrorism and in natural disaster response. Terrorists use these marketing techniques often and almost as a means of practice. Emergency managers generally do not.

With a keen eye on the flow of information and ideas along the diffu-sion of innovation (see Chapter 8), Pattern Recognition Specialists watch trends move and influence individual choices. They see the next choice

Figure 6.3 Mashups can be found in music, digital media, and computer pro-gramming, but the most unmistakable example of a good mashup can be found when a DJ combines two songs from separate eras to create a completely "new" piece of music.

a person will make before that person will make it. They are not afraid to use computers to model this behavior. In fact, many retailers are now using SKU numbers on items you purchase to bring up a screen in the store that tells the checkout person what else you might like based on a rich flow of information created daily. It is important to note here that there is a similar rich flow of a very different type of data happening in cyberspace right now with terrorists, and on the ground with emergency response across an array of both private and public systems. However, we are neither harnessing it nor computing it as aggressively as marketing firms in the consumer goods space do.

When one idea does not work as well as expected, (i.e., a certain display shows blue jeans at the Gap with a red sweater but the data shows that more people are buying the blue jeans with a white sweater) that data is mashed up, and the in-store display is changed as soon as possible. Emergency managers and terrorist intelligence agencies are rarely that adaptive to the changing needs of victims or the constantly evolving intentions of would-be terrorists.

With the understanding that Pattern Recognition and trend spotting are an art assisted by the "science" of market intelligence and test marketing, these companies are not afraid to cut or paste as needed. They cut by taking items off the rack and abandoning them completely to the dusty aisles of discount stores like Ross or TJ Maxx, but they also paste in new items as soon as they "cross the chasm"[12] from the early adopters into the early majority. If a company like Urban Outfitters is highly aggressive and fashion forward, they do not even have the traditional seasons of summer, fall, winter, and spring inventory every year. They cut and paste into their inventory base eight to 16 times a year. How often do we cut approaches that are not working and paste in ones that will work based on our results? We do not do it as often as we should.

When everything is going smoothly and the Pattern Recognition Specialist, the designer, and the store are running at high volume with minimum changes to their inventory or approach, these stakeholders instantly start looking for an opportunity to broaden their sales and increase their profits. When Grateful Dead shirts are selling at Urban Outfitters, they will find a Grateful Dead picture book, bobblehead, or some other Grateful Dead merchandise and synchronize it into that moment. As Emergency Managers, how often do we leverage what is working in an additive way, not to increase profit, but to increase results?

Perhaps the biggest insight to be taken from marketing is the new idea of the **gnarl**. Like a knot in a growing tree, it is a point at which ideas and products aggregate and morph into one another. It is a place of deep growth and market adaptation that looks like a swarm, or a gnarl along the diffusion of innovation. This is where the real money is. A gnarl indicates a high likelihood that any similar product can be added and will sell. That any similar approach can be added and enhance the recovery effort. Or, that any similar intervention of a terror cell will work again. How often do we spot the gnarl and capitalize on it?

In reality, for all the standard reports, ad hoc reports, queries, drill downs, statistical analysis, forecasting, extrapolation, and predictive modeling we are doing in our daily work as emergency mangers and counter-terrorism experts, we are working on too many systems and not asking the right questions or optimizing our data results. Today there is not even a system-side DHS interface to indicate that emergency managers who looked at a possible attack in San Diego also looked at any person, place, idea, trend, or thing connected to shipping to San Diego harbor or the frequency of other emergency management power users looking at the same data! It is critical that we begin using our systems to make us competitive *now*. If business-marketing systems use data like a contact sport, then the systems that support emergency response, counter-terrorism, and the operators behind them are working at the serious business of life or death.

The truth is, pet projects and stand-alone, ad hoc funded, computational systems will not sustain a war on terror or affect a more agile response capability for emergency managers. We must advocate beyond our "turf" for the greater good and highly integrated intelligent systems that deliver the goods: from intelligence to communications.

The following is an unconfirmed story that circulates in the emergency management field. It is repeated here to simply raise a point about the necessity for independent thought and verifying work at all levels in our field.

A first responder to the attacks of 9/11 placed an order to the acquisition desk for stakes to mark the location of bodies during the first two days of the response. Within eight hours, three or more trucks had blocked the traffic of important supplies arriving to the wharf. He went out to solve the problem and asked why there were three refrigerated trucks full of steaks on his dock! It was not time for a barbecue or party, he had work to do. The communication system did not catch the misspelling of the acquisition requests and he got his "stakes."

Whether this incident truly happened or not, little mistakes similar to this *do* happen, and when they evolve into big mistakes it negatively affects the entire response effort, possibly even causing new concentric rings in the Disaster Halo Effect. This is untenable and *every first responder,* emergency manager, and counter-terrorism specialist should be enraged by this story, and demand the finest tools and personnel available. Furthermore, by applying marketing approaches to our systems and learning from companies like Apple and Amazon, *we will do better,* and limit the number of easily preventable mistakes. Just think about how much more effective you will be as a responder!

Numerical calculations of probabilities, including the possibilities in our scenario-building and decision-making, and demanding better computational tools while understanding the limitation of them, lead to a simple prescription. We must develop deeper expertise in gut-level thinking. Pattern Recognition and intuition must be embraced. We do not need to be right 100% of the time, neither can we be, but *we do have to be agile.* We have to dare to be experts in intuitive thinking and accept that sometimes our instinct will be wrong. Being wrong some of the time is a necessary companion to being right more often. In short, any team that expects excellence must expect to fail if they are building on innovation to win, whether it is in markets or in the field of terrorism and disaster response.

For almost the entire history of humankind, philosophers, sociologists, and historians have debated why and how humans think. A broad consensus that has been reached in all of these fields is that humans are unique amongst all creatures because we are greater than the sum of our physical parts. We have a capacity for reasoning, greater cognitive thinking, and even greater, yet untapped, potentials. Behind the zeros and ones of even the best "pipe dream" system for sharing intelligence about attacks and aid-giving, there must stand men and women who are more than just players on the team. They must be master players, top of their game champions, and all-source data analysts. They must be Emergency Managers.

We have proven to have an innate sense of history, somehow linked to our evolution, to imagine, reason, and thereby create completely new avenues of capabilities based on instinct, experience, knowledge, and Pattern Recognition. Why not use this instinct actively like marketing professionals do in order to aggressively press our advantage? What would our profession look like, and how much more effective would we be if we apply marketing approaches to terror intelligence and emergency response? As Emergency Managers, we do not need to be afraid of the limits of our imaginations regardless of how many pundits and naysayers choose the current, and inadequate, status quo. For most of us, when it comes to protecting our nation, institutions, and ultimately our citizens, the status quo will just have to accept that it is going to be transformed by experts in informed intuition: *the leaders of gut.*

We need ways of extending expertise into situations where those skills have not yet caught up to our practice. Consider Aristotle's remark in his *Nicomachean Ethics* that "it is a sign of sound intuition in a philosopher to see similarities in things far apart." Expertise in recognizing similarities calls for a broad base of experience on which to draw that makes the study of cases critical. Awareness of typicality may degenerate into stereotyping, with disastrous effects.

With training and reflection, one may need to correct for bias and passion, or may have to correct their training based on a bias for results and passion. Trade-offs are inevitable. Some people are more naturally suited to generate change than others are; some have that capability more than others do. These people so often mold public sentiment and policy. Their metaphors, which express an uncanny perception of similarity and lead to still deeper discovery of the situation, have a profound effect on our perception of risk, crisis, opportunity, and ultimately our practice.

We ought to expect those working at building and sustaining our culture to be proficient at metaphor and analogy, and not simply for the sake of persuasion. Apt metaphors are necessary in order to help mobilize our capacities of perception, enhance our habits of attention, and bring poise to our dispositions of response. We should then employ methods of developing this ability with those whose vocation is the exercise of prudence with respect to the common good. Their effectiveness will depend largely on their skills of rhetoric—the ability to bring together the concrete particulars that seem disparate, in order to extend new skills into old domains.

This allows the opportunity for a procedural kind of approach to change that is often necessary in tricky situations, as well as for communication among team members about possible courses of action. Just as Pattern Recognition is a powerful aid in the perception of risk and opportunity, so is the capacity to build imaginative scenarios on those metaphorical foundations to propose states of affairs for consideration.

We would be closer to our mark if we just started talking about retraining our habits of perception and sensitivities to include the human element of invention. Suppose that instead of looking at the proposed changes and approaches, we collaborate with management, acting as mentors and models of the kind of skills that go into creating scenarios, and instead create incredible workarounds and improvement? The construction of the scenario (or a better way) would involve the manager in the kinds of concern and interpretive imagination *that distinguish public safety leaders from public safety workers.*

A small step forward is better than our current state of affairs. Even better is several small steps forward.

6.7 IN REAL LIFE: THE BOXING DAY TSUNAMI AND HAITI

Tilly Smith was 10 years old when she spotted signs of an impending disaster at Maikhao beach near Phuket, Thailand. The tide rushed out, the water began to bubble, and the boats on the horizon started to bob violently. All of the tourists and locals watched in amazement. Tilly Smith, like many others affected by the 2004 tsunami, did not feel the quake, but she knew she was in danger.

The young and inexperienced girl felt something strange, and to her naked eye, it was completely out of character with what she knew. The tide was rushing out away from the shoreline where she and her family were enjoying their vacation. It reminded her of something... and as local children, fishermen, and tourists alike ran out onto the newly exposed sea floor to collect shells and fish, Tilly became ill at ease.

It is normal for the sea to recede before a tsunami disaster. According to Melissa Block,[12] "Around the Indian Ocean, this rare sight reportedly induced people, especially children, to visit the coast to investigate and collect stranded fish on as much as 2.5 km (1.6 mi) of exposed beach, with fatal results."

In the distance, past the throngs of people moving out toward the newly exposed sands, Tilly Smith saw something that terrified her: a piece of a much larger puzzle that she instantly put together. She said, "I noticed that when we went down to the sea the sea was all frothy like on the top of a beer. It was bubbling." The sight terrified her. She said, "Seriously, there is definitely going to be a tsunami."[13]

A geography class two weeks before Tilly Smith's vacation had given her all the insight she needed. Her teacher, Andrew Kearney at Danes Hill Preparatory School in Oxshott, Surrey, has been credited with her ability to spot the signs of the impending wave.

Tilly liked geography, and Mr. Kearney taught it well. Her mother, Penny, said she was proud of her daughter's quick thinking, as she herself had not seen the danger signs. "I just thought that it was a bad day at the beach, it was very unusual," she said. "Tilly just started going on about this froth on the sea and started getting hysterical, saying that she had seen a video about the one in Hawaii in 1946."[13]

Tilly recalled for the BBC exactly how it came to her, "I was having visions from the Hawaiian videos that I had seen two weeks before." She told her mother, who had helped with her geography homework, and her father, who alerted a security guard. "Me and my mum were down on the beach away from the hotel. I was hysterical. I was screaming, I didn't want to leave my mum in case it would come."[14]

"I said, 'Seriously, there is definitely going to be a tsunami' but we were walking further and further away from the hotel." She persuaded her parents, seven-year-old sister, and other tourists to flee their beach and hotel. According to Tilly, her mother was the hardest to persuade: "I went, 'Right, I'm going to leave you, I know there is going to be a tsunami.' My mum was taking it in more."[14]

The images of the Hawaii tsunami were powerful. In the video, Tilly would have seen the tide go out and then rush back in, leveling Hilo and everything else in its path. The scene before her, when matched to the data in her mind from the Hawaii tsunami, was enough for Tilly to take two dots and make the connection: Danger.

Tilly's generation, known as "millennials" or Gen M, have grown up in a completely digital age and have very different worldviews and approaches to problem-solving than Baby Boomers, or even Gen X. Much of what they think and do is influenced by the rules of the Internet and gaming. While there is no direct evidence that Tilly was involved with either, her value system and choice-making skills were developed in a peer group of similar-aged children with these values.

These are ideas set forth by John C. Beck and Mitchell Wade, the authors of *The Kids are Alright*.[15] The idea is based on the theory that the "boss" in a video game is the hardest obstacle to get past; and that normally, it takes an inside perspective to win. This is where the strategy guide comes in handy. These are usually free, written by peers, and published on the Internet. They have "cheat codes" and "walkthroughs" that guarantee success. You can win almost any level in any game using a good strategy guide. The authors of these guides earn immense credibility. The strategy guide is not viewed as cheating by these youth, but as a means of sharing what you know, and collaborating in order to beat the odds that are stacked against you.

Returning to Tilly, a mere school girl, who was willing to leave her mother to make her point, she successfully marshaled the inner strength to confront the "bosses" around her and raised the alarm. She had seen the "strategy guide" in her geology class. She knew what was going to happen next and was not afraid to confront the "boss," her mom. Her actions ultimately saved approximately 100 tourists from the tsunami that killed at least 200,000 people in 13 countries. Tilly has received several awards for her life-saving actions on that day.

In December 2005, Tilly was named "Child of the Year" by the French magazine *Mon Quotidien.*[14] On the First Anniversary of the Official Tsunami Commemorations at Khao Lak, Thailand, on December 26, 2005, she was given the honor of closing the ceremony with a speech to thousands of spectators, which read in part, "It wasn't devastation or death that won the day. It was humanity that triumphed, the shining victory of generosity, courage, love."[14] Tilly Smith was not afraid to innovate and be an early adopter. Because of her bravery, she saved more than 100 lives.

In emergency management, we talk a lot about "connecting the dots." Tilly did not need to connect an array of information to arrive at a conclusion well before catastrophe struck. She connected *two dots* and took *action*. This says a lot about early adopters and Pattern Recognition. Most importantly, it says that experts in intuition and gut-level thinking get there first, understand what is next, and can save lives—if they are trusted.

Consider the response to the recent earthquake in Haiti. On the third day, many response teams piled up on the tarmac of the Port-au-Prince airport waiting for trucks that had little diesel to get them into town so they could assist. Meanwhile, Israel was already in full action:

> The first Israeli delegation landed in the capital of Port-au-Prince on Friday evening (15 January) and *established its operation center in a soccer field near the airport.* On Tuesday night (19 January), an additional team joined the IDF forces operating in Haiti since the earthquake, consisting of GOC of the Home Front Command, Maj. Gen. Yair Golan, CEO of the Ministry of Health, Dr. Eitan Hai-Am, and the Chief Medical officer, Brig. Gen. Nahman Esh. After landing, the team arrived at the IDF field hospital and was updated on the current situation regarding the treatment of victims.
>
> Israeli Ambassador Amos Radian and Maj. Gen Yair Golan, head of the IDF Home Front Command, met with the Prime Minister of Haiti and toured the demolished UN headquarters and other disaster areas in order to assess the continuation of Israeli aid.
>
> During its stay in Haiti, the medical delegation treated more than 1,110 patients, conducted 319 successful surgeries, and delivered 16 births including three in cesarean sections. The IDF Search and Rescue force has rescued or assisted in the rescue of 4 individuals.[16]

Even the Israeli Prime Minister, Benjamin Netanyahu, was caught off guard,

> On January 13th, tragedy struck Haiti. Approximately forty hours later, maybe even thirty-six hours later, when I requested that a delegation be sent, they were already on their way! Less than one day later, they were already in the field. The plan was to erect the field hospital within twenty hours—it took just ten. The 240 members of the delegation— officers, regular soldiers, and reservists—began working in record time. The Chief of General Staff told me that the other armies were in awe, expressing their amazement at how quickly our soldiers arrived and were ready to work.[16]

6.8 CONCLUSION

Coolhunting, trend spotting, and Pattern Recognition can have an immensely positive effect on our profession if we change the way we *think* about our profession. To demonstrate this, we will take a look at some examples of these marketing practices, and technology in general, at use in the field.

First, terrorists use on-the-ground judgment, open source tools, and the most basic of communication networks such as consumer-grade cell phones and basic Internet Web sites. They observe their environment and make changes based on their successes and failures to adapt and overcome the obstacles against them. The luxuries they do find in technologies are exploited and celebrated. Just look at any YouTube video before a martyr's death (a recruiting video) or Osama bin Laden's use of video or press warnings just before the major attacks in the early part of 2000.

Back to the good guys now, and on the other side of the spectrum of technology and marketing adaptation—after the devastating 9.0 Japanese earthquake of 2011, Google created a Crisis Response webpage[17] to provide the latest news on the tragedy and up-to-date information for all those affected. One of the tools available on the Web site was a Person Finder, an aspect of which used Google's photo storage and sharing service, Picasa. People uploaded lists of victims and the name of the shelter in which they were located. This information was then crowdsourced and became a searchable database for missing people. While it was treated as a novelty, it worked. Now compare that to the effectiveness of taping photos and names to walls and buildings. Seeing how efficient and productive this response was, does it not make sense for DHS and FEMA to adopt the same or similar approach in the United States?

Similarly, the use of Twitter during the Santa Clara cable outage on April 9, 2009, went from "genius" to "cute" in our profession. Few, if any, suggested using social networking during response activities. The reason this approach has been ignored was that many argued that such large-scale events would make the Internet irrelevant. By looking at the numerous recent dramatic revolutions in Iran, Egypt, Libya, and the freedom movement in China as case studies, we can see how untrue this has become. The Internet may be the most resilient and relevant invention known to man.

What are we waiting for to start implementing the Internet and marketing tools and practices in our workflows today? A study by the National Institute of Standards and Technology (NIST)? Further proof of good works and effective alternatives?

Our field does not make it a practice to embrace the Internet or other new forms of communication and problem-solving. In fact, it does not have a standard guideline in place that even suggests that emergency managers use social networks to their advantage, though FEMA Director Craig Fugate has been a vocal advocate for the use of new technology. The reason for this unresponsiveness is because we just do not have the guts to popularize or promote something we do not own and cannot control—*even though it works*! What irony. If you consider that a doctor would use a pen out in the field for an emergency tracheotomy, you can see how failed our logic is. Modern marketing practices combined with the powerful communication methods of the Internet are serious contenders in emergency response that do not have to be commoditized and controlled to help our profession. Indeed, any effort to do so would only slow and hinder the results.

Emergency managers must consider using these new tools during our initial assessments. We have to make it official and incorporate it into our collective toolkits. It is a proven alternative communication method for many large catastrophic events that should be leveraged and encouraged immediately by Emergency Managers. For example, just consider that the names of missing persons should be of public record. The post that you make should be public record as well by quickly vetting them through your Public Information Officer. Social networks are great tools, and once activated, yield results in minutes. In addition, loose agreements and information sharing with Google, Facebook, and Twitter in advance will speed the process and should be investigated as part of the planning process.

Using marketing practices in our fields will enable us to make quick and effective judgment calls because, like the terrorists mentioned at the beginning of this section, we will be aware of our environment and making decisions based on what works and what does not, and effectively adapting and overcoming the obstacles in front of us (see Figure 6.4). Even better, we will be preventing a good many of them!

In the Market State world, we do not have the luxury of deliberating on these clearly effective uses of technologies and immediately issuing guidance policies that merely place them on the plate of *possible* options due to our over-the-top fear that it might not work one day. In terms of trusting Coolhunting, Trend Spotting, Pattern Recognition, and open sources like the Internet, there is nothing ventured in our field when it comes to our good, old-fashioned, press release mindset.

It is now the twenty-first century and now is the time for us to get caught up with the world around us.

6.9 END OF CHAPTER QUESTIONS

1. What are the characteristics of a believable story?
2. List the patterns consistent with a natural disaster you are familiar with. Do the same with a man-made incident.
3. What advances can be made in the day-to-day practice of your profession by adopting the current marketing practices of Trend Spotting, Coolhunting, and Pattern Recognition, and implementing them into your workflows?
4. If you were to begin using social networking tools at your existing job, what advantages would you perceive? Are there any

Figure 6.4 Thinking about the Market State and how we might apply marketing techniques to the fields of counter-terrorism and emergency management is more than a comparative exercise. This chapter has illustrated real-world applications of marketing techniques to our practice.

disadvantages, real or perceived? How would you encourage those above and below you to begin using these tools?

5. Consider everything we have covered up to this point in the book. How do you see the individual topics and practices we have covered combining to form a whole? How has this material changed your view of Emergency Management?

NOTES

a. Edward De Bono introduced the concept of lateral thinking in his book *The Use of Lateral Thinking*.[2] His work is also available at http://www.edwdebono.com/, http://www.debonogroup.com, and http://www.debonoconsulting.com.

b. Another similarity to cautionary tales/urban legends is the difficulty to track the origin of this commonsense.

c. Early adopters are early customers/users of a given product, or technology. In politics, fashion, art, and other fields, they are usually called trendsetters. The term originates from Rogers.[1]

d. Crossing the chasm is a term introduced by G. A. Moore. It entails crossing the chasm between early adopters and the early majority.

REFERENCES

1. Rogers, Everett M. *Diffusion of Innovations*, Fourth Edition. New York: The Free Press, 1995.

2. De Bono, Edward. 1967. *The Use of Lateral Thinking*. London: Jonathan Cape.

3. Department of the Army. "Federation of American Scientists." *Field Manual No. 3-24 Counterinsurgency*. December 15, 2006. http://www.fas.org/irp/doddir/army/fm3-24.pdf (accessed March 15, 2010).

4. Lang, Josephine Chinying. "Managerial concerns in knowledge management." *Journal of Knowledge Management* 5, no. 1 (2001): 43–59.

5. Popper, Karl R. *Objective Knowledge*. Oxford: Oxford University Press, 1972.

6. Bernton, Hal, Mike Carter, David Heath, and James Neff. "The terrorist within: The story behind one man's holy war against America." July 7, 2002. http://seattletimes.nwsource.com/news/nation-world/terroristwithin/ (accessed March 15, 2010).

7. National Commission on Terrorist Attacks Upon the United States. *The 9/11 Commission Report: Final Report of the National Commission on Terrorist Attacks Upon the United States*. New York: W.W. Norton & Company, 2004, 427–428.

8. Smith, Yves. "Debunking Michael Lewis' subprime short hagiography". March 25, 2010. http://www.nakedcapitalism.com/2010/03/debunking-michael-lewis-subprime-short-hagiography.html (accessed March 27, 2010).

9. Nance, Malcolm. *The Terrorist Recognition Handbook: A Manual for Predicting and Identifying Terrorist Activities*. Boca Raton: Taylor & Francis Group, LLC, 2008.

10. Poole, H. John. *The Tiger's Way: A U.S. Private's Best Chance for Survival*. Emerald Isle: Posterity Press, 2003.

11. Baum, Dan. "Battle lessons: What the generals don't know." *The New Yorker*, January 17, 2005. http://www.newyorker.com/archive/2005/01/17/050117fa_fact (accessed March 17, 2010).

12. Moore, Geoffrey A. *Crossing the Chasm: Marketing and Selling High-Tech Products to Mainstream Customers*. New York: Harper Business, 1999.

13. Block, Melissa. "Indian Ocean Tsunami." "*Voices In the News*, NPR. Jan. 2, 2005. http://www.npr.org/templates/story/story.php?storyId=4254871 (accessed October 6, 2011).

14. BBC News. "Award for tsunami warning pupil." *BBC News*. September 9, 2005. http://news.bbc.co.uk/2/hi/uk_news/4229392.stm (accessed July 17, 2011).

15. Beck, John C., and Mitchell Wade. 2006. *The Kids Are Alright*. Boston: Harvard Business Press.

16. Israel Ministry of Foreign Affairs. "Israeli aid to Haiti, field hospital set up." January 17, 2010. http://www.mfa.gov.il/MFA/Israel+beyond+politics/Israeli_aid_arrives_Haiti_ 17-Jan-2010.htm#17jan (accessed March 16, 2010).

17. Google Crisis Response. *Resources related to the 2011 Japan Crisis*. April 30, 2011. http://www.google.co.jp/intl/en/crisisresponse/japanquake2011.html (accessed April 26, 2011).

7

Putting the Market State to Use: Application, Practice, and Understanding

7.1 KEY TERMS

7.2 CHAPTER OBJECTIVES

In this chapter we will highlight key elements of basic cultural marketing theory on an event-by-event basis. After reading this chapter you:

- Will be able to identify and describe a major difference between the cultures discussed in Chapter 7 and what the United States could learn from these cultures to enhance pattern recognition.
- Describe how pattern recognition can be enhanced through the tactics of the *blink* and the use of *thin-slicing*.
- Describe Areas of Dominant Influence and how using them can impact response planning and communications in the emergency management culture.
- Consider Copycats, Reverse Engineering, Swarm Effects, and Kiddie Tactics and describe the threats they pose beyond those noted in the condition of the Market State.
- Discuss how risk continues to evolve even as the Market State condition applies itself to our geopolitical situation on a much more micro, and local, scale.

7.3 CHAPTER INTRODUCTION

In this chapter we will highlight how certain nation-states are prepared to move into the Market State more readily as a result of tragic events in their history and national investment in emergency preparedness. We will also see how this has led to the practice of a heightened state of pattern recognition. It is also important to know that pattern recognition can evolve into the ability to *blink* and even *thin-slice* scenarios in a matter of seconds as our skills in this area are sharpened. *Areas of Dominant Influence* can both enlighten our planning efforts and inform our decision-making when it comes to conveying key messages to core stakeholders in emergency management. We will see how Copycats, Reverse Engineering, Swarm Effects,

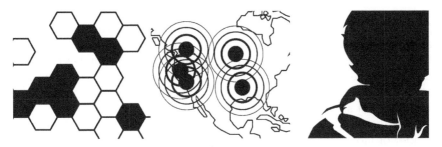

Figure 7.1 In this chapter we will discuss the application of pattern recognition, areas of dominant influence, and how a myriad of popular social engineering trends including Kiddie Tactics can catch us off guard.

and Kiddie Tactics can catch us off guard (see Figure 7.1), and finally take a look at how new risks are increasing even as we consider the new face of risk as part of the Market State condition.

7.4 AMPLIFYING PATTERN RECOGNITION

A Regional Perspective: Israel and Japan

From a regional perspective, looking at Israel and Japan as leaders in the international effort to build better emergency management and homeland defense capabilities is highly useful. Both countries could be said to have an "apocalypse" culture that has matured their approach to dealing with terror and disasters over hundreds, if not thousands, of years.

Japan has reflected on Hiroshima and Nagasaki with a fetish-like pop sensibility that has woven the notion of apocalypse into their culture as well as their policies. Israel is a nation composed of people that are compelled to embrace scenario planning based on tragic events. Perhaps the nation did not want to have to engage in an on-going, near real-time threat assessment lifestyle, but tragic events, both historical and modern, have compelled them to, and in the process, they have become masters of the First Cause Scenario, the Disaster Halo Effect, and a lightning-fast response. However each of the countries has reacted, it can be said that theirs are the most threat-adverse nations in the world, and their people are more indoctrinated toward emergency response and terrorism than any other Western countries.

Japan

Relatively small compared to the United States, Japan has a total landmass approximately the size of the state of Montana. It is the contemporary history of disasters and nation-state changing events that makes modern-day Japan the emergency management-oriented culture it is today. The atomic blasts of "Little Boy" over Hiroshima and "Fat Man" over Nagasaki were the first and only uses of atomic weapons in warfare.

While the dropping of the bombs resulted in the unconditional surrender of Japan's Pacific Theater operations during World War II, it also left a scar on the sociological fabric of the nation that is still present today. To better frame the impact on the collective psyche of the Japanese people, these bombings killed between 90,000 and 160,000 people in Hiroshima. Nagasaki death tolls range as high as an additional 80,000. The effect of these bombings is expressed in cultural forms from Godzilla movies of the early 1950s (Godzilla was the H-bomb Monster) to the anime and manga of today. Anime and manga are comic books and cartoons, both hugely popular in Japan, that feature themes of apocalypse, survival, self-determinism, and National heroics.

This national fixation on terror is extended by frequent natural disasters, including massive earthquakes such as the 1703 Genroku quake that killed 108,000, to more recent events such as the 1995 Hanshin quake that killed 6,434. We would be remiss not to mention the 9.0-magnitude earthquake off the coast of Fukushima on March 11, 2011, that has enveloped the country in tsunami and radiation Disaster Halo Effects. As of this writing, in mid-2011, the official death toll is more than 12,000 and there are still an additional 15,000 missing. In terms of frequency and size, Japan may be the earthquake center of the world, with 6.0 to 9.0 magnitudes being more frequent than not. This new event, along with the historical focus in Japan around emergency preparedness, includes all manner of government and public response and education programs.

There are emergency drills that include primary school-age children learning how to set up mobile toilets and hand out bottled water. The Disaster Imagination Game (DIG) emphasizes creative foresight in school children by having them draw a map of their own school area and marking temporary shelters, evacuation routes, hydrants, and discussing the range and magnitude of tsunamis and earthquakes. As is a tradition in Japan, community residents clap two bamboo sticks together to warn of potential fires. There is even a popular "Fire Fighting Kids Club." The Maiko High School in the Hyogo Prefecture of Japan has an Environment and Disaster Mitigation Course, and there are Prefecture-level (state level) volunteer organizations that are made up of large volunteer bases.

A recent earthquake response test included the participation of 650,000 people, many of them civilians. UNESCO created a comic book style pamphlet called the *Tsunami Rescue!*[1] to educate children about the dangers of tsunamis. Underscoring the federal position on Emergency Management in Japan is the Fire and Disaster Management Agency, which reports through the Ministry of Internal Affairs and Communications. The strong emphasis on public education, formal education, and international aid through the Japanese International Rescue Team (IRT) is a pronounced and novel approach to emergency management, especially when compared to the United States' approach to emergency management.

In fact, the Japanese Constitution itself, established on November 3, 1946, after the World War II surrender, seems to summarize Japan's position on preparedness. The Constitution is known as the "Peace Constitution" because of Article 9 which states, "Aspiring sincerely to an international peace based on justice and order, the Japanese people forever renounce war as a sovereign right of the nation and the threat or use of force as a means of settling international disputes."[2]

Perhaps because it is without a national desire to wage war outside of its borders, Japan is fixated on maintaining defense within its borders. After 9/11, Japan formally created the Anti-Terrorism Special Measures Law that would allow it to support and affect cooperation internationally in anti-terrorism affairs. The Japan Self Defense Force, (JSDF or SDF) reports to the Minister of Defense and the Prime Minister. There are three branches—the Ground Self Defense Force, the Maritime Self Defense Force, and the Air Self Defense Force. In total, Japan has five armies, five maritime districts, and three air defense forces.

A completely volunteer force, all members of the SDF are civilians and are not classified as members of the services, but rather special civil servants who are subordinate to the ordinary civil servants that run the Ministry of Defense. The Defense Agency in Japan, aware that it cannot accomplish many of its programs without popular support, pays close attention to public opinion and often uses the SDF in emergency response and anti-terrorism activities to protect the Japanese homeland.

As we write this, the impact of the March 11, 2011, earthquake and the numerous Disaster Halo Effects that followed are just starting to sink in. The series of events following the quake certainly underscores the Disaster Halo Effect at work, given the number and frequency of aftershocks, two major tsunamis, and the nuclear incident at Fukushima. To call the series

195

of quakes that happened after the initial quake of 9.0 aftershocks (according to most scientists, although Japanese seismologists initially placed the quake as a 7.9) is a fantastic understatement. There were no less than a swarm of quakes that lasted for a week after the First Event Scenario and ranged in intensities as high as 6.0.

The resulting tsunamis were devastating. There were reported wave heights from five meters (16 feet) at Ishinomaki, to an unofficial report of a 30-meter (98-foot) wave at Ryori Bay. Entire cities and farms were devastated, and what only made the tragedy worse is that several thousand people were struck by the tsunamis in areas designated as tsunami evacuation sites.[3] Here are some numbers describing the damages:

- Tens of billions of dollars were estimated to be lost within the first few days.
- Some 2,800 people were declared dead within two days, and the numbers quickly rose to over 10,000 fatalities in one province alone. Ultimately, the total loss of life could be well over 100,000.
- Three nuclear power generators lost the ability to cool their cores, threatening nuclear meltdown and exposing thousands to radiation.
- Two million households were left without power on day two of the event, and 1.4 million homes were without water.
- By the second day, gasoline was being rationed nationwide.

All of this happened in a country that was more prepared for an earthquake and tsunami trigger event than any other in the world. The scale of the global response could only emphasize the massive scale of the disaster. Over 500,000 people were placed in shelters. Japan's Self Defense Force deployed 100,000 troops. Teams from 13 countries poured into the Island. The USS *Ronald Reagan* (CVN-76) offered medical assistance, and was the first U.S. warship that has been allowed into Japanese territory since World War II.

The massive earthquake affected the entire northeast coast of Japan, caused rolling power outages in Tokyo, and even affected world markets with $1.6 trillion being pulled out of Japanese companies viewed as unstable because of the disaster. Going forward, it has been suggested that as much as $200 billion will be spent by Japan's government just on basic infrastructure. The damages have also caused a slowing of chip manufacturing, including the Far East movement of watches (popular with fashion brand, lower cost watch manufacturers like Seiko), vehicles destined for U.S. shores, and other goods. Further, supplies of these and many other items have been constrained for weeks, if not months. Computer memory could be slow to rebuild its base of stable pricing internationally for as long as three quarters, slowing the speed with which new devices—everything from smartphones to digital cameras—enter the world market.

Japan's thriving and resilient culture has pushed it to the top when it comes to emergency management. The *New York Times* featured a headline that swam directly upstream against the other news agencies, "Japan's Strict Building Codes Saved Lives."[4] This is very important to remember! When we do our jobs with the consistency, thoroughness, and attention to detail it requires, the impact we have on the effects of a disaster are beyond measure, even if we are not immediately able to see the good it has done. Japan was unquestionably prepared. What would this look like had it happened in San Francisco, or at the New Madrid Fault Zone? As we look back at this defining moment in Japan's history, we must ask ourselves, are we underestimating our own preparedness as individuals, businesses, and a country?

Israel

The awareness of risk and emergency is embedded in Jewish life; every year at the Passover Seder, Jews recite a quote from the Haggadah (the traditional book of prayer and blessings used at the Seder dinner) by Rabbi Shimon Apisdorf, "In each and every generation they rise up against us to destroy us." Like Japan, Israel is a small country with a total landmass about the size of the state of New Jersey; it also shares a rich history of disasters and wars. However, unlike Japan, Israel's history of catastrophes is ancient—spanning millennia, and emergency management is a cultural affair.

In 1099, Crusaders herded Jews into the Jerusalem Synagogue and burned it to the ground. In 1290, Edward I expelled all the Jews from England with the Edict of Expulsion. In 1348 and 1349, Jews in Europe were blamed for the black plague and many were tortured and/or murdered from Spain to Poland. During the Spanish Inquisition in 1483, Spain expelled nearly 300,000 Jews. The Cossack massacres in the Ukraine from 1648–1649 resulted in the murder of 100,000 Jews. Ultimately, during World War II, it was the genocide of six million Jews at the hands of Nazi Germany that instilled a deep interest in self-preservation and preparedness in the Jewish People. By far the largest loss of human life in history, Hitler's genocide was bound to create a culture of deep fear, deep preparedness, and a strong appetite for self-defense.

Unlike Japan, Israel is not rife with natural disasters. While drought and mild earthquakes are frequent, they are not on the scale of those in

Japan. However, the level of national awareness around terrorism is very high. There have been countless terror attacks in Israel. Car bombings, market bombings, and mass casualty shootings are part of the Israeli national fabric. It is with great external pressure from neighboring nations and internal pressure from years of persecution that Israel orients itself toward emergency management.

Israel Military Industries (IMI) is a government-owned corporation that supplies firearms and technology to the Israel Defense Force (IDF), as well as anti-terrorism training and emergency response training. The IMI has a partnership with the Metropolitan College of New York (MCNY) that offers a Masters in Public Administration in Emergency Management and Homeland Security. The Israeli government maintains extensive public education and awareness programs. The public is educated on how to handle and report suspicious activities, persons, and vehicles; the reports from civilians are treated as seriously as if they came from a first responder. The Israeli town of Sderot has built a vast playground that also serves as a bomb shelter. There are concrete play structure tunnels that are designed thick enough to be bullet and blast resistant, should immediate shelter be necessary. All play structures are built with a priority toward quick egress, allowing children enough time to meet the 15-second rule for entering the bomb shelter. The Israeli view is that the public is not a victim of emergencies or terrorism, but a partner in preparing and militating against such catastrophes. Open and transparent communications are encouraged at all levels.

Supporting the deep public involvement in emergency preparedness and anti-terrorism is the Israel Defense Force, including a youth corps, and women conscripts. All Israeli citizens are conscripted into one of the branches of the IDF upon turning 18 years of age; two years of mandatory service are required for women, and three for men. Some exemptions are granted for the purpose of study, religious works, or other reasons; however, service in the IDF is considered a measure of patriotism and involvement in the country.

What is notable for U.S. anti-terrorism agencies and emergency managers is what is shared between the Japanese and Israeli cultures surrounding events:

1. A deep commitment to public education and awareness of terrorism and disaster preparedness that starts early and continues into adult life
2. A deep commitment to homeland security and defense that emphasizes preparedness and patriotism

3. A strong orientation toward preservation and preparedness at the public level
4. A strong orientation toward preservation at the national level
5. A culture of catastrophic awareness that leads to deeper pattern recognition

Of note is the education of primary-school-age children in creating threat assessments, and the seriousness with which public reports of suspicious activity are taken by Israeli first responders. Perhaps this explains why Israel has never had a hijacking or airborne terror attack originate from their international airport. "Today, this morning, there's going to be an attack." This mindset is what makes Ben Gurion, Israel's international airport, arguably the safest airport in the world. Israeli sky marshal, Mordechai Rachamim, feels Americans should take note of Israel's security successes.

Ben Gurion Airport Security is comparable to the U.S. Secret Service. Once a ticket is purchased, the buyer's name is sent to Israeli intelligence and Interpol to be researched and cross-referenced with terrorism databases. Upon entrance, armed guards inspect cars and talk with their occupants, and 50% of all the airport staff consists of armed undercover agents. Trained profiler agents question and screen travelers, intuitively looking for suspicious activity, body language, and behavior.

Meanwhile, in the United States, a decade after 9/11, U.S. airport security remains obstinately focused on intercepting bad things—guns, knives, and explosives. It is a *reactive* policy, aimed at preventing the last terrorist plot from being repeated. The 9/11 hijackers used box cutters as weapons and this yielded the banning of sharp metal objects from carry-on luggage. Would-be suicide terrorist Richard Reid tried to ignite a bomb in his shoe, so now everyone's footwear is screened for tampering. Mid-2006, British authorities foiled a plan to blow up airliners with liquid explosives and as a result, liquid substances like toothpaste, cologne, and deodorant are limited to three ounces for carry-on.

Of course, the Israelis check for bombs and weapons too, but always with the understanding that terrorists are the threat and not inanimate objects—and the best way to detect terrorists is to focus on how people behave. To a much greater degree than in the United States, security at El Al and Ben Gurion depends on intelligence and intuition—what Rafi Ron, the former director of security at Ben Gurion, calls the human factor.

The TSA screens for threatening objects and reported confiscating 13,709,211 items in 2006 alone. Instead of focusing on finding objects like knives and guns, Israel feels that, "the best way to detect terrorists is to focus on intercepting not bad things, but bad people."[5] Israeli airport security focuses on profiling behavioral patterns. They consider their historical threat patterns, but also assume that any person can be a threat. Moreover, the screening does not occur at one checkpoint, but at several points of interaction once the passenger has entered the airport. From the moment you are greeted by the gate guard to the time you board the plane, your behavior is watched. Israeli security does not hesitate to act once a threat is perceived, and there is so much observation happening that suspicious characters are quickly rounded up and assessed for true threat potential.

In 2005, the United States implemented Screening Passengers by Observation Technique (SPOT). SPOT is a derivative of Israel's security operations, which trains security personnel to identify specific microexpressions. This technique, developed by renowned psychologist Paul Ekman, PhD, has generated some debate.[6] The technique is not completely accurate because other factors influence behavior and expressions such as mental disorders and medications, but it is currently being developed further.

However, security expert Bruce Scheneir feels differently about these efforts. He says,

> Instead of wasting money [on airport security], we would be far safer as a nation if we invested in intelligence, investigation, and emergency response... We need to defend against the broad threat of terrorism, not against specific movie plots. Security is most effective when it does not require us to guess. We need to focus resources on intelligence and investigation: identifying terrorists, cutting off their funding, and stopping them regardless of what their plans are. We need to focus resources on emergency response: lessening the impact of a terrorist attack, regardless of what it is.[7]

Whichever view you take, whether it is the proactive stance of Israel or the broad approach of U.S. emergency management and counterterrorism, pattern recognition is one of the keys to effective prevention. The notion that Americans are victims of disasters and terror attacks is not as compelling as that of a nation of citizens that view themselves as active participants in prevention and response. Education, awareness, and involvement heighten public participation and the ability for more eyes and ears to spot patterns that may go missed otherwise. It may be that the United States lacks the deep experience with disasters and terror that Japan and Israel do; therefore, more emphasis on awareness is needed.

7.5 BLINK AND THIN-SLICE

Blink

It is hard to separate the hype from the facts when real world emergency management experience is hard to come by. In fact, if you stack up what you *know* about emergency management and counter-terrorism from television shows versus what you *know* about our field from first-hand experience, it is easy to see why choosing and implementing the right plans, tactics, and solutions can be such a tough job.

In Malcolm Gladwell's book *Blink*,[8] there are numerous examples of the power of first-hand experience and practical knowledge. Gladwell illustrates how the Getty Museum spent an enormous amount of time on vetting the purchase of a $10 million Greek marble statue (a kouros) from 600 BCE. The investigation involved art historians, geologists, the analysis of a core sample of the statue using electron microscopes, mass spectrometry, X-ray diffraction, and X-ray fluorescence. All of the data supported the purchase, which was wonderful because the Getty's curators wanted to hear it was real.

Too bad the Getty ignored the advice of Evelyn Harris, one of the foremost experts in Greek sculpture. When she found out that the Getty was about to finalize the purchase, she said, "I'm sorry to hear that." The problem with the statue, Mrs. Harris said later, was that it looked "fresh" and fresh is not a word you want to hear when buying an allegedly 2,600-year-old piece of art![8]

In the fall of 1986, after an expensive purchase and restoration process, the statue went on display. There was only one problem—it was a fake.

In the summer of 2000, Operation Millennium Force, a war game put together by the Joint Forces Command (JFCOM) set out to, "test a set of new and quite radical ideas about how to go into battle …" according to Gladwell.[8] The test used both simulated and actual munitions, men, planes, and ship deployments. It cost millions of dollars to script and execute—and it was rigged.

The Blue Team in the game (normally representative of U.S. Forces) was given every technological advantage: they had a supercomputer running Operational Net Assessments that broke down the Red Team's military, economic, social, and political systems and created a matrix that revealed the interconnections and vulnerabilities in those systems. They were given Effects-Based Operations, which directed them to think

201

beyond the conventional military method of simply destroying military assets. They were given a comprehensive, real-time map of the theater of war called the Common Relevant Operations Picture. They had a tool for joint communication. They had information and intelligence from every corner of the U.S. Government. They had advanced weaponry and satellite. And in spite of the plethora of advantages, they also were decimated.

Paul Van Ripper, the commander of the Red Team understood that war is messy, that people get confused, and that the fog of war obscures the facts. He exploited opportunities and ancient technologies and he won—*against the odds*. He did not use traditional warfare strategies. He ignored the advice that his systems and game coaches gave him. He relied on his past experience and practical knowledge. The risk rewarded him the victory.

This is to say, at the end of the day the strategies and tactics you deploy will be based on the raw, human instinct of your *gut*.

As much as we would like to think that analytics and data come into play when making tough (and expensive) risk choices, most of us tackle multiple variable choices with which we have limited first-hand experience based on our intuition, our gut. These gut feelings have fashionably become called the **Blink**. Malcolm Gladwell's book of the same title was a number one national best seller[8] and captured the imaginations of many top performers in industry and commerce. The mantel of blink expertise is that of the "seers," people with well-developed "sixth senses," or wide peripheral vision. However, the notion of blink also hinges on deep wisdom and experience. It confirmed what many of us always knew: when all is said and done, we consider all the evidence, including the sales hype, chatter, and talk, and we just choose; not based on the facts or promised "value," but based on intuition. This is not to infer that data collection and analysis are not integrated as full components of our practice, but that intuition and wisdom have an important and weighted role in emergency management decision-making.

Intuitive, rapid cognition decision-making is natural, and therefore, inevitable. We are guided by our past experiences, beliefs, cognitive models, states of mind, and practical intelligence to come to the decisions we make.

Past experiences cannot be influenced because they are already ingrained in our psyches. In the business of emergency management and anti-terrorism, practical experience is usually based on misguided marketing messages and has little to do with our own personal experience with the subject matter. Where we have deep personal experience with a subject, "blinking" a solution makes perfect sense. However, if we lack personal experience and real, practical knowledge in a subject area, trusting our gut can be expensive, if not dangerous.

Thin-Slicing

Related to blinking is **thin-slicing**. Thin-slicing is essentially the process of "blinking" with cognition, or of making a snap-judgment using rapid cognition, which is defined as subliminal information processing in the first seconds of evaluating a situation. The small "slices" of information that are assimilated instantaneously are enough to trigger accurate and instinctive decisions. Everyone naturally thin-slices situations and makes decisions based on slices of dense data and rapid cognition. This is because our evolved "adaptive unconsciousness" aids in decision-making through the instant filtering of massive amounts of data. Even cooler—it is always at work. Thin-slicing harnesses the adaptive unconsciousness, allowing us to make decisions based on minimal information and minimal deliberation. The key to thin-slicing is the presence of experience and practical knowledge.

Can we use the tactics of thin-slicing data and comparing it against real-world experience and practical knowledge to recognize patterns instantly and derive highly accurate solutions? Certainly. Given that we have an understanding of how blink works and that we have real-world experience to rely on. A person with deep, personal experience takes a thin-slice of data and compares it against his/her real-world experience and practical knowledge; then rapid cognition occurs and an intuitive solution comes to mind.

Intuitive rapid-cognition-based decision-making is natural, and therefore, *inevitable*. The predominant factors that guide intuition are past experiences, beliefs, cognitive models, states of mind or emotion, and practical intelligence. Past experiences, which cannot be influenced because they are already ingrained in the psyche, generally guide decision-making through an application of practical intelligence.

How we amplify blinking, thin-slicing, and pattern recognition has more to do with broadening the public's role in emergency preparedness than it does with simply training our existing emergency managers and counter-terrorism thinkers on how to use our intuition. *Without a culture invested in self-preservation*, the emergency managers and counter-terrorism specialists may find themselves without public support as our need to make decisions in a more rapid, intuitive, and informed manner increases.

7.6 AREAS OF DOMINANT INFLUENCE (ADI) AND EMERGING MARKETS

As we have discussed, strong intuition, pattern recognition, and gut play a huge role in our ability to exhibit mastery of emerging risk. We have held out examples such as Tilly Smith, Agent O'Neil, and others as recognized masters of intuition prior to catastrophe. We have looked to the cultures of Japan and Israel as examples of resilience and fruitful grounds for pattern recognition and *gut* being used as readily as research and analysis to move their state of readiness forward. What are worth considering now are the roles of the Areas of Dominant Influence and emerging markets. **Areas of Dominant Influence** (ADIs) are key markets or geographies that influence the buying behavior of broader regions. It is a common marketing term that is used to describe both macro (large regional) and micro (small local) market behaviors (see Figure 7.2).

Our friends who created Tecktonik in Chapter 5 were keen to areas of dominant influence when they rolled Tecktonik out in a dance club in Paris. They were aware of it as they slowly penetrated other markets based on the influential status of French techno music at the time.

In fact, music is a great way to better understand ADIs. Did you ever notice how songs that are popular in New York or Los Angles (the two biggest ADIs in the industry) are soon rolled out to Dallas, Los Angeles, and other markets? Have you ever seen something you would love to buy at a major retailer in New York and know that it would be a season or

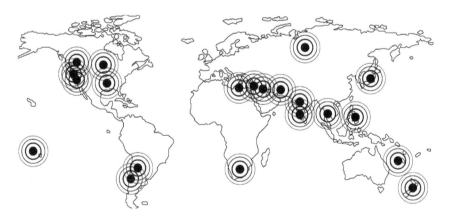

Figure 7.2 A global perspective of areas of dominant influence by city, with regional influences inferred by the concentric circles.

so before it reached the same retailer in your neighborhood? These are examples of ADIs at work.

ADIs are known to influence the markets around them, and therefore, are used by marketing professionals as test markets prior to committing to national distribution. A **test market** is a limited geographic region or demographic group to gauge the success of a new marketable product. ADIs, in turn, are the geographical version of early adopters. If a song becomes "hot" in a club in Los Angeles, radio stations will start experimenting with that song in other markets of influence and spread the song out in both the number of plays and the number of markets until it is in full rotation and eventually dies out.

Understanding test markets and ADIs when preparing for disasters and catastrophic events is vital to crafting a strong response. Populations in different markets respond differently to assistance in disasters. These differences in trust level and resiliency have been met time-and-time again by first responders and emergency managers. Here is what we have been missing: people in New Orleans will respond to assistance differently than those in Texas, and perhaps, may cope with disasters in completely different ways. At the macro-level, or regional perspective, emergency managers may find communities or organizations very open to the notion of preparedness and helpful during actual events. They may also find that other regions may not be helpful at all.

Areas of high crime, low income, and distrust for government can, and will be, very resistant to aid. On the other hand, micro-level subcommunities, such as church groups, public aid groups, and school communities may be very helpful. The fact that we do not leverage demographic data and in-depth market testing to better understand the high degree of variance that we might experience when planning for response and building scenarios is troubling.

If radio stations can use information from ADIs to better understand what songs will play well in certain markets, and subsequently influence other markets to do the same, why are we not looking for similar data to use in our field? In the private sector, disgruntled employees may be of little help recovering from a disaster. In the public sector, citizens may be more threatening than helpful in an event. At the national level, states may be more of a hindrance than a help when seeking Federal aid during a disaster.

Emerging Markets

In the Market State, local events now impact organizations across the world. From the tsunami that reached from Japan to California, to a chip factory in Mexico taking an outage that halts production globally for a major computer manufacturer, there are no such things as so-called "emerging markets." These markets, where cheap labor, parts, or other sourcing can be found are not emerging—they have *arrived* as a core component of our now fully globalized business supply chain. They are single points of weakness, with lower standards, higher risks, and have every bit as much, if not more, impact on the business we are protecting than if we took a direct hit at the U.S. headquarters.

Understanding the areas of dominance in your business, state, or county is key to crafting appropriate First Event Scenarios and the human element of the Disaster Halo Effect on a site-by-site basis. To better accomplish this, we recommend the use of survey tools, onsite interviews, and discussions with key stakeholders to better understand the cultural biases held by the community you are serving, and the value-at-risk at remote and overseas locations. We also advise the crafting of appropriate scenarios and response plans based on the cultural differences found within these emerging markets and the areas of dominant influence they serve.

Reverse engineered, the areas of dominant influence that are aligned to disaster response can be leveraged to influence those that are not, popularizing the concept for First Event Scenario planning and response planning by positioning it with agencies or offices that are considered "cool" by other locations or offices. Consider this, a First Event Scenario planning session and the resulting planning may be very uncool if it is announced, "We are doing this because it is coming down from HQ in New York." While on the other hand, if it were announced that the same First Event Scenario planning task was being rolled out based on what worked for the design and research group in Copenhagen, it could produce a completely different response.

Finally, if you doubt that areas of dominant influence and emerging markets play a role in the sustainability of any national or organization-wide emergency response program, consider this: markets are easy to overlook. What works in HQ, or Washington, rarely works on the ground as planned. The 2010 census demonstrated this concept clearly. In some states, census workers feared for their lives due to local anti-Federal sentiments, while in others, it was easy going.

In the dialogue around Narco-Jihad, there are multiple states that are areas of dominant influence in the conversation. Texas, New Mexico, California, and Arizona are among them. However, a simple study of the attitudes in Arizona, plus some analysis of legislature currently being considered there, would place Arizona head and shoulders over the other states in terms of influence in this area. Emergency managers can choose their battles and plan accordingly if they would only look to the areas of dominant influence and the emerging markets that impact their assumptions in First Event Scenarios every day. Areas of dominant influence impact our understanding of markets both near and in far off regions; this is why it is important to consider them in the overall mix of our scenario building.

7.7 COPYCATS, REVERSE ENGINEERING, SWARM EFFECTS, AND KIDDIE TACTICS

In marketing and manufacturing, just as in emergency response, you are bound to come across four realities that will catch you off guard. First is the copycat. **Copycats** are individuals or organizations that adopt a "me too" attitude and can easily disrupt your emergency planning efforts—from First Event Scenarios to response—simply by taking on this view. What is more, any copycat terrorist—or someone who is in the majority, late majority, or even a laggard (see Chapter 8)—can simply copy a tactic used by another terror organization and use it against us. Next is the notion of **reverse engineering**, which is the concept of taking something apart and using it to create the opposite effect that the original design was meant for. Consider a fire truck being used as a bomb, or a police car being used by a terrorist to get to a secure location. This concept came about quite accidently in Mumbai, when terrorists accidently found themselves firing their weapons from a stolen police car. However, with reverse engineering in mind, the next time first responders turn out to be first attackers will not be an accident at all. Third is the concept of **swarm effects,** in which groups of people take on a "swarm" mentality and react indiscriminately and out of fear. Hospital surges during a pandemic are a prime example of this. Finally, there are **Kiddie Tactics,** which are incredibly dangerous attacks that can be performed by any deranged child with an Internet connection and the will to abuse it. As emergency managers, a deeper understanding of each of these types of behaviors is required to truly understand emerging risk.

Copycats

The copycat problem has been witnessed multiple times in terror attacks. From early bombings of clubs, to the more mature, multiple bombings and gunning down of innocents in Mumbai, we believe that similar attacks, because of their success, will be "copycat" crimes in the United States soon. The problem with copycat crimes is you do not need the sophistication, planning skills, or affiliation we would commonly associate with the Taliban. A copycat in this case could simply be the boy next door—for instance, Jared Lee Loughner.

This 22-year-old man had no formal ties to any terror group, and acted as a "lone wolf." Only if there had been Orwellian-style surveillance of his Facebook page and other social media sites, would we have been able to perceive the threat. On January 8, 2011, Jared Lee Loughner walked freely through, and opened fire upon, the crowd gathered at a Tucson Safeway hosting a political event. Single-handedly he killed six people and injured 14 others, including the near-fatal shooting of U.S. Representative Gabrielle Giffords. His tactics were the combination of two or more nearly identical crimes. One close cousin to his brazen, multiple-weapon attack would be the Tower Shootings at the University of Texas. Another similar attack would be that of the Columbine shootings. However, the most interesting thing is that Loughner saw himself as something of a terrorist, and may have simply realized that what had been done at Beslan or Mumbai could be just as easily accomplished in Tucson.

While first responders and emergency managers speak of "lone wolf" attacks, we do not track the type, style, and tactics used in attacks across the diffusion of innovation (see Chapter 8); therefore, they fall off our radar as something that could "never happen here." Copycat crimes are as old as crime itself, and now, with foreign and domestic terrorism taking the main stage, we are not using fundamental, proven approaches to tracking the trends in means and methods of attack and applying the concept of copycats to the International stage.

Reverse Engineering

With regard to reverse engineering, it is exactly what made the attacks at Beslan so terrifying. The trucks and armored vehicles, assumed to be part of the celebration or some type of training, turned out to be full of terrorists waiting to attack innocent children. We currently are not prepared for an event like this in the United States. There are only a few cities that have adopted rapid means of changing their identifying badges or uniforms if they have been breached by an organized effort to reverse engineer emergency response and infiltrate our most trusted institutions. Most, if not all, major cities in the United States would not be able to tell who was the bad guy and who was the good guy during a coordinated attack that used official-looking vehicles or uniforms. By reverse engineering first response, terrorists could actually slow the ability of the true first responders . . . and much worse. They could undermine public trust as they did in Beslan (see Chapter 5), and in our race example in Chapter 1, and put to task all emergency managers with the dual challenge of fighting the actual enemy while dealing with a general public who thinks they are the enemy themselves.

In the private sector, simple employee badges, visitor badges, or just a good power suit and some social engineering can get you nearly anywhere you want to go. A disgruntled employee can reverse engineer their customer service job into a customer nightmare by simply trashing your brand with the access they have to names, addresses, and phone numbers of your clients. Private sector companies do not do enough to secure and compartmentalize such data! The banking and health care industries do because of required regulation, but most privately held or unregulated businesses do not. The emergency manager who does not understand that anyone with easy access to data, or who looks and seems like an employee—let alone the potential threat of a supposed first responder—has a blind side advantage so large that one disgruntled person can easily cause great damage in an unsuspecting environment. *God help the emergency manager who has to respond to a crisis that has never been considered as a First Event Scenario!*

Swarm Effect

Swarm effect, when not factored into a First Cause Scenario, creates a Disaster Halo Effect that is often *much worse* than the initial event. A fairly good example of this is people swarming into the Superdome during Hurricane Katrina. The outrage experienced by people when hospitals experience surge beyond capacity, and are then unable to take additional patients sickened by a pandemic, is another example. Swarm effects have overrun all international aid workers in Haiti, Japan, and Chile as they simply try and to hand out food and water to survivors after a trigger event. We keep deploying such resources without security forces as a standard at the risk of harming, if not killing, our first responders. Not including security as part of post-event aid distribution is no longer acceptable! Any emergency manager who considers the past ten years of major catastrophes, and assumes public order will prevail, is out of touch with reality and in the wrong field.

The scenario of a nurse giving out inoculations for a pandemic virus from pods that are geographically disbursed, or at schools without parents present, is inviting public violence and unnecessary bad press. There is also a possible scenario of injury to first responders as a simple lack of foresight in our field. Swarm effect behavior must be considered. In this case, our hindsight is so poor that it has not even touched our ability to foresee the swarm effect as a natural extension of a large-scale event that requires security planning in conjunction with aid distribution.

Kiddie Tactics

This leads us to Kiddie Tactics. Here is the simple reality: there are hacks available on the Internet right now that any 14 year old can apply to his Xbox 360, that cause the motion sensing camera to track and command anything—even a gun. There are computer hacks for businesses, instructions for building bombs, and enough radicalized "literature" online right now that one could simply decide that they were having a bad day, pick a religion or fundamentalist attitude, become totally convinced that he or she is doing the right thing, and attack with incredible effect—before reaching the age of eleven.

An 11-year-old boy and his 13-year-old friend perpetrated the Westside Middle School shooting in 1998 that killed five and injured ten. Kiddie tactics are not just for the United States either. Whereas U.S. children may be influenced by TV, movies, video games, and the Internet, the kiddie tactics deployed in Mexico, Latin America, Darfur, Sudan, and other parts of the world may be informed by much more hands-on experience. Our insistence to ignore these attacks as juvenile offenses puts the blinders on once again and leaves soft targets like highly populated schools ill prepared for events like Columbine. Most emergency managers do not plan for kiddie tactics, and the few who do rarely run joint exercises with police, fire, and emergency response crews as well as parents, teachers, and school staff.

The Secret Service has done much research in the area of kiddie tactics. What they found is chilling. First, and foremost, profiling does not work. Most of these students are not "loners." They are "followers" looking to fit in. "These children take a long, considered, public path toward violence." [9]

In the Market State of Palestine, the long, considered public path toward violence is amplified by incessant reinforcement of Hamas terrorism tactics on children's television programming. A breathtaking example

210

can be found on Al Aqsa TV, where a clearly trademark-violating likeness of Mickey Mouse teaches children how to—among other things—become suicide bombers. When left to their own devices, children around the world experience some sense of alienation in their pre-pubescent years. What a shame that those would promote killing and violence against innocents are using this natural insecurity to their advantage by leveraging the media. Even in the United States some have questioned the influence of violent video games and films in youth violence.

In these four areas—copycats, reverse engineering, swarm effects, and kiddie tactics—emergency responders find themselves limited in their imagination and capability to foresee First Event Scenarios. Yet, as we consider the evidence, we should start to realize that these blinders must come off. We have to begin developing emergency response plans and First Event Scenarios in which the horrible can, and will, happen, lest we get caught with our pants down again for lacking foresight.

7.8 NEW RISK, REASONED

Perhaps at the heart of this book is the simple issue of risk and reason. Merriam Webster defines reason as that which is "a statement offered in justification." Further, it is based on "a rational ground or motive" and has "a sufficient ground of explanation or of logical defense…"[10] Reason and its close cousin, rationality, are often used in the fields of science, mathematics, and philosophy, when we perceive there are reasonable decisions about risk that can be made—such as cause and effect, truth or lies, or good and bad judgments made by reasonable people.

The challenge with reason is that it relies on some law, fact, experiment, or logic to become widely regarded as reasonable. Simply stated, we have witnessed many disasters and terror attacks that are not at all "reasonable." They defy probability, what we consider to be humane, and sometimes, what we consider to be possible. They do not operate within a "rational ground" of justification, nor do they rely on a "sufficient ground of explanation or…defense." However, we want our field to be reasonable because we associate reason with the sciences and the practice of law.

In fact, our leadership often demands we exercise reason when crafting First Cause Scenarios and response plans to them. Much of the guidance for Business Continuity and Disaster Recovery within the private sector is based on the legal (read: liability) term "reasonable best effort," which is often why some emergency managers in the private sector are

211

left only viewing those things that can be proven and based in rationality. Moreover, the public sector, with its bureaucracy and tendency for some semblance of order, seeks to constantly fight the unreasonable with reason, often forgoing the plain truth that disasters and terror attacks do not exhibit any reason at all as the Disaster Halo Effect spreads out; thus, we are surprised by so-called rogue outcomes.

Risk, when reasoned, is certainly subjective; meaning that it is mostly based on what an individual or group thinks about what is reasonable, and in particular, what is reasonable to a given person or organizational outlook. We often take an objective-based reason as being the real nature of something, or the truth of its essence. However, here again, we are surprised when our hindsight biases and lack of imagination catch us off guard. Can disasters and terror attacks really be reasonable and subject to a collective reality? Well, they are, but is it the best method of practice? Perhaps not.

Some private sector businesses will tender risks all day long that others will not. Banks simply will not take risks that bakeries take every day. Manufacturers of commercial automobiles are willing to take the risk that the makers of weapons systems and rocket ships will not. Armies and governments will not take the risks that guerillas and terrorists will take time and again. Drug dealers will take the risk that school teachers would never consider. The more we think about risk as being reasonable, something that is based on laws and truths and widely agreed upon, we start to realize that *risk is highly subjective*. Therefore, the management of risk is a tricky thing to do, that is, *if* we are to practice in such a manner as to keep all of our varied stakeholders happy. Often, this is fine for individuals in their early years of practice in emergency management. It is easy to take the "safe" road, the reasonable road, and keep all of the stakeholders happy...at least until the reality of the Market State rears its ugly head.

In fact, many emergency managers stay in this zone of safely practicing for much of, if not their entire, careers. A certain status quo sets in; conference after conference goes by with few or no new insights, even though the risks we are supposed to manage are changing rapidly. In Chapter 2, we talked at length about Emergence and the rise of the Market State. We covered areas such as the new face of risk in the form of a new set of tactics being deployed, and a completely new view of disasters we call the Disaster Halo Effect in which all downward events can be tied to the first event, but may not be expected. We recommended 25 core areas of threats and vulnerabilities that fit within five constructs that we view as First Event Scenarios.

To the practitioner of emergency management, who has simply done what is needed to get by and stuck within the "reasonable" categories of risk, these concepts were probably quite a shock. But as we moved into later chapters, we clearly illustrated that there are better methods for considering emerging risk—methods borrowed from disciplines other than science and law. We explored marketing theories, the diffusion of innovation, and pattern recognition. We looked at ways in which individuals in the emergency management field made more than reasonable choices in the face of emerging risk—they made the *right* choices.

Some facets of emergency management will certainly remain in the classical fields of the rational, such as the sciences of meteorology or geophysics. On a broader scale, political science will continue to play its role. However, what we have added to the mix of multidisciplinary studies includes other areas of rational science, including consumer studies, the science of marketing, diffusion, and innovation. We have rolled up our sleeves and looked at additional, rational, yet unconventional, areas of study to meet the new challenges of emerging risk with new tools.

These tools are good, solid methods for dealing with risk. Many would argue that what we have suggested is that practitioners in the field of emergency management would be doing something more akin to art than science if they applied these commercial approaches. They would be right because, in fact, art itself is considered to be rational. After all, rationality is often described as using a decision-making process that is not just rational itself, but is also the *best* or *most optimal way* of solving a problem.

The best and most optimal way is often not taught, but is learned later, in practice across an array of fields of work. It is why doctors do internships and master makers have apprentices. The best and most optimal way is sometimes referred to as tacit knowledge, which is very different than common knowledge. **Tacit knowledge**, experience from the field, is often referred to as know-how; much of what has been discussed in this text has to do with the application of the rational used in other fields of study to expand on the reasoning on which emergency management has been based. Sharing this type of knowledge is often difficult. Many believe that tacit knowledge cannot be transferred at all, but must be experienced.

Nonetheless, the problem at hand is simple: either we continue our work in emergency management yielding to years of business as usual, or we embrace new, rational concepts from other fields to deal with emerging risk. It is a bit of a creative venture and requires innovation. However, given the stakes, we believe there is little choice but to reconsider what is given as rational in our field and push it to the next level.

213

As it turns out, many organizations and fields of study are now grappling with what they once considered "rational" in this new era. Science, medicine, and computer technologies have leapt forward in the past decade. Politics have become more dynamic and fluid than they have been in generations past. We are seeing the rise of innovation across a broad array of industries— including ours. There are many new innovations in software and technologies to assist in protecting the homeland and responding to disasters.

The hardest thing to change, however, is that what we once took for rational thinking in our space now must be met with an extension of that thinking toward greater innovation and the inclusion of other rational sciences and areas of thinking. *We must extend our concept of what is reasonable into the range of creative innovation and foresight to combat new risks and consider new methods of scenario creation and response.*

Richard Florida, in his book *The Rise of the Creative Class*, states it simply, "Creativity must be motivated and nurtured in a multitude of ways, by employers, by people themselves and by the communities where they locate..."[11] He continues, "long run growth requires a series of gradually accumulating changes in the organizational and institutional fabric of our society, taking place over perhaps half a century."[11] The reason Florida sees this massive rise of the creative class as part of a larger change in society is the same reason the lessons in this book are so important. "The deep and enduring changes of our age are not technological but social and cultural. They are thus harder to see..."[11]

But we *have* seen them. In the past decade, emerging risk is no surprise. We have witnessed disasters and terror attacks unthinkable prior to the new millennium. So now, having seen them, we must extend our thinking about risk beyond the rationale of the "company man" of the 1950s and orient ourselves to a type of emergency manager that is closer to us in terms of chronology and the logical progression of time. Meet the emergency manager of 2020. This future emergency manager will have fully embraced the range of ideas not only presented in this book, but new technologies and techniques bound to arise as our field experiences a boom of innovation in the wake of massive change and the emergence of the Market State.

7.9 A NEW WORLD, NEW RISKS

Almost monthly, we are faced with new risks and new areas to protect. Consider Unalaska. Unalaska is the last U.S. Island in the Aleutian Chain that separates the Bering Sea and the Pacific Gulf of Alaska. This chain stretches between Russia and Alaska and is closer to Seoul than to New York. You may know it from the Discovery Channel television show that is filmed there called *The Deadliest Catch*. During fishing season, this small town of 18,000 blooms to a population of 80,000 for a six-month period.

Here we have the best deep-water inland harbor in the Arctic Sea, making the area attractive for fishers, and now, with the planned drilling in the Chukchi Sea off Northern Russia, it is a perfect spot for Royal Dutch Shell's new circular rig and the only oil spill containment area in the North Pacific, the Nanuq. The airport, while frighteningly small, is serviceable, and the other infrastructure in the area is good, including the U.S.-operated ferry system known as the Alaskan Highway. The problem is the Internet connection; it is an antiquated dial-up line that makes doing business very problematic.

Royal Dutch Shell just invested $3 billion into their initial port and docking areas, with more money on the way. Furthermore, the Internet challenge is about to change with the completion of the Arctic Link, a fiber connection underwater cable pull that will connect North America to Russia, China, and points south such as Japan, that is planned to be completed in 2012. This will make the small island an essential hub for all Pacific Rim data traffic.

This mega-project is one-upped only by the opening of the Trans-Arctic shipping route expected to occur sometime in the next twenty years as the ice of the Arctic cap continues to defrost, making it possible for ships to pass cargo quickly from Upper Asia to Alaska year-round. Today, the small port called Dutch Harbor takes in more fish in terms of tonnage than any other port in the world, with much of it being shipped to China and Japan.

Unalaska is just about as nasty a place as anyone would ever want to visit. It is near freezing with an average temperature of just around 38°F, and high-speed wind gusts nearly every month of the year. However, this small island is opening up a new, faster means of moving goods to China, Russia, and other Asian countries from the United States, and vice versa.

Some people are going to have to go up there and work for these companies and public sector agencies as emergency managers. The threats they face will be new. The world they will work in will be new. The disasters and terror threats they will face will look nothing like Katrina or 9/11. We are further from those catastrophes now and closer to the unforeseen emerging risk of Unalaska, and hundreds of new choke points. **Choke points** (narrow, strategic routes) are areas that will be soft targets for interrupting international trade. Choke points that affect international oil trade alone are "the Straits of Hormuz, Strait of Malacca, Abqaiq processing facility, Suez Canal, Bab el-Mandab, Bosporus/Turkish Straits, Mina

215

al-Ahmadi terminal (Kuwait), Al Basrah oil terminal (Iraq), LOOP (United States), Druzhba pipeline (Russia)."[12] New choke points are being created worldwide to speed the transfer of goods, data, and people. Other choke points such as the enlargement of the Panama Canal and the proposed Baja Canal are due to come online in the next decade as well. These are real projects, changing the way goods and people move across territories in the Market State. The new risks are real, and the new definition of "rational" presented in this text has been designed to prepare for these and other emerging opportunities and, potentially, emerging dangers.

7.10 CONCLUSION

In this chapter, we have reviewed how certain nation-states are more prepared for disasters and emergencies as a result of tragic events in their history and national pride in emergency preparedness (see Figure 7.3).

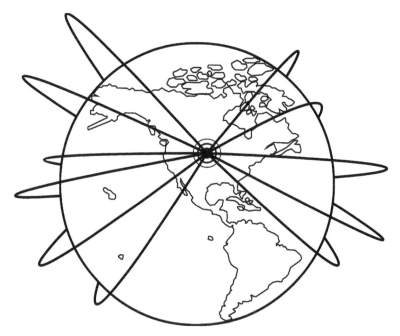

Figure 7.3 In this chapter, we considered how some nation-states prepare for emergencies and terror attacks, as well as how areas of dominant influence can enlighten our emergency management strategy.

We explored how pattern recognition can evolve into the ability to blink and even thin-slice scenarios in a matter of seconds. We looked at Areas of Dominant Influence that can both enlighten our planning efforts and inform our decision-making when it comes to conveying key messages to core stakeholders in emergency management. Finally, we reviewed how Copycats, Reverse Engineering, Swarm Effects, and Kiddie Tactics could catch us off guard, even with a Market State World view. Finally, we took a look at how a world of new risks is challenging the practice of emergency management to extend itself. What can be drawn from this chapter is that, while we have much to learn, there is much to learn from—if only we approach our practice with an open mind.

7.11 END OF CHAPTER QUESTIONS

- What are the major differences between the Israeli and Japanese cultures discussed in 7.4? What are their similarities? What can the United States learn from these cultures to enhance pattern recognition?
- How can pattern recognition be enhanced through using the tactics of "blinking" and "thin-slicing?"
- What are the Areas of Dominant Influence? How can implementing these impact responses and planning in our profession?
- How do copycats, reverse engineering, swarm effects, and kiddie tactics pose threats? How do the threats they present compare to those described in the condition of the Market State?
- Considering the Market State, how does risk continue to evolve and what kind of impact does it have on the micro (local) scale?

REFERENCES

1. Asia/Pacific Curtural Centre, *Inamura no-Hi, Tsunami Rescue!* New York: UNESCO, June 2007.
2. The Constitution of Japan. 1946. http://www.kantei.go.jp/foreign/constitution_and_government_of_japan/constitution_e.html.
3. Elliott, Michael. "Sea Of Sorrow." *Time*, January 10, 2005. http://www.globalsecurity.org/org/news/2005/050110-tsunami.htm (accessed October 6, 2011).
4. Glanz, James, and Norimitsu Onishi. "Japan's strict building codes saved lives." *New York Times*. March 11, 2011. http://www.nytimes.com/2011/03/12/world/asia/12codes.html?_r=1&hp (accessed April 5, 2011).

5. Jacoby, Jeff. "What Israeli security could teach us." *The Boston Globe*. August 23, 2006. http://www.boston.com/news/globe/editorial_opinion/oped/articles/2006/08/23/what_israeli_security_could_teach_us/ (accessed July 4, 2011).
6. Dwinell, Joe, and Natalie Sherman. "TSA to put Hub fliers on the spot." *Boston Herald.com*. August 2, 2011. http://www.bostonherald.com/news/regional/view.bg?articleid=1355725 (accessed August 4, 2011).
7. Schneier, Bruce. *Movie Plot Threats in The Guardian*. September 4, 2008. http://www.schneier.com/blog/archives/2008/09/movie_plot_thre_2.html (accessed June 8, 2011).
8. Gladwell, Malcolm. *Blink!*. New York: Little, Brown and Company, 2005.
9. Kirk, Michael, director. "The killer at Thurston High." *Frontline*. PBS. January 2000. http://www.pbs.org/wgbh/pages/frontline/shows/kinkel/profile/ (accessed March 8, 2011).
10. Merriam-Webster.com. *Reason*. http://www.merriam-webster.com/dictionary/reason (accessed April 2, 2011).
11. Florida, Richard. *The Rise of the Creative Class*. New York: Basic Books, 2002. p. 5.
12. Lehman Brothers. "Global oil choke points." *Deep Green Crystals*. January 18, 2008. http://www.deepgreencrystals.com/images/GlobalOilChokePoints.pdf (accessed April 7, 2011).

8

Tracking Memes: Data Trends and the Diffusion of Innovation

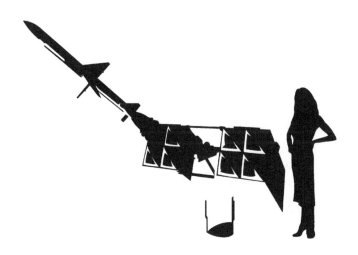

8.1 KEY TERMS

8.2 LEARNING OBJECTIVES

After reading this chapter, you should be able to describe:

- How memes are translated into real actions by emergency management professionals and by terrorists
- How understanding the diffusion of innovation illuminates the timeline under which new memes move through popular culture and the professional culture of emergency management
- What we can learn from the diffusion of innovation when we know who the stakeholders are and how to communicate with them
- How to use the diffusion of innovation to enable better narratives around risk and response in the emergency management field

8.3 CHAPTER INTRODUCTION

In traditional marketing, innovation is the ability to take a novel meme or product and present it to the market. The media plays a powerful role, as well as public relations. The same is true if we use a market approach in emergency management. Innovation gives way to invention and the dynamics of the diffusion of innovation (see Figure 8.1). The **diffusion of innovation** is a theory that explains the adoption rate of ideas and products (new memes), and how long it will take for that product or idea to reach market saturation. Everett M. Rogers wrote *Diffusion of Innovations* in which he defined this spreading of ideas as, "the process by which an innovation is communicated through certain channels over time among the members of a social system."[1]

We have already discussed how data becomes memes and how memes can help kick-start the narrative around risk and response in Chapter 5 of this book. This chapter will discuss how new memes can be translated into real threats or response tactics, and how they grow and morph over time (diffusion). We will also learn who the key stakeholders in diffusion

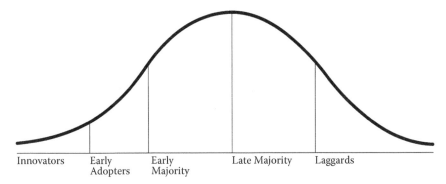

| Innovators | Early Adopters | Early Majority | Late Majority | Laggards |

Figure 8.1   The diffusion of innovation breaks down the groups who adopt new products across five unique categories.

are and some ways that understanding the diffusion of innovation can help build better narratives in emergency management.

Key areas in diffusion research are the innovation of the new idea, the types of communications channels used, the time rate of adoption, and the social system that frames the innovation decision process. Many of the theories of innovation stem from early social science theory and classic social learning theory and are highly applicable to emergency management in the context of emerging risk in the Market State. In *Diffusion of Innovations*, Rogers breaks the groups who adopt new products and memes into five unique categories:[1]

- Innovators
- Early adopters
- The early majority
- The late majority
- The laggards

These are groups placed across an adoption scale (see Figure 8.2). It is important to consider that **market share** (how much of the complete market for a product or service the new product takes) or ideologies are of little difference. Rogers is clear that there are opinion leaders and early adopters who are influential in communicating their negative or positive experience with an idea or product. These opinion leaders have access to change agents, broader social circles and networks, and are generally more adept at utilizing media. A **change agent** is something, usually a person, which brings about change by having influence in their organization. The techniques they use, in one form or another, are the techniques

221

Figure 8.2 In this chapter, we will discuss the diffusion of innovation, stakeholders in innovation such as the early majority, and how some memes become viral and act as change agents.

of *persuasion*. Whether it is for corporate purposes, the natural diffusion of innovation, or to spread a new idea within a culture, change agents are people that other people pay attention to—whether they know it or not.

The diffusion of innovative memes is something that terrorists understand completely. As we will see, emergency managers would do well to understand them as completely as terrorists do in order to better track risk potential, and to understand and to communicate with stakeholders throughout the emergency management process. The process by which an innovation is communicated through a social system is key to creative foresight and planning for disasters and terror attacks. It is also why many terror attacks have caught us off guard. Terrorists have simply adopted the tactics more quickly than intelligence, law enforcement, and emergency managers have identified them. In many cases, neither emergency managers, nor intelligence agencies have been able to foresee and disrupt such attacks. Considering the first decade of the twenty-first century (without casting disparagement on the good work of the CIA, FBI, DHS, FEMA, and other agencies in thwarting many plots), we have simply not anticipated or prevented as many attacks as we would like.

We will also explore the anatomy of risks and response in terms of cultural and marketing phenomena and describe how data is collected and disseminated in the competitive world of marketing. We will present a discussion regarding the challenges facing change agents in any industry. Finally, we will be describing how emergency managers can use the three-up storyboard technique to track key ideas in emergency management.

8.4 TRANSLATING MEMES AND DIFFUSION

The diffusion of innovation provides us with a reference and a baseline for the currency of our practice today as well as the effects and potentials of threats and responses of tomorrow. Using this model we can map who knows what—the location of the new tactic or idea (on the diffusion of innovation curve)—and what the arch of usage will be in an attack, a disaster, or our response to an event (see Figure 8.2). However, first we have to understand how a meme is translated and arrives on the timeline of diffusion of innovation.

Translating a meme (see Figure 8.3) means to co-opt, or move a meme from the novel to the mainstream. It is a little bit like translating a foreign language into a native tongue. When first exposed to a new language you are not able to understand it. By using an interpreter you are granted access to something that is foreign and you are able to make sense of it. In the case of memes, a change agent is this translator. The Change Agent takes the new meme and crosses it over by making small adaptations to it so that it is changed enough to be understood by a broader audience. In this example, the Change Agent is the innovator and the original broader audience consists of the early adopters. The mechanics of translation are the keys to the evolution of a meme.

The most important actors in the translating of a new meme to a broader audience are the Change Agents and Early Adopters. Change Agents can make a meme work for them to match their agenda. The term *translating* in this context comes from the marketing world where memes are translated into fashions, cars, and other consumables. As an example, a Coolhunter or pattern recognition expert may see that touch screens have become a huge meme because of the iPod Touch. By applying that meme and translating it, the interior of the new Lexus may feature a touch screen for controlling and monitoring other aspects of the man-to-machine interface, such as the air conditioner, GPS system, or even maintenance records.

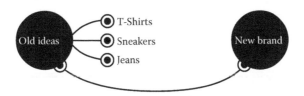

Figure 8.3   Here, a Change Agent has taken a set of memes from T-shirts, sneakers, and jeans, and translated them into a completely new brand.

223

All emergency managers are Change Agents, particularly when it comes to communicating First Event Scenarios and gaining the necessary support and cooperation needed to plan for them. Emergency Managers are naïve if they feel that such activities are best left to policy makers or "think tanks." According to Aristotle, there are three basic ways to effect change. One is to apply logic. For example, all earthquakes over 7.0 magnitude are bad; there was a 7.0 magnitude earthquake in Los Angeles; therefore, it was a bad earthquake. These three logic statements are called the major premise, the minor premise, and the conclusion. However, we have warned in this volume against sloppy logic, as it will create falsehoods. Here the same example reveals flawed logic: All earthquakes over 7.0 are bad; there was a 7.0 earthquake 500 miles off shore in the Pacific; therefore, that was a bad earthquake.

The second way to effect change is to appear to be ethical (e.g., smart, hardworking, licensed, or interested in the welfare of our clients). An ethical appeal for change may take the form of a statement such as, "I have my Masters in Emergency Management and I would be remiss if I did not point out the potential for a Disaster Halo Effect from an earthquake in Los Angeles." The final technique Aristotle presents is that of using emotions or "emotional proof." These appeals take the form of emotional statements such as, "you wouldn't want to have a bad plan for an earthquake in Los Angeles would you?" or "think of all the lives we could be saving by looking at the potential for a First Event Scenario this way." While Aristotle considered logic, ethics, and emotions to be the three pillars of change, the field of marketing has evolved many other tools that are now available to emergency mangers and use slight variations of these age-old teachings.

When marketing experts get together to discuss change and new memes they often look at the challenge from a macro-level. For instance, using black rubber as a clothing material might be a new meme. The next step for those who want to create stories about the black rubber meme is to attach key words, phrases, and images to the meme. This is called creating a storyboard, or just storyboarding. A **storyboard** (see Figure 8.4) is a series of images used to visualize the main points and direction of a film, TV show, commercial, or a Web site. It is used in marketing to do the very same thing—highlight the key points of visual change in action. A storyboard is usually supported by good narratives and storytelling, which we will discuss later in this chapter.

The marketing storyboard starts to connect key words and phrases to the meme and frame them with other images. Once the high-level ideas presented on a storyboard are digested and read, the next step is a very

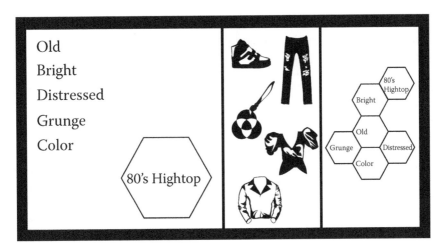

Figure 8.4 This marketing storyboard captures '80s grunge rock trends on the far left and arranges them into a translated product line in the meme cluster on the far right as a means of telling the story.

natural question, "Can this meme be translated?" Change Agents and Coolhunters will help designers translate the meme so that it applies to the market or product required. By showing the original meme—in this case black rubber—used in product mock-ups, prototypes, or other commercial applications, the audience is able to foresee the natural movement of black rubber from an innovative trend into a new product that they can make and sell. Typically, a meme cluster is developed in the final panel in a three-panel marketing storyboard and shows how the new product or line of products would resonate, with representations of key memes from other trend areas supporting the product.

This third and final panel may be the most important of them all. It is simple to imagine a Coolhunter spotting a street trend and translating it, or turning it into a possible new product; mock-ups are cheap and easy to make. Psychologically, the question of *if* we can take a new idea and translate it into a product is easy to answer. Most of us, at a gut level, know that we can make almost anything, and that applying a new twist to an average product, say a thick rubber strap to an average watch, is a simple fact of life. But the third panel, which shows the meme cluster surrounding the new product, gives the idea *context*. The *in context panel* (the panel that shows the new product surrounded by other memes that support it) is the psychological kill shot.

This mental leap is a bit harder to make. Most private and public sector decision makers are uncertain of what people will think of new ideas or innovative approaches; some may even be risk adverse to doing or making things that are new. The third panel suggests that the market *will accept* the new idea and that it will show up on billboards, magazine covers, TV ads, the news, fashion models … that it will *be commoditized and successfully translated*. The third panel helps the blind to see, and as the saying goes, "seeing is believing."

Using the same approach in emergency management, a meme can also be illustrated on one page that shows the key terms, phrases, and relevant data visualizations. From this storyboard, a discussion can develop around how the meme can be translated into a broader audience, a wider group of adopters. This is important to understand as it assists the emergency manager in telling the story about how a meme can become a real action (see Figure 8.5).

In this example, we have taken the meme of narco-jihad used in the fourth scenario of Chapter 1 and storyboarded it. Because a storyboard forces all of the key elements of a meme (images and data) onto one page, it helps the viewer better understand what is possible by enabling them to visualize the facts. Using a storyboard approach, the reader can create a mental image of the key words, phrases, and data in the first panel that connects the dots around a new ideology and groups of people, tactics, and possible targets. This mental picture pops out at the viewer and assists the presenter in beginning a conversation about the meme that is forming.

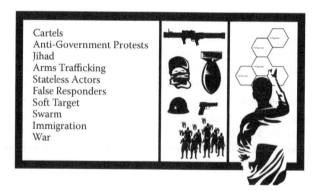

Figure 8.5 Emergency management storyboard. The narco-jihad scenario has been illustrated using the marketing storyboard approach.

The storyboard then indicates how the meme has been translated and how deeply it has taken root by presenting a second panel that indicates surveillance images, background data, and even earlier attempts from other cities or places to use the same meme to do harm. But that is just the beginning of the story an emergency manager has to tell. Showing that the meme has been, or can be, translated *and* where it sits on the diffusion of innovation scale is what is needed to really tell the story. This comes in the third panel.

In the third panel, a scenario is presented that ties the translation of the early memes and current translation of those memes into real action in the form of a meme cluster. Possible targets are indicated. People of interest are shown. A possible timeline is indicated. The tactics and possible approach of the terror cell is presented. Just like the marketing storyboard, the emergency management storyboard helps leadership to *see a possible view* of the future in which the dots connect, the memes aggregate, and the scenario becomes real. In business, as in life, a picture tells a thousand words. And while an accompanying narrative is key, *the storyboard is a must* for any emergency manager who takes the job of presenting scenarios seriously.

Critically re-designed with an emphasis on the frequency of events, we can use the original diffusion of innovation map as part of the third panel to create a better illustration of how memes have taken hold and what the current adoption state and future usage will look like over time. The diagram that follows is the diffusion of innovation as applied to emergency management known as the Emergency Management Diffusion Map. The **Emergency Management Diffusion Map** is a modification of the original diffusion of innovation illustration (see Figure 8.6). It illustrates two key differences that lend it higher utility in emergency management than the original diffusion of innovation illustration. It also allows for the identification of novel or invented ideas *before* innovators apply them. Finally, the Emergency Management Diffusion Map focuses on the reasonable likelihood of event frequency based on adoption—not market share, as does the focus of consumer marketing.

Now that we have a means of storyboarding a meme to begin the narrative and a map on which to place key memes, we can look at events with a different view. A perspective of how ideas get passed along that provides us with a clear picture of the diffusion of innovation allows us to become more predictive and less reactive. Keep in mind that a good narrative, or briefing, should accompany the storyboard. However, before we dig deeper into emergency management narratives, the reader will have

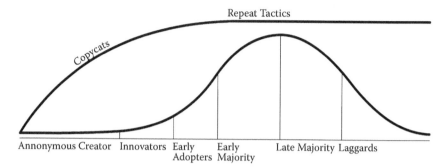

Repeat Tactics

Copycats

Annonymous Creator   Innovators   Early   Early   Late Majority Laggards
                                   Adopters   Majority

Figure 8.6   The Emergency Management Diffusion of Innovation Map considers the possibility that market penetration may stay high after the initial introduction of innovative technology based on Copycats and a repetitious use of tactics.

to take time to learn a bit more about the stakeholders in diffusion and the important role they play.

8.5 STAKEHOLDERS IN DIFFUSION

The most important stakeholder in the process of the diffusion of innovation is often overlooked: *the innovator*. An **innovator** is defined as the original artist or creator of an idea, or alternately, the one who translates an old idea into the market of cultural imagination. We often assume that memes start of own their accord and are not attributable to any one inventor or invention. However, the birthing of a meme is often not simply the aggregation of old ideas, but the creation of something altogether new. Novelty or a new invention is neutral. New inventions do not hold negative or positive impacts unto themselves; it is how they are translated that causes positive or negative outcomes. When an invention is truly new we understand it as being extremely novel. Many inventions are also aggregations of old ideas placed in a new order or reverse-engineered to be used in novel ways.

The reason the innovator is the most important stakeholder in the diffusion of innovation is simple. This person, or group, is the root cause of the diffusion of innovation. The reason for this is that where there is no innovation, there is no new meme. Where there is no new meme, there is nothing for early adopters to latch onto; and, therefore, there is nothing for us to track on the diffusion of innovation timeline. Be sure that you

228

keep in mind that the translator or designer of an innovation can also be considered the innovator. The creative act of figuring out how old memes can be used in new ways is an act of innovation unto itself.

The reader may be focused on memes that are negative and thinking about a myriad of "bad" inventions and their impact on our practice. It is worth highlighting that the act of innovation and applied invention is central to improving our "game" in the emergency management field. Since new inventions and innovative ideas are neutral, the emergency manager can apply them with positive effects. As an example, the Israeli Army recently upgraded the Merkava main battle tank (MBT). Considered one of the best tanks in the world, it took a beating in Lebanon in 2008 when Hamas and Hezbollah started targeting the tanks with heavy missiles. The Israeli Defense Force (IDF) lost 130 to 140 of the tanks. Sometimes only a good beating necessitates looking for innovation.

A company well known for advanced defense systems was called in to see if they could improve the Merkava's antimissile and active defense systems. Reportedly, Rafael Advanced Defense Systems had an interesting demonstration in mind for their new Trophy Active Protection System. They placed a crew of IDF tank specialists in a tank outfitted with the Trophy system and fired a rocket at it. The rocket was destroyed by a barrage of explosive projectiles within three to four yards of the tank and no one inside was injured—a perfect demonstration!

The Trophy uses a system that fires a shotgun-like blast of explosive projectiles interfacing with four flat panel radars that use a computer to calculate the range of incoming fire before propelling its load of buckshot. It has a very small kill zone so as to not endanger nearby troops. It has proven so highly effective that in 2010, a deal was made that will put the system on all of the IDF's tanks.

The amazing innovation behind this defense system is a meme that can be traced back to early science fiction and Japanimation (Japanese cartoons). Advanced defense systems were imagined in shows like *Star Wars* and cartoons such as *Robotech* in the early 1970s. Using the meme of computer-controlled, self-targeting, and self-deploying anti-artillery systems seen in these early fictional works, Rafeal, in partnership with others, translated the meme into a meaningful and very real defense system. Their creative knack for commoditizing the unbelievable does not seem to be stopping there.

The Kinetic Energy Penetrator (KEP) is a type of armor piercing weapon that does not use explosives or chemicals to do damage. It simply uses mass and velocity to shred through anything in its path. Much like the swords, spears, or axes wielded by the Mecha (a piloted tank/ robot combination) of Anime culture, the KEP is an old-school weapon, powered by very modern propulsion and targeting systems. It seems that translating memes from fiction to reality is clearly a part of meme tracking, and these two examples, in the hands of the right armies, can be seen as great examples of real-life meme adoption into the mainstream.

While often missed in discussions regarding the diffusion of innovation, we must keep in mind that it is the initiator of invention themselves—the inventor, designer, or translator—who triggers the innovation and has the highest stakes in the diffusion of innovation.

When it comes to innovators there are two types: the Anonymous Innovator, and the Iconoclast. The **Anonymous Innovator** is someone or something that creates without any credit or celebration that may bring attention to the creator. A great example of this is the Che Guevara meme, a graffiti glyph (see Figure 8.7), that is based on a facial caricature created by Irish artist Jim Fitzpatrick. The icon is used for mixed meanings and messages, everything from revolution to hipster cool. This legacy image

Figure 8.7 The Che Guevara meme is the product of a little known and iconoclastic creator that has morphed over the years to have many meanings. The image most closely resembles a little known painting by Fitzpatrick, but varied interpretations arise time and again.

resurfaced in the late 1990s and within nearly two years could be spotted in any major metropolitan area in the world.

The image of Che's face could mean anything to the person or people who placed it there—from a deep appreciation for Che's revolutionary character, to a real affiliation with his politics (see Figure 8.7). However, most likely the image is completed depolarized at this point and is simply a "cool picture." It did not take long for the Coolhunters to track this highly adaptable meme down and translate it. Within months, the image of Che's face was on everything from T-shirts to Zippo lighters. A huge part of the appeal with the Che meme is that it is highly malleable and can be easily translated and interpreted based on its context in media and audience. While the T-shirts today are still selling like hotcakes and the image is still found on products targeted at rebellious youth around the world, no one has stood up and said, "I made this iconic and viral graffiti because. ... "

Many youth believe this free image, lacking any corporate or state identity, represents globalization and a bucking of the marketing system that controls and manages the dissemination of such information and images. Moreover, the anonymity of the maker creates room for urban legend to flourish, and for nearly anyone to lay claim to the meaning or the message behind the image. It turns out, quite simply, that memes that cannot be traced back to an original source or creator have much more credibility, and spread more quickly, than any meme that is put into the market by someone taking credit for it.

In marketing, as in emergency management, this creates a problem. The belief that the innovator is the source of all strong memes is true, but the most influential innovators do not directly advertise their influential powers of innovation. This is why Osama bin Laden had risen to nearly saintly heights within the radical Muslim world. He innovated, often by proxy, allowing middlemen and others to take the fame, while he simply spun his ideology. His hand in 9/11 was one of the Wizard of Oz, or "man behind the curtain" roles. In other attacks, he was completely anonymous, and let others spread his viral memes without crediting him at all. While we know he was the source, he was a source that was not seeking the limelight; therefore, he was a very innovative adversary, and difficult to locate until his death on May 1, 2011.

In emergency management, the even more anonymous innovators are Theodore Kaczynski (the infamous Unabomber) and the Beltway Snipers (John Allen Muhammad and Lee Boyd Malvo). Both crimes of terror went on for a long while without anyone understanding their motives or underlying ideologies. No credit was sought. No spotlight asked for. Kaczynski was not captured for nearly 17 years. Muhammad and Malvo killed nine people and went undetected for months. Because there was no innovator, or creator of the "sniper" meme, the attacks were mistakenly mixed in with the 9/11 attacks by the general public and some journalists.

From 1978 to 1995, Ted Kaczynski's bombings went unsolved even though we had many of our best intelligence professionals working the case. It was not until April of 1996 when he published his "manifesto" through two major outlets and laid claim to the meme he created—the Unabomber—that we were able to catch him. Similarly, the tarot cards, long notes on Jihadism, and even calls to the police during the Beltway Sniper Attacks were so cryptic that it took months of good police and investigative work to capture the two criminals. This was in spite of the fact that the media had devoted massive amounts of airtime to the attacks, covering each new shooting with near hysteria, and tying the terror of the shootings to the terror of 9/11. The anonymous innovator is a dangerous thing for emergency managers trying to proactively stop terrorism. There is no clear motive, mode of tactics, or method of deployment. The meme is there, but we have a hard time linking it to the innovator.

On the other hand, the **Iconoclasts** of innovation, whether for good or evil, are easy to "get a bead on." They have an agenda; they *want* people to know why they are doing what they are doing. On the positive side of the ledger, one only needs to think of Steve Jobs, the current CEO of Apple and his launch of the iPad as an innovation to see how clear his motives are and what he expects. On the negative side, there are figures like Timothy McVeigh, who proudly sought out support for his bombing at Oklahoma City. He was sloppy, gaming for attention, even proud to be arrested. The Iconoclast, while innovative and a meme creator, is much easier to understand and track than the anonymous creator when using the diffusion of innovation.

The mythic qualities bestowed on innovators by marketers, the public, and the media make the Iconoclastic interesting and the Anonymous fascinating. This characteristic of fascination with the anonymous has caused many eager attackers to withhold their intention, or even their hand in the innovation that created the meme in the first place. And we believe that the trend toward anonymous innovation in terrorism will rise over the coming years. We discussed the concept of Copycats in detail in Chapter 7.

Given that we operate in a Market State world, innovation is the operative word of the decade, if not the millennium. Innovation cannot be outsourced. It is not easily accomplished. It requires organizations that have common goals and values to sustain. *It is the competitive edge that everyone is looking for.* Whether you work for the good guys, the bad guys, or just the guys who clean up the mess, we all know that innovation is the be-all, end-all in today's globally competitive landscape. So much so that if one is not innovating, it could be said that one is not competing at all.

Large corporations that use designers to translate memes into new products are highly invested in the diffusion of innovation of the products of their labors. Politicians who translate a meme into a campaign slogan or advertisement are highly invested in the diffusion of that type of innovation. Policy makers that aggregate a set of ideas into a new meme and express that meme as a policy position are invested in the diffusion of innovation. Terrorists who translate old tactics into new approaches or angles of attack are highly invested in the diffusion of innovation. Finally, and one of the main points of this work, emergency managers who discover new ways of meeting evolving challenges in the risk landscape are invested in the diffusion of innovation. In short, if the reader wants to *identify* the most important stakeholder in the diffusion of innovation process, it is the inventor, translator, or designer of the meme itself. *That is the person or group with the most to lose and gain.*

From the inception of a new meme or innovation, the highest priority task of the innovator is to influence the early adopters. They are the real change agents in the diffusion of innovation process. Early adopters are the individuals, groups, or influencers who have important "go/no-go" power in the narrative that occurs as memes move along the diffusion of innovation timeline. They are the curators of the new idea, the first in, and often, the least invested. Early adopters are fickle, move from one meme to the next, and often lack focus.

As such, their influence is crucial in starting the diffusion of innovation, but it is typically short-lived. Consider this: who are the most important people an innovator has to convince to move a new idea or meme forward? It is those who can change the thinking of a broader majority. If an innovator succeeds in impacting early adopters, even if only for a short time, an early majority will follow. This is why inventors place so much emphasis on finding and influencing early adopters—because they, in turn, influence broader and deeper decision makers.

It should be noted that Geoffrey A. Moore contested the notion that the diffusion innovation theory provides a smooth ramp from early adopter to early majority in his work *Crossing the Chasm*, published in 1991. Moore believes that there is a difference between early adopters who are visionary and enthusiastic, and the early majority who are more pragmatic. His work suggests that there is "chasm" between the two groups that must be considered in marketing.[2]

While Moore's theories are focused on disruptive and discontinuous consumer innovations, he raises an important point. Early adopters are very different than early majorities. However, if all of our work in emergency management and all terrorist activities took place in the early adopter space, the problems we are facing today would be just as pronounced, novel, and dangerous. Furthermore, we are already witnessing the diffusion of terrorist ideologies and tactics in practice.

Perhaps the bigger issue is that, as the emergency management diffusion of innovation shows, we tend not to look forward toward the repetition of events and copycats that will come later. Unlike hindsight bias, which is covered so well in books like *The Black Swan* or *Normal Accidents*, or the notion of creative foresight, which is tackled breathlessly in the book *Blink*, the most frightening gap in the Emergency Management Diffusion Map shown here is that we do not expect another event like a plane bombing or vehicle attack—even though it is clear that they are more likely to happen as a result of adoption and diffusion of innovation.

Whether or not the early majority follows seamlessly from the influence of early adopters is really the outcome of the evolutionary nature of the meme itself. A strong, viral, and adaptable meme will easily translate itself "across the chasm" into the early majority stage. Once a meme enters this stage of diffusion, most bets are off. The innovation is now ramping quickly as an early majority adopts the new meme into their lifestyle, business culture, or product buying choices. The same is true for new ideas or memes in the emergency management space. Once the early majority adopts an idea it is well on its way to becoming a new "best practice" or standard. This is because the early majority *is* a majority, and the ramp of adoption peaks with smooth transition from early majority to a late majority.

The late majority are often stakeholders who are holding out for one of three basic reasons:

1. They do not like new ideas until many other people have tried them.
2. They cannot afford to take on new memes until they look like they have staying power.
3. They lack the self-confidence and leadership skill to be part of an early majority, but will follow along gladly once the early majority is established.

Whatever their reasoning, the distinction between the early majority and the late majority is that the former is more apt to spend more, take more risk, and stay on the cutting edge. Whereas the latter, while willing to try new things, is constrained by their own lack of imagination, outside factors such as budget, or a lack of leadership capability.

Many people who look at the diffusion of innovation for the first time are apt to think that the peak of the adaptation of invention is at the end of the late majority adaptation phase. Because of the distribution in the graph it seems like that is where the most power is located, but nothing could be further from the truth. Once an idea tips over the top of that graph and starts down the ramp on the other side and through the group known as the laggards, we can see that the composition and distribution of power is just as high in the laggards' area as it is in the early majority area.

While this idea may be counterintuitive, it is very important to our field. In his book, *The Long Tail*,[3] Chris Anderson presents some new thinking in this space and suggests something even more interesting— **the long tail**. The concept of the long tail suggests that time does not cut off abruptly in the diffusion of innovation map at all. He goes on to propose that really good memes have a shelf life that often goes on and on at a low penetration point, but for a very extended period of time. For instance, if you placed a Big Mac cheeseburger on the diffusion of innovation timeline, it would not stop being adopted at the end of the laggards' phase, but go on and on in time with a certain group of the population continuing to enjoy them.

Here is what is so important about the long tail idea; if you stack up the small percentage of people who keep doing the same thing, buying the same product, or acting out based on the same original meme, the long tail can aggregate over time into a much bigger market share than all of the other phases in diffusion combined. Apply that idea to emergency management: If the roadside bomb was invented in Afghanistan and IUDs then traveled successfully through the early adoption, early majority, and late majority phases in the 30 years that followed, it would be the next 100 years of use that this type of attack would hold in the diffusion model—the long tail would do the most damage and would lead to the highest body count.

Understanding what is important to each of the stakeholders in the phases of diffusion is an important key to understanding how the diffusion of innovation works (see Figure 8.8). What do each of the stakeholders want, what motivates them, and how does one reach them?

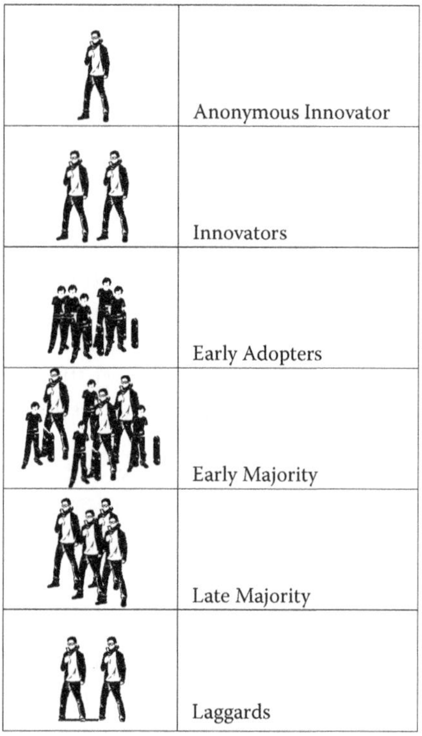

Figure 8.8 In review, the stakeholders in diffusion are the anonymous innovator, the innovator, the early adopter, the early majority, the late majority, and the laggard.

8.6 THE "SHOW AND TELL" OF DIFFUSION

To get back to the notion of creating a narrative, or telling the story in order to get in front of the challenges facing the emergency management field, this chapter has suggested that the storyboard is an excellent method for describing all manner of innovation and meme potentials. Next, including a visual description of how the meme might translate or adapt to be malicious or magnificent is an important step in helping stakeholders understand what is possible with the meme. Finally, the emergency management diffusion map can be applied to any terror plot, attack, and disaster or response effort and project the adaptation rate and diffusion of the meme over time.

There are two additional ideas we would like to add to this basic concept. One is *that visual communication is paramount to gaining traction and sharing this type of information.* We live in a visual age and the saying that "a picture tells a thousand words" applies to this type of communication in a very important way. Capturing a new meme on a storyboard, describing how it is being translated and distributed, and showing how it will be spread, or is expected to spread, across the diffusion of innovation can be accomplished in three slides or less. We recommend that communicating these types of ideas is accomplished first through the use of a few slides and supported by a deep, graphically intensive report. This allows stakeholders to capture the key points of a meme first, understand the potential, and then dive deeper into the ideas by reading the report after the presentation. Using visual communication methods allow you to share a lot of information, and the story all but tells itself to the viewer.

Prior to emphasizing the importance of solid reporting and a good narrative relative to a First Event Scenario, we want to take a moment to highlight what we consider to be one of the biggest gaps in emergency management—*a lack of graphic artists.* While many budgets in the private and public sector pine for more analysts and systems with little or no business case for the investment, the real problem seems to be that we have plenty of data (if not too much), but we are just not good at communicating it. This is where the need for strong visualizations to come into play. Masters of emerging risk understand that we live in a visual age, and when asked if they would rather have another analyst or an artist, they say, *we should pick the artist.* An artist will fast-track the visual storytelling of an emergency management program, improve communications, and ultimately, increase the performance and budget of the program. However, that artist will need solid narratives, like a good script, to work from.

A good narrative is the output of good analysis. Good analysis does not yield lengthy spreadsheets or incomprehensible charts and graphs. The message must be simple and easy to read, and so too, must be the narrative that is found in the data—this is accomplished visually. Like the storyboards discussed earlier, good narratives start with three key components—a beginning, middle, and an end. Have you ever read a story that does not have these three elements? It is tempting to simply extract data and hope that our stakeholders will understand the dump of information we lay on their desks. But that is a hopeless, and often fruitless, endeavor. We have to use a better approach to communicate this volume of information in layman's terms.

Mapping out the Narrative

First, we have to explain where the data came from and how it is connected. Second, we have to show how it is changed, or how it is about to change given a new tempo, atmosphere, or recent development. Finally, we have to show what the result of this change in the data means currently, or in the future. Simply stated, we need to take the data and show it in three states, the beginning state, the middle state, and the end state. This is a fairly straightforward proposal while developing First Event Scenarios.

The Beginning of the Narrative

The beginning of the narrative should clearly have a set of facts (the data) that will support the translation of the concept into a scenario. As previously suggested, these data sets can be presented as memes, which is to say that we might not know *exactly* who, what, or why, but we know that the idea or tactic *exists*. With the memes connected in a meaningful initial story of how "this" connects to "that," the last part of the narrative should have a clear problem statement. A **problem statement** is a crisply written paragraph that explains the conclusion the data leads to. It is important that each of the memes, or facts, that precede the problem statement have either caveats or assumptions that set them in a realistic context.

The Middle of the Narrative

The middle of the narrative should provide, like the storyboard, a clear picture of how the problem statement is changed, or translated, given new information or data germane to the location for which you are writing the First Event Scenario. There should be a clear statement of assumptions or caveats here that indicate the likelihood or the possibility of change, and/ or clearly indicate that a change that has occurred taking the data set of memes in the beginning and changing them in the middle of the story. Simply put, the middle of the narrative must show how the memes have been translated and transformed.

The End of the Narrative

Finally, at the end of the narrative, there should be a powerful resolution of the translated memes. That is to say that the ending should be strong, clear, and concise. It should be a natural and obvious conclusion of the beginning data and memes, and the middle translation of the memes. With the given caveats and assumptions made, the end of the narrative should present the only realistic outcome.

Narration in Action

This natural and realistic outcome is referred to as an airtight script, and this is how it works:

Have you ever seen a movie in which, during the opening scene, you know something bad is going to happen? Let us say that a doorbell rings and the heroine answers the door. You are a critic, so right away you are screaming at the screen, "Don't open the door, you idiot!" Okay, sorry, this is *not how an airtight script works.*

What we need here is a compelling reason, the suspension of disbelief, so that, as a viewer, you believe she *has* to answer the door.

This is how you solve the problem: You plant the assumption, the suspension of disbelief, during the opening credits that she is excited that her six-year-old son is on his way home from summer camp and she cannot wait to see him. Soft and suggestive assumptions and caveats that make her rush to answer that door make this beginning *bulletproof.*

Next, in the middle of our script, she and her son are kidnapped. In a chance moment, they take an opportunity to escape. As the viewer, we know that there is *no way* she is going to escape just because she found an unlocked car while her captors were in hot pursuit. But we use a flashback as a storytelling device allowing us to implant a small caveat that makes this escape attempt entirely believable. Her husband was a chop shop mechanic (conveniently, this also explains why she would be in so much trouble). Incidentally, he was murdered during a scuffle with a few car buyers.

Our heroine recalled a first date with her husband, during which he asked which of the cars in the front of a fancy hotel she would like to go home in. Thinking nothing of, it because she expected nothing, she chose a Lamborghini. To open the car, her husband used a tennis ball with a hole in it to reverse the pneumatic door locks, and popped them open with air pressure. Then he jammed a screwdriver into the ignition to start the $300,000 vehicle. Her fond memory of that night saved her right when she needed it. She scooped up the screwdriver lying on the floor of the warehouse and imitated his action. Our belief is suspended, the caveat is there, and the scenario is *bulletproof.*

Finally, at the end of the story, she has evaded her captors and arrived at the old beach house she shared with her murdered husband. We are amazed when she walks in and sees her husband on the balcony; silhouetted by the setting sun, he turns toward her with a warm, loving smile.

What? This was supposed to be the bulletproof script! We said he was dead. Nope—here is the caveat; we thought he was dead—we assumed he was dead, but he was not! He managed to flip himself onto the floor below after being shot at and escaped. He was only slightly injured and had to go on the run while the bad guys kidnapped his wife and son. Now that our heroine has bravely fought off her attackers, he is back.

In all, three assumptions (caveats) were used to make the unbelievable, believable and the unanticipated, explainable. Thus, the script is bulletproof. Simple concepts closed the doubt loop and suspended disbelief so that the story could be told without interruption from the audience, or loud questions from producers.

This is an example of how emergency managers *must work* (less the cowardly husband running away while his wife and son outwit and defeat the bad guys). Our narratives have to be bulletproof. Our assumptions must be used to make our narratives *airtight*. Those assumptions should be carefully chosen to make the stories we are telling lead to natural outcomes. The reader should know where we are going and be able to accept it before we get there. Any surprise should be covered with something they have already heard, something they believe to be possible. The result should be that a bulletproof narrative with carefully considered assumptions results in a believable and actionable scenario.

We have to be this good. We have to be *this right*. We are using memes, facts, data, and assumptions to generate the First Cause Scenario narratives about the future of risks. We cannot afford for our stories *not to be believed*. The same rules apply to solution planning, recommendations, and emergency response planning.

To recap, here is a list of what every good narrative must have:

1. A believable beginning with real facts and meme clusters
2. A solid middle that illustrates how the memes change, or have changed, to dramatically alter the probability or possibility of the result
3. A strong ending that is a natural result of the existing memes, any given assumptions, and the change from the middle

8.8 TELLING THE STORY

As we have said, the failure of imagination can be overcome. A better way to integrate, communicate, and tell the story about upcoming First Event

Scenarios and better emergency response models can be had. The key is using strong communication methods. We have outlined several methods in the past few chapters:

- Pattern Recognition
- Trend Spotting
- Memes
- Meme Clusters
- Storyboarding
- Narratives

However, even with these tools, we cannot forget the old axiom, "know your audience." It is as important in emergency management as it is in any other profession. Using the diffusion of innovation, we can be much more effective at telling our story. Many texts and standards within our organization suggest "going straight to the top" with *everything*. We contest this notion and think that the best approach is to know your audience, and to use that knowledge to your advantage.

Having read and mastered the material in this book, you will be in command of some of the most cutting edge techniques and thinking practices in the emergency management space. Building consensus in your organization around these new approaches will be paramount to your success in renewing and invigorating your field. Start with early adopters in your workgroup and find the people who are eager to talk and think about new risks and new ways of adapting to deal with them.

Listen closely to their ideas and input. Test the assumptions and caveats built into First Event Scenarios or new response solutions. Have fierce conversations about the ideas—do not personalize the outcomes. Build on the knowledge you gain and the shared views you create with other early adopters to form an early majority. Increase awareness of new memes. We would even go so far as to suggest hanging a bulletin board in your organization's work area called "New Threats" and pinning newspaper and magazine articles to it in order to foster conversation about events around the world.

Always ask the early adopters and early majority if they think a certain scenario could impact the organization that you are serving. Discuss the threats with an open mind and use the techniques found in this book to brainstorm the common memes, meme clusters, the assumptions, and caveats that would translate those data points into a First Event Scenario for your group. Notice that we have neither suggested that you ask permission, nor take this to the top right away.

If you follow the guidance laid out here, the top will come to you. Use storyboards and narratives to show and tell your most compelling First Cause Scenarios and/or new response solutions (see Figure 8.9). Have your early adopters chip in (even if they are not from in the market, but work inside your organization). Build a grass roots movement that *fundamentally changes the way your organization looks at the new face of risk.* This is not optional. If we are to survive the threats of this new millennium, strong, smart, and brave emergency managers will have to adopt new tactics and adapt to the new realities of the Market State and Emerging Risks. To do this, they will have to be Iconoclasts and change makers.

8.9 CONCLUSION

Memes allow us to group ideas, tactics, ideologies, and other concepts into meaningful units of measure and then to replicate and adapt them into useful analytical and operational tools using the four meme potential metrics we have identified: 1) proximity and similarity to other memes; 2) the tactical advantage of a meme; 3) the popularity of the meme; and 4) whether an adaptation in the meme would yield positive or negative outcomes for emergency managers.

We have reviewed how memes have the potential to create new tools such as virtual worlds and better real-time assessment tools (see Figure 8.9). We have also illustrated the outcomes of memes, stressing that when they are reverse engineered or applied in a creative way, they can lead to terrible results such as they did at the siege at Beslan. Understanding that memes can be utilized in a deterministic fashion, or evolve in a random way, as discussed early in the chapter is also paramount to mastering the process of building strong scenarios.

8.10 END OF CHAPTER QUESTIONS

1. Take the idea of Unified Communications using multiple media vehicles. What is embodied in the term and how would you illustrate it as a meme?
2. Given a current possible scenario in your workplace, can you identify the memes in the scenario? Are there more than one?

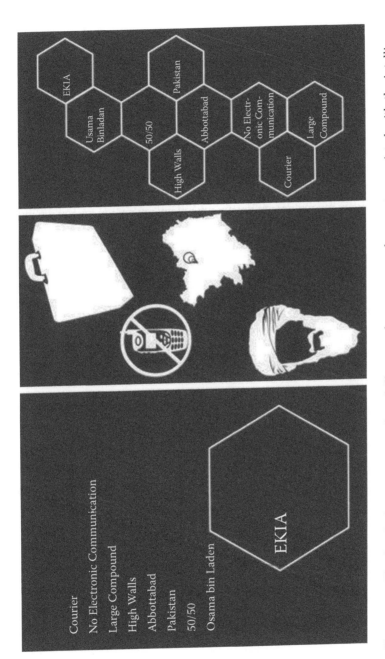

Figure 8.9 This bin Laden capture storyboard illustrates key memes and concepts associated with the intelligence available prior to arriving at death. Note the 50/50 odds prescribed by intelligence officials at the time of the raid and the resulting Enemy Killed in Action (EKIA) meme—that became viral in the days following his death.

3. Reflect on your personal experience—have you spotted a cultural meme that has an impact on the field of emergency management or anti-terrorism work? How could this meme be beneficial and/or harmful?
4. Looking at the various stakeholders in your workgroup, are there individuals who are more likely to think about scenarios in terms of the memes that compose them? What makes some people more apt to think in terms of groups of data points that can be orchestrated (memes) instead of charts and graphs with limited detail?
5. Consider meme clustering. Write a two-page proposal on a new approach to emergency response planning that utilizes meme clustering to identify and track a current scenario or potential event.

REFERENCES

1. Rogers, Everett M. *Diffusion of Innovations*, Fourth Edition. New York: The Free Press, 1995.
2. Moore, Geoffrey A. *Crossing the Chasm: Marketing and Selling High-Tech Products to Mainstream Customers*. New York: Harper Business, 1999.
3. Anderson, Chris. *The Long Tail*. New York: Hyperion, 2008.

9

Engaging in a New State of Practice

9.1 KEY TERMS

245

9.2 CHAPTER OBJECTIVES

After reading this chapter you will be able to:

- Describe the impact of the Market State on emergency management practitioners' lifestyles.
- Describe what personal traits and characteristics will make up emergency managers of tomorrow.
- Describe the meaning of the Brand of Self.
- Describe the professional practices necessary to incorporate into the field of emergency management in order to enhance the value and legitimacy of our field in the global Market State era.

9.3 OVERVIEW: THE NEW FACE OF EMERGENCY MANAGEMENT PRACTITIONERS

The Market State condition of our new century has changed not only the practice of emergency management, but fundamentally ourselves—if we expect to keep up with our rapidly changing world. Our lifestyles will have to transform along with our work. Whether we are public sector employees working for small towns or the federal government, or we are private sector employees working for small or large companies, the impact of the Market State is being felt in the practice of emergency management and, thus, necessitates changes in how we do our work and how we conduct ourselves. This book has outlined various means and methods for confronting the change in how we do our work with determination and will. In this chapter, we will consider the changes needed in our lifestyle to personally embrace and become *the new face of emergency management*. However, prior to discussing life changes we need to make, we are going to review the practice changes we have recommended in this book.

As first responders, disaster plan developers, emergency managers, investigators, or business continuity and disaster recovery professionals, these personal lifestyle changes are critical to transforming the overall practice of emergency management so that it can fall in sync with the modern realities of the Market State condition. In short, it is time for change. These personal lifestyle changes are as necessary to our future success as the practice changes we have discussed in this book.

We will have to reconsider our approach to conversations, the impact of the marketing culture on professional demeanor, and the rise of the new face of emergency management professionals.

To understand the new face of the emergency manager, this chapter will consider changes to our lifestyle, the traits and characteristics of the globally competitive emergency manager, how marketing culture has necessitated the **Brand of Self** (how effective messaging and meaningful dialogue is used to highlight the new way of business and values), and the necessary demonstration of *mastery* in the professional practices already described in this book (see Figure 9.1). A failure to *personalize* the concepts in this book is a failure to recognize that emergency management has changed at all in the past ten years. We must leverage that change to our *personal and professional advantage.*

9.4 THE EMERGENCY MANAGEMENT LIFESTYLE

We are closer now to the emergency manager of 2020 than we are to the seminal figures of emergency management such as Kahn and Wack. Pierre Wack's work, as you will recall from Chapter 2, is said to have peaked in the late 1970s. The emergency manager of tomorrow will be informed by a whole new set of data garnered from new disasters, terror attacks, and global events such as the 2011 earthquake in Japan (the most scientifically documented natural disaster in history), the terror attacks in Mumbai (the most documented terror attack communications in history), and the recent fall of several autocratic nation-states in North Africa and the Middle East including Egypt and Libya.

By 2020—only 8 years away—our profession will be transformed to be globally oriented, time zone agnostic, and technologically savvy.

Figure 9.1 In this chapter, we will discuss the mastery of counter-terrorism and emergency management practices using memes, as addressed in prior chapters, the personal lifestyle changes that are critical to transforming our profession, and the need to create a Brand of Self.

Holding on to the lifestyles of yesterday's practitioners does *nothing* to move us forward. Emulating the senior rank and file of our practice does *nothing* to propel us toward the personal choices we will have to make to compete in the coming decade.

Simply look at the boom in emergency management in Northern Europe and Southeast Asia. These are young, entrepreneurial, *creative* professionals in the practice who are willing to question everything in light of what they consider to be a normal state of affairs—the Market State. The question at hand is, "Who are you going to be now that there is a New Face of Risk? One who holds onto the practices of yesterday, or one who *lives* in the practices of tomorrow?"

Personal Lifestyle and the Global Orientation

Not all of us will be called upon to travel the world or to lay our own eyes on the risks our organizations face abroad. Regardless, even those of us who are not going to be traveling *must become more globally informed*. What happens half-a-world away is changing emergency management *right now*. For example, we already realize that the tsunami damage done in the wake of the Japan earthquake means that our current models for a tsunami triggered by a fault line rupture along the Cascadia Fault in Northwestern America *will be more intense*. We have learned that a 15-foot wall of debris and water pushes vehicles, boats, and small appliances as high as 70 feet into the air and deposits them onto buildings or *into* buildings, depending on the topology over which the tsunami is traveling. While this has often been a *theory* that has been argued, it is *fact* and we have it on video.

We know this if we are paying attention to *in-depth coverage* of the story from sources ranging from PBS to the BBC. We have to read deeper and more globalized material, from sources beyond our borders. We have to watch coverage of current events beyond the sound bites of the five o'clock news and seek out programs that include commentary from Israeli thought leaders all the way to Al Jazeera reporters in order to truly understand the depth of sectarian violence and genocide that may come in the wake of the revolutions of 2011 in North Africa and the Middle East. CNN and NBC are fine if we want a *purely* U.S. take on these events; to truly master the Market State world and the risks that come with it, *we must move out of the bubble of nation-state commentary and into the commons of global dialogue*. Change the channel. Pick up foreign relations magazines. Search out local points of view on the global stage!

Read international magazines such as *Monocle, Wired, The Economist,* and *Foreign Affairs* to better understand the Market State and what most of the world already takes for granted—a merging of market and design culture with business culture. The reason we mention *Monocle,* is that its editor, Tyler Brûlé, is seeking out the same fusion of marketing culture and political affairs as we are. This may have something to do with his being shot twice by a sniper while covering Afghanistan for *Focus* magazine, and that he later launched his own global fashion magazine, *Wallpaper,* to much critical success. (The magazine was purchased by Time Inc. in 1997.) He is as fascinated by travel, international design trends, and consumer goods as he is by politics, war, and disasters.

The irony of a revolution started by 11– to 14–year-old boys writing graffiti slogans in a suburban part of Syria is lost on Brûlé. He is a Coolhunter and Pattern Recognizer who sees the impact of popular culture on politics as a memetic membrane that was crossed long ago. The ten boys were arrested for writing, "The People Will Overthrow the Government" in Daraa. The boys were then taken to Damascus until the parents and many of the people of the city of Daraa demanded their return. This was handled by a transition team, but quickly turned into another bloody slaying of innocent lives similar to smaller uprisings that had occurred sporadically since Hasan Ali Akeleh poured gasoline and burned himself to death in protest, the same way that Mohamed Bouazizi had in Tunisia.

In fact, the uprisings across the Middle East and North Africa share a memeplex that *Monocle* and Brûlé are best suited to cover—that of a youth culture shut out from the world of Google, Facebook, and social networking sites by autocratic governments. This leads to protests. The rulers of Egypt, Tunisia, Libya, Algeria, Bahrain, Yemen, and even Oman meet these protests with Machiavellian treatments of human rights abuses. The world *has* become flat, as Thomas L. Friedman warned us in his book, *The World Is Flat,*[1] but it turns out that the kids are the ones who want it to stay that way. Tyler Brûlé, like other Coolhunters, sees that what the "kids" want, they usually get—for they are too young to fear the existing systems of cruelty and punishment that their parents fear.

The lesson here is something akin to the 1960s peace movement in protest of the U.S. military in Vietnam, which simply amplified the situation and emboldened the young demonstrators' need to prove that it was wrong for the United States to be in Vietnam. Back then, the FBI agents, police, and scenario planners would have been better off if they understood the crowd dynamics and were thinking of the youth they were trying to control. Today, *we will be better off* if we understand the market dynamics of technology and the energy of a booming Eastern Hemisphere generation gap that is driving freedom and the hope of democracy into countries where we could not have imagined them less than a year ago. Certainly, this was nothing even hinted at in U.S. news, but Brûlé and some others got it. Sociologist Patricia Martin in her book *RenGen: The Rise of the Cultural Consumer—and What It Means to Your Business,* "explores the conditions that are giving rise to a generation on the verge of a second renaissance. Years into the knowledge economy, the context in which we live our daily lives is no longer a twilight zone of change. Who we are and what we care about is taking shape with an emerging set of imperatives, products, behaviors, and ambitions." [2]

It is amazing that we allow the highly discontented and polarized worldviews of some U.S. networks and newspapers to shape our worldview as emergency management professionals, when sociologists, urban planners, and even scientists in the field of business management are already documenting a radical change afoot as the United States ages and emerging countries are booming with youth. *Continuing to stay tuned to the sound bites of U.S. networks and ignoring the voices of sociologists and others will severely hamper our local success at understanding the Disaster Halo Effect, let alone our global capabilities to protect our enterprises.* You are what you study. Reading this book alone will not completely prepare you for an emergency management career in the Market State world. *Living a more globalized lifestyle that includes listening to and reading the international voices in the news and media will.*

Own Private Time Zone (OPTZ) and a Change in Our Business Hours

Those of us who practice emergency management in businesses or in the government and are required to travel for work, either within the United States or around the world, should become accustomed to what we refer to as your **Own Private Time Zone**. This type of attitude toward time ignores the 9:00 a.m. to 5:00 p.m. paradigm completely and takes the 24/7 mentality to a new level. For travelers, it is the equivalent of setting your watch to GMT and *forgetting* any other notion of time. It comes in very handy for those of us who want to stay on top of emerging Market State events in order to be the most informed person in the room when it comes to the unfolding events so we can demonstrate mastery in the workplace.

For those of us who do *not* travel as a practice, the private time zone approach is still highly recommended as a key lifestyle change if we want to master our knowledge of emergency management in the new era. Here is the reason why: If we are still approaching our workday as a nine-to-five proposition, we are not *practicing emergency management*. In this scenario emergency management is just our job. We go in, we work for a solid eight hours, and we go home. If we live in California, we are three to four hours behind events on the East Coast all day long. We are in what is called the **925 Club**, a group of DR planners, business continuity planners, and emergency managers who do not see deeply past the eight-hour day in the time zone that we devote to our job.

The 925 Club is so committed to their job as emergency managers that they arrive at work with nearly military precision, promptly at 9:00 a.m. They may have caught 20 minutes of *Good Morning America* while eating their Wheaties, and they heard a little of the news on their way to work. While they think they are informed, truth is, they are as informed about the possibility of a North American tsunami strike in the United States as the secretary that sits outside of the CEO's office. They shut down promptly at 5:00 p.m. (17:00). Despite the fact that they "carry enough communication devices to run a small military campaign," as Tyler Brûlé says, they still post messages that say "out of office and away from my cell phone"[3] when they go to conferences or take a day off from work.

We say these people do not fall into the area of emergency management practitioners because, by definition, they *do not practice it*. How could they? By definition, a practitioner is someone who *practices* a learned profession. To practice, we must be available as disasters strike in order to observe and analyze information *as it happens*. We have all heard the complaints of 925ers that hate the 3:00 a.m. call from their boss who asks, "Did you hear about the earthquake in Japan?" The so-called emergency manager says, "No. I *was* sleeping." They do not use Twitter feeds, news alerts, or breaking news alerts on their smartphones. They do not monitor the world 24/7 by maintaining a global network of associates who know they will pick up their phone whenever it rings. The 925ers in emergency management *do not* act like professional emergency management practitioners and constantly demonstrate, through their actions, a lack of timely information, a lack of availability, and a lack of knowledge in our field.

For every 925er in our field, there is a loss of faith by CEOs and leadership in our profession. We do not confidently or happily *engage* with the 24/7 world around us; and therefore, as 925ers, do not demonstrate professional knowledge about events when they occur, and sometimes worse, only long after they have. Do you have a colleague in the field that has been asked at 11:00 a.m. about events in the Middle East only to hear them respond "they had no idea"? This is embarrassing not only to our field, but also to our department within our organization.

On the other hand, if we are practitioners who fall into the "Own Private Time Zone" club, or the OPTZ group, you are not afraid to wake up when your phone vibrates on the bed stand at 3:00 a.m. and read a Tweet about the quake in Japan. You get out of bed; you start tracking events on Twitter, CNN, BBC, and everywhere on the Internet. You burn the midnight oil. You work around the clock, arriving to work the next morning sleepy, but totally aware of the in-depth coverage that has been ongoing for the past five hours. You are a proud member of the OPTZ Club and your depth of practice makes you a true modern emergency management practitioner.

You have a response when the CEO calls. You have the details the next morning in the office and you are monitoring the unfolding events on several Twitter news feeds and have the latest information at your fingertips. You already have the early reports of damages and have seen it on YouTube. You board planes and change global time zones without the fear of jet lag. You sleep when you can and are awake and functional when you need to be. You are also professional enough to know that sleep matters and that you have to take shifts during a crisis. You find downtime when there is no crisis at hand to stay mentally alert and balanced. You do not take the time on your watch as seriously because the GSM phone is automatically updating via satellite. (Originally Global System for Communication, the French Groupe Spécial Mobile created the European standard for mobile phones.) You are focused on a balance that keeps your batteries charged, your lifestyle healthy, and your life engaged with global events as they happen.

Again according to Brûlé, who writes in "Do the Business—Global," for *Monocle*,

> As more economies rely on everything from logistics and final assembly to wire transfers from South Korea, Taiwan and Singapore, the Asian working day is starting to impact on working hours in Stockholm, London, Madrid and New York more than ever.[3]

He is right. This book has illustrated these connections in our global economies and the resulting need for emergency managers to live in the OPTZ. The emergency manager who lives the OPTZ lifestyle enjoys the benefits of a career that grows as their ability to respond increases. In fact, as their knowledge and availability skyrocket, their careers launch with them. We know there are many of us who feel we are too old for this type of lifestyle, and we will not argue that. However, as unsustainable as being highly available as an emergency manager seems, Western economies (and workers) are going to have to break with old habits to become more responsive to the Market State that is increasingly influenced by Northern Europe and Southeast Asia.

Get Into and Stay in Shape

Here is the third point on our view of the emergency management practitioner of tomorrow: they get into, and stay in, shape. This is a fairly simple concept. Your body has to be taken care of to respond to the strange hours that come with the work of emergency management practice. We should appear as if we were designed in a wind tunnel for a fast-moving global business culture. We should be able to get on a plane and arrive rested in another country ready and able to recover a business unit once we hit the ground. We should look like we are ready to *run*.

Part of this concept is purely self-defense. If our practice is on a trajectory toward more global business and more uncertain local business based on the scope of events that we are responding to, we ought to be in shape. For the public sector emergency manager, this is a simple and obvious statement. However, in the private sector, we do not take this seriously. Travel into so-called emerging markets can be dangerous. Learn basic self-defense. Learn to be streetwise. There is nothing more damaging to a response effort than an emergency manager who becomes part of the emergency.

We understand that there are many body types in the industry and we have equal respect for all of them, but here is the brutal truth: If we are out of shape, we are signaling that the profession of emergency response is more about sitting behind a desk than it is about being in the field. For some in leadership or high-level executive roles near the end of our careers, this is probably acceptable. For those of us who are building a better, deeper knowledge of current world conditions and want to understand the risk exposure to our whole enterprise, it is not.

However, for those of us who are young enough to do something about it, we owe it to our families and ourselves to eat better and exercise. Even to get some sleep as we live in the OPTZ. We owe it to the profession to shift the perception of emergency managers from desk jockeys to adrenaline junkies who are ready, willing, and capable of using our strong bodies and healthy habits to keep us sharp, functioning, and alive during the course of our work. Above all, get into physical as well as

253

mental shape. Both NASA and our military know the importance of good rest, think time, and the ability to keep a consistent sleep rhythm while working strange shift hours and performing during high-output periods. We can, and need to, learn from them.

Work It

The emergency manager of the Market State world *works it*. We know how to dress for the job we want, not the one we have. Here is the value of a good tailor: we do not need an expensive suit when a good tailor can make the difference. Everything is in the fit and finish. Sensible shoes are important, you know; something we can run in. We will also need a suitcase that is ready to go when we need to go. We have a smartphone and the ability required to exhaust it before we are exhausted. We have a power network of other emergency managers or business continuity and disaster recovery professionals who are as strong and committed as we are. We have the audacity of experience to stand up for what is right, what is humane, and what promotes the true values of our profession. We have the gall to believe we are the protectors of freedom. We have the foresight to act upon First Event Scenarios that may threaten the safety of not only our nation, but also all freedom-loving people.

Stop and think about what we are saying in this section. Perhaps it strikes a nerve; perhaps it does not seem appropriate to write about media consumption, time management, fitness, and dress habits in one textbook. The premise of this book is that emergency management has lost its edge as the Market State has unfolded beneath it, and the Disaster Halo Effect has become larger and larger with urban density and the connectivity of the Market State. It will take real work for us to regain that edge!

Personally Commit to Reclaiming the Esteemed Status of Our Profession

This is our chance to reclaim the power of our profession. This is our chance to reposition the *practitioners*, not the salespeople, as the thought leaders. This is our time to reinvent and reenergize our field with the best, brightest, and most marketable skills we have when they are needed the most. We could leave it at simply developing mastery over the New Face of Risk, but that is not enough. We have to commit ourselves to change, to keeping up, to pushing ourselves collectively to higher heights. We can become more than the failed naysayers of our age.

Few of us have *earned* mastery of the new face of risk through true, first-hand experience. However, those opportunities are expanding as fast as U.S. organizations are spreading their operations out into the world. We either get on with it now, or stand on the sidelines for another 30 years. To truly master emerging risk we *must dig deep individually and change the perception of our field one person at a time.* To do this, we have recommended the following lifestyle changes for the emergency management professional:

1. Create a personal Global Orientation by consuming media differently and sourcing international news, design culture, and marketing information.
2. Join the OPTZ Club and stay in front of breaking international events and the possibility that you will have to respond to them. If not, at least be fully informed of them.
3. Get into and stay in shape, including learning self-defense, and building a support group.
4. Work it by dressing for success.
5. Personally commit to reclaiming the esteemed status of our profession.

Managing emerging risk is about more than becoming aware that the world has changed because of the Market State and that we should be incorporating market theory into our practice. This book is about remarketing our profession so that we can emerge as risk is emerging, and become representative of the *new face of emergency management.* In the competitive world of emerging markets, if we do not lead the change at a very personal level here in the Americas, ASIA-PAC will happily take the leadership role. *It is up to us individually to master emerging risk and become the new face of emergency management.*

9.5 THE PERSONAL TRAITS AND CHARACTERISTICS OF TOMORROW'S EMERGENCY MANAGER

Managing Emerging Risk has discussed two seemingly opposed views of emergency management. On the one hand, military language and views were expressed as worldviews and geopolitics. On the other, the language of marketing theory informed our discussion of what managing emerging risk means and how it is accomplished. This admixture of military and marketing language exposes the underlying traits and characteristics of the *new face* of emergency management professionals. These personal traits and characteristics are best captured in archetypes of military and marketing lore and two Greek legends.

On the one hand, we have Cassandra, who in Greek mythology was granted the gift of foresight by Apollo. Interestingly, Apollo himself is associated with medicine, healing, prophecy, and plague, as well as foresight. Cassandra, who was so beautiful that she was granted the gift of foresight, is associated—as is this book—with two opposing forces: namely war (the infamous battle for Troy and the legend of the Trojan horse) and marketing. She was so beautiful she was sought after by both Trojans and one who would sack the city, namely King Agamemnon.

In both the *Iliad* and the *Odyssey*, Homer characterizes Cassandra's gift from Apollo as a curse. Cassandra saw many things about the fall of Troy, considered to be the greatest of fortified cities of the era. In Homer's legend, she foresaw the use of the Trojan horse, her own death, and the death of Agamemnon. However, the gift Apollo gave her was also a curse, as she caused his wrath by ignoring his passions for her, and Apollo ensured that *even though she could see the future, no one would believe her.*

Today, the saying "to be a Cassandra" is associated with being a person who claims to foresee many horrible things (like disasters and terror), but who is not believable and is not providing actionable information besides the incessant whine that bad things will happen. Cassandra is the archetype of someone who knows the future but is never believed because they are viewed as insane; their stories of future events are disjointed, incomprehensible, and too rambling to be understood at all.

The character of the gifted individual with foresight being ignored for many reasons appears throughout historical literature and folklore. A close cousin to Cassandra, of course, is the tale of "The Boy Who Cried Wolf." He too is not believed when he truly sees impending doom, but for altogether different reasons. He has simply lied too many times, and is too young and inexperienced to be believable. His insistence in having seen a wolf in the past becomes too tiresome to be taken seriously anymore, and no one paid any heed to his cries, nor rendered any assistance. The Wolf, having no cause of fear, at his leisure lacerated or destroyed the whole flock."[4]

These memes, "the Cassandra" and "the Boy Who Cried Wolf" have endured for some 3,000 years. They are deeply engrained in our cultural knowledge and skepticism toward any foretelling of the future. **Skepticism** is loosely used here to imply those who require evidence before they place belief in anything that, paradoxically, is impossible when it comes to the shape and form of emerging risk and the true results of the Disaster Halo Effect.

To be incoherent, out of sync with reality, vilified for being wrong or raising false alarms—and unable to tell a coherent story about the future—are all characteristics of Cassandra and the Boy Who Cried Wolf. We have all met emergency management professionals who offer nothing more than loose theory and alarmist sketches of disasters and attacks yet to unfold with no clarity, basis, or method. These traits lead to the emergency manager becoming something of a pariah, or outcast, and every single emergency manager who exhibits these traits does fantastic harm to our profession. Specifically they:

1. Create baseless, unbelievable futures
2. Present them in incoherent ways
3. Rant about horrible futures
4. Are inexperienced
5. Have been proven wrong over and over again.

Unfortunately, baseless unbelievable futures, presented in incoherent ways, and rants about horrible futures are a great way to sell short-term solutions to meet the long-term challenge of emergency management. Inexperienced and consistently wrong sales people who offer simple solutions dominate much of the conversation in our field today. *These sales people are undermining the very profession they claim to be knowledgeable in.* Their consistent hyping of every past event and the ever-present cry of "Wolf!" are traits and characteristics that no professional in the industry wants anything to do with.

It should be said that at the very top of hardware manufacturing and solution building organizations are sound, educated, and professional emergency managers who are qualified to create innovative solutions. They cannot often be painted with the same brush as the salesperson who has been using scare tactics to sell the newest solution. We simply wish to point out that people in the industry with little more to offer than a single type of scenario, plan, or product, who exhibit the traits and characteristics associated with Cassandra and the Boy Who Cried Wolf, are *not the personalities that will be the future of emergency management if it is to become the profession it once was, and needs to be again, in the face of emerging risk.*

As we mentioned, the traits and characteristics we are looking for align themselves with military and market theory. Unlike Cassandra and the Boy Who Cried Wolf—who both had military aspirations regarding their visions of the future and the need to protect something of market value (their virtue or their sheep)—we must search for another archetype. The archetype we are seeking is able to understand the future and successfully navigate it with determination, inspiring trust, leadership, and action.

This is the archetypical Greek hero, Odysseus. In some academic circles, Odysseus is described as a Greek cultural hero, suggesting he is the hero of the Greek culture itself, although this distinction varies. What does not vary, however, is that part of his namesake was a descriptor that inevitably followed his name in both The Odyssey and The Iliad. Depending on which side of the Trojan War we are studying (that of the Romans or that of the Greeks) he was either "the cruel" or "the cunning, intelligent one." The latter term is associated with the Greek word *metis*, which translates into cunning intelligence.

Odysseus is credited with the creation of the Trojan horse, an act of cultural reverse engineering if ever there was one. After Troy was finally taken, Odysseus is also credited in some Greek literature for throwing Astyanax, the son of Hector, from the high city walls to his death to ensure that the boy would not grow into a man and avenge his father. This strategy ensured that the Greek victory was complete and everlasting with no one to avenge Hector, Paris, or the sacking of the city. However, it is after the battles of Troy that we learn of Odysseus's most intelligent and cunning exploits.

In the 20-year journey home from war, Odysseus is driven off course by storms. Along with his crew, he is visited by lotus-eaters, captured by the Cyclops, angers Poseidon who threatens him with more malice on the sea, is visited by the witch-goddess Circe who turns half of the men into pigs, and nearly reaches home but is blown back by the wind of Aeolus. Then Odysseus skirts the island of the Sirens by tying himself to the mast, and passes between the six-headed monster Scylla and the whirlpool Charybdis. All of his 12-ship fleet is destroyed, and all of his men are drowned by a storm caused by Poseidon. Odysseus is washed ashore and saved by Nausicaa, princess of the Phaecians, who helps him return home. Through much of this Athena guides him, and in the end, recommends a peaceful return home even as Odysseus is tempted to kill the suitors to his wife Penelope.

It is this *metis*—the cunning intellect informed by foresight, the self-control, the debating skills, and the mastery of strategy—that Odysseus demonstrates that frames him as such an excellent archetype for the practice of emergency management. Metis, that cunning intellect, is rooted in wisdom, skill, and craft. Metis is also said to be "wise council" and prudence by Stoic scholars.

These are the true personal traits and characteristics of the new emergency manager:

1. Cunning
2. Intellectual
3. Wise
4. Skillful
5. Crafty
6. Strategic
7. Self controlling
8. Skilled debater
9. Wise counselor
10. Prudent

Prudence by itself may be the most important of all of these traits. It comes from the Latin *prudentia*, which means foresight and insightful knowledge. It suggests exercising sound judgment in practical affairs, and is considered to be a virtue. It is the opposite of being reckless and cowardly. Even though in modern English the word is increasingly associated with being overly cautious, it is Aristotle who takes the word to its most appropriate philosophical definition and best suits it for our use here in the *Nicomachean Ethics*, in which prudence is simply **practical wisdom**. Practical wisdom, by definition, is of course won by experience.

The list of ten traits that the new emergency manager should exhibit is important, but it is the simple concept of practical wisdom we should focus on. Practical wisdom, as demonstrated by Odysseus in all of his battles and the long journey home, is the thing that gives him the foresight and resilience to see his journey through to the end. This is what we are after—practical wisdom that informs sound decision making in the practice of emergency management. *Our field would certainly be better off populated with men and women exercising practical wisdom and delivering wise council than it would be if populated by Cassandras and Boys Who Cry Wolf.*

9.6 BRAND OF SELF

Changing the perception of the emergency management discipline to meet the needs of the Market State means changing the **Brand of Self**. As master emergency managers, what are we worth? A lot of this depends on how we market ourselves. If marketing is anything, it is *branding*. When we think of sodas, we may think of Coca-Cola. When we think of electronics we probably think of Apple. When we think of cars, we probably think of Chevy, and on it goes. All of these are name brands, recognized not only by their name, but the array of lifestyle images and stories we bring together in our mind around each name.

This memeplex has been edited, some marketing professionals would even say cultivated, to bind certain qualities and traits to the brand name. The memes are simple, like taglines and stories (advertisements) that reinforce the lifestyle the brand brings to us. Coke is the real thing. Apple Computers are personal. A Chevy is tough. Marketers use all sorts of mediums to convey these ideas, from TV advertising, to flyers and brochures, to new media such as YouTube videos, Web pages, blogs, Twitter, Facebook ads, and user groups. One of the amazing things about the Market State is that most of these outlets for building corporate brands are now within our personal reach.

The Brand of Self is the memeplex that surrounds us—each individual practitioner of emergency management—by leveraging new and traditional media to tell our personal story. Our memeplex starts with our professional résumé. It may be that we have worked for the same company for many years, or worked for several. It could be that we are free agents, consultants, or full-time employees. Whether you are in the job market or not, it is important to keep your résumé open and continually fine-tune it. A recent survey found that the average emergency manager will work for 14 companies in the course of their career—and those are the practitioners who are looking for full-time employment!

The two things that build the Brand of Self in a résumé are 1) where we have worked, and 2) what we accomplished. Who we have worked for is important because it informs something about our brand. It is a kind of professionalism by proximity. Our military experience, our professional experience in large corporations, our practical experience with smaller, local companies, and our travel experience all matter when considered as part of our own Brand of Self. The organizations we have worked for have reputations and a brand of their own that rubs off on our brand, helping us to differentiate ourselves from other emergency management practitioners based on what we may have been exposed to when working with this or that organization.

Our résumé should also tell people about what we accomplished while working for these organizations. Whether we worked as a free agent and were only there for three months or as a full-time employee that worked at the same organization for 13 years, our accomplishments along the way should tell a story—a narrative as we described in Chapter 8, about who we are and what we have accomplished in our emergency management career. Have we completed risk assessments? Have we done scenario planning? Drafted plans? Managed programs? Have we planned for, and responded to, real events? Anything we have completed or managed should be included. Each new position should show us taking on more responsibility and deeper challenges along our career path. When considering new job offers ask yourself, "Does it enhance the Brand of Self or is it just a new job?"

Finally, we should mention every seminar, user group, paper, and class that we have given, every degree that we have earned, and every personal experience we have had that enhances the story of our Brand of Self. These accomplishments, from being in the high school ROTC, to writing a professional article for a conference, are part of the story of who we are: professional emergency managers. Sometimes, the tipping weight in the scale of making hiring decisions is not just the years of experience at certain companies or the professional certification and education, it is a little personal detail—the study of military tactics, or a passion for geopolitics—that can be the difference in how our personal brand can help us get the job.

The personal interest section of a résumé is a great place to show what the Brand of Self identifies with and what one values. Community achievements, public speaking, volunteering, scouting, or hobbies such as graphic arts or math puzzles are memetic clues about our personal brand that can seal the deal. In today's Market State world, however, if we are going to talk the talk, we had better walk the walk.

The Market State age means that employers will be using Google. Google yourself and see what you get. It should be a memeplex that is consistent with your résumé. In fact, in branding, nothing is as important as consistency. Your professional profile on networking sites like LinkedIn should be an exact replica of your résumé, with as many positive client testimonials as you can garner. Your profile on job boards like Monster, Dice, and CareerBuilder should have exactly the same message as your résumé. And it does not stop with your professional brand. No—there is more.

Your personal network should reflect relationships you have built with other emergency management professionals, clients, teachers, and instructors. Here, with networks like Facebook that are commonly researched now as part of the hiring process, we might add to the core of our brand some personal experiences that enhance the Brand of Self—a love of our family, our personal values, our hobbies, even the types of music and art we love.

That said, we should also beware. Personal networks do not allow us to manage the content our friends post about themselves or us. As a rule, we should never "friend" someone who is posting dangerous or unflattering things about themselves or us that might hurt our brand. We want employers and peers to find out more about our personal brand in terms of our taste, our interests, and our values than we do about our mistakes and misadventures. There is a lot of brand damage that can be done if one of your friends posts pictures of themselves being foolish and it shows up on your personal network!

We often ask other professionals in the emergency management field what their own personal brand is. In conversations, it is natural to inquire about where they work, where they live, and what they are interested in. We do it all the time in conferences and at user group meetings. The real test in the Market State age is a much simpler question, "What does Google tell me about you?"

Google is the meme aggregator. If we get an emergency management professional with great connections on LinkedIn, a consistent story about their career and their accomplishments, a personal network of like-minded individuals, and a great family life we are probably on the right track. If we get photos of the person working out, riding mountain bikes, practicing martial arts, or speaking at a conference, we are on the right track. If we get videos of speeches, articles in professional journals and magazines, even posts to blogs about people who disagree with the other person's opinion on a professional issue we are on the right track. We have found an emergency management professional who cares about their brand and is managing the Brand of Self. If we Google the person and get nothing, well, there it is...nothing.

Using tools such as professional, social, and photo sharing networks may intimidate people. It requires some time to get used to them. However, they are incredibly user-friendly and are consistently being used by professionals in the human resources industry to get to know potential candidates. There is not a separation between your career and your personal life online, and if you are not managing your online reputation then you are not managing your Brand of Self.

This applies to how you network at conferences as well as your behavior at them. Many view a conference as a chance to get away from work and dress accordingly. Many attend parties and act as if they are at fraternity initiations. We have to find it hard to take a person in Bermuda shorts with a drink in his or her hand seriously as an emergency manager. Whether we are at the office, in the field, or in cyberspace, the way we carry ourselves, the image we maintain, and the way we carry our professionalism are all parts of the Brand of Self. While you may not think you need to be concerned about this today because you have chosen to stick with the same firm for the next ten years, do not be so secure. The market is shifting, as this book has demonstrated, and your next career move could depend on how diligently you have managed the Brand of Self.

By extension, applying the concept of the Brand of Self to professional emergency managers who want to fully embrace the challenge of managing emerging risk, we are extending the *new face of emergency management* out to the public, to our peers, and to our customers. We are each change agents in a large movement that positions emergency management as it once was—an honorable and valuable profession that meets danger and uncertainty with determination, will, and values consistent with democracy and humanitarianism.

We all have a role to play. Every top official in Homeland Security and federal emergency manager has said this at one time or another. However, the role of the emergency manager is one of the biggest, and is in need of the most attention we can muster, to bring sanity, security, and a sense of professional pride back to our profession. Recent events in the Market State world have given this opportunity to us, and we should take the challenge very seriously.

9.7 THE NEW PROFESSIONAL PRACTICES OF THE MARKET STATE WORLD

In Chapter 1 of this book, we presented fictional, but believable, scenarios that were fresh, intense, and backed by real-life events and trends. We challenged ourselves to think of a world in which systems are reverse engineered, memes collided/combined, and havoc resulted. We illustrated through the scenarios that the terror attacks and disasters of tomorrow will be influenced by new developments in world affairs and the current era in which we live.

In Chapter 2, we outlined why we believe that the new professional practices of emergency management must evolve, mainly because of the rise of the Market State and a clear realization that the Disaster Halo Effect is at play in all scenarios. We outlined the history of emergency management and how it has diverged into many areas of specialization and away from its roots in contingency planning. We also discussed emergence and downward causation, presenting the view that terrorism and disasters are evolving, and so too must our ability to create First Event Scenarios and appropriate responses that fit the new realities of our world. Chapters 1 and 2 firmly established that the professional practice of emergency management would have to evolve to stay abreast of the *new face of risk.*

In Chapter 3, we explored the three main components that frame a sound emergency management program: policy, strategy, and First Event Scenarios. We distinguished the new face of risk management as a fundamental difference among various approaches to emergency management scenarios and strategies. We discussed the most pragmatic approach for developing scenarios for emergency management and the four "must haves" for scenarios given the new face of risk. The measures for these scenarios are:

1. Firmly rooted in one of five discrete, Location-Based Risk Assessment areas
2. Have been peer-reviewed and have met a standard of measured likelihood
3. Can either be remediated or mitigated
4. Are not limited to likely events but also include zero sum scenarios

Finally, in Chapter 3, we illustrated how to differentiate among scenarios, strategies, and tactics. We described the meaning of the Zero Sum Scenario and why it is an important consideration in the practice of emergency management today.

In Chapter 4, we discussed the difference between data sources and data handling systems in the world of emergency management. We described classified and unclassified data sources and the limitations of existing counter-terrorism and emergency management systems and modeling tools. We illustrated how probability mathematics, in and of itself, may leave us shortsighted, and what the term possibility means when applied to counter-terrorism and emergency management in the current age given issues such as User Bias and Power Users.

Chapter 5 introduced the use of marketing theory into the practice of modern emergency management and demonstrated how memes aggregate ideas and concepts. We outlined the four potentials of memes and how they might adapt into new First Event Scenarios. We illustrated what we can learn from memes when we use them to create meme clusters. We discussed why most disasters have memes at play and how memes can be used to better understand and communicate the dynamics of a situation. Finally, we showed what the cutting-edge application of meme clustering means to the fields of anti-terrorism and emergency management.

In Chapter 6, we looked at how Coolhunters identify memes and apply them to their field. We define the role that Coolhunting and pattern recognition can play in emergency management and preparedness. We showed how early adoption is the fundamental quality of meaningful narratives and leads to change in complex systems. We concluded with why the strongest pattern recognition specialist should be recognized as an all-source data specialist, and should be responsible for creating a forward-view story.

In Chapter 7, we reviewed regional perspectives from Israel and Japan to better understand resilient cultures. We propelled the conversation around intuitive knowledge, the "blink," and pattern recognition, so that it can be easily adapted to our field of practice. We added the concept of thin-slicing data and making short work of analysis to arrive at meaningful conclusions regarding evolving situations. We discussed Areas of Dominant Influence and how they can be leveraged to better respond to disasters and to identify and communicate to the most important of stakeholders prior to an event.

In Chapter 8, we illustrated how the diffusion of innovation is applied to emergency management to track key meme clusters and the evolution of terror tactics and response innovations. We demonstrated how memes are translated into real actions by emergency management professionals and by terrorists. We illustrated how understanding the diffusion of innovation illuminates the timeline under which new memes move through popular culture and the professional culture of emergency management. We discussed what we can learn from the diffusion of innovation when we know who the stakeholders are and how to communicate with them. Finally, we brought these important concepts together into an actionable method of using the diffusion of innovation to enable the creation of effective narratives around risk and response in the emergency management field with storyboarding

In this final chapter of *Managing Emerging Risk*, we highlighted the importance and impact of the Market State on emergency management practitioners' lifestyles. We described what personal traits and characteristics will make up the emergency managers of tomorrow. We illustrated the meaning of the Brand of Self and outlined important steps each of us in the field must take to forward the sound practice of emergency management (see Figure 9.2).

Figure 9.2 By using the techniques in this text, the practitioner becomes more than an employee, and we hope evolves to become a trusted counselor in the field of emergency management or counter-terrorism. And as such, the practitioner will have more than a seat at a table and will engage in meaningful, one-on-one dialogue with key stakeholders.

Taken together, these *are* the professional practices that will be necessary to incorporate into the field of emergency management to enhance the value and legitimacy of our field in the global Market State Era.

9.8 CHAPTER SUMMARY

Looking back on this chapter, it should be clear that emergency management professionals have the highest stakes in understanding the Market State. We discussed key changes to lifestyle, the personal traits and characteristics of the emergency manager of tomorrow, illustrated the Brand of Self concept, and described how to incorporate these concepts into our own professional lives. Finally, we reviewed the whole intent of *Managing Emerging Risk* and stressed the importance of these professional practices being applied in the Market State world.

9.9 CONCLUDING QUESTIONS

1. Looking back, how has the rise of the Market State raised the stakes for Emergency Managers?
2. Describe the varied lifestyle changes suggested in this chapter, and pick one that you think you should apply to your own life. Explain the reasons for your answer.

3. What is the most important trait or characteristic—to you—of the emergency manager of tomorrow, and what impact do you think it will have on the practice going forward?
4. Describe the meaning of the Brand of Self and discuss a goal you have set for yourself to improve your own brand.
5. Reflect on the overall messages within *Managing Emerging Risk* and describe the most important facet of the book relative to emergency management and the role you play in your organization. Use critical thinking and comparative literature to support your answer.

REFERENCES

1. Friedman, Thomas L., *The World Is Flat: A Brief History of the Twenty-First Century*, New York: Picador/Farrar, Straus and Giroux, 2007.
2. Martin, Patricia. *RenGen: Renaissance Generation*. Avon: Platinum Press, 2007. p. 2.
3. Brûlé, Tyler. "Do The Business—Global." *Monocle*, March 2011.
4. Aesop, "The Boy Who Cried Wolf." East of the Web. http://www.east oftheweb.com/short-stories/UBooks/BoyCri.shtml (accessed October 12, 2011).

INDEX

52 scenario school, 84
9/11, *see* September 11 attack
9/11 Commission, 77
9/11 Commission Report, 149
925 Club, 251

A

All hazards planning, 47
All Hazards Risk Assessment Report, 107
All-source data specialist, 166, 265
Amplifying pattern recognition,
    193–200
Anonymous innovator, 230–231
Areas of dominant influence (ADI),
    204
    and emerging markets, 204–207
Artificial intelligence (AI), 115
The Art of War, 38

B

"Battle Lesson: What the Generals
    Don't Know," 177
Beslan Massacre, 141–143
The Big Short, 118
Bin Laden capture storyboard, 243
The Black Swan, 234
The Blind Side, 118
Blink, 201–203
Blink and Thin-slice
    Blink, 201–203
    Thin-slicing, 203
Boing Boing, 126
Bojinka, Operation, 75–79
Boxing Day Tsunami and Haiti,
    183–186
"The Boy Who Cried Wolf" meme,
    256–257

Brand of self, 259–263
Building security and egress
    standards, 112
Business continuity, 40
Business continuity and disaster
    recovery (BC/DR), 40, 45, 211,
    246
    industry, 41
    as "necessary evil," 42
    origin, 40

C

Capabilities of modern smartphones,
    memeplex, 138
"To be a Cassandra" meme, 256
"Causal chain" approach, 139
Central Intelligence Agency (CIA), 46
    from 1970 through 2000, 46–49
Change agents, 221–223
    emergency managers as, 224
    from memes, 223
Choke points, 215–216
Civil unrest and terrorism risk data,
    108–111
Climatological hazards data, 108
Clustering, 136
Communication, 174
Complex systems, 143–145
Computer and computational systems,
    role of, 115–117
Consumer behavior, predicting, 116
Contingency planning, 37
    at the beginning of new
        millennium, 48
    as business concept, 39–46
    as government concept, 46–48
    as strategic concept in Sixth
        Century BCE, 38